WILDERNESS BEGINNINGS

Rose
Hertel
Falkenhagen

Caitlin Press Inc.
Prince George , B.C .

Wilderness Beginnings
© 1997 and 1995 Rose Hertel Falkenhagen

Caitlin Press
Box 2387
Station B
Prince George, BC • V2N 4E1

Caitlin Press acknowledges the support of the Canada Council for the Arts for our publishing program. Similarly we acknowledge the support of the Arts Council of British Columbia.

Page design and layout by David Lee Comunications
Cover design by Warren Clark Graphics
Index by Katherine Plett
Printed and bound in Canada

Canadian Cataloguing in Publication Data

Falkenhagen, Rose, 1940–
Wilderness Beginnings

ISBN 0-920576-67-2

  1. Hertel, Paul 1910– 2. German Canadians—British Columbia—Biography.
    3. Immigrants—British Columbia—Biography. I. Title

FC3850.G3F34 1997   971.1'00431   C97-910467-X
F1089.7.G3F34 1997

Contents

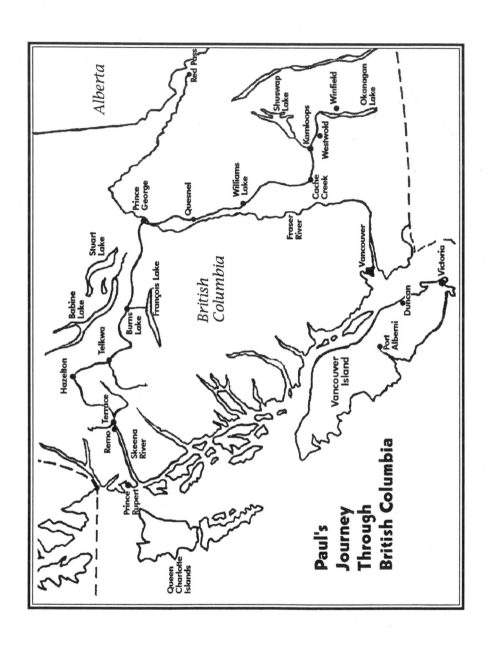

Paul's
Journey
Through
British Columbia

Dedicated
to
MARGARETE
HERTEL

SPECIAL THANKS TO—

George Hertel of Qualicum Beach, BC
Thomas Hertel of Port Alberni, BC
Catharina Kurucz of Port Alberni, BC
Henry Joseph of Babine Lake, BC
Monica Joseph of Babine Lake, BC
Ron Michael of Vancouver, BC
Marge Troger of Victoria, BC
Joe Klein of Penticton, BC
Jack Boudreau of Prince George, BC
Grete Davidson of Prince George, BC
Harry Weaver of Prince George, BC
Emil Froese of Remo, BC
Floyd and Aileen Frank of Terrace, BC
Dora Samuelson of Vanderhoof, BC
Klein Gusti of Rehau, Germany
Hans Griesshammer of Rehau, Germany
Christl Rank of Rehau, Germany
Irma Hertrich of Rehau, Germany
Helga Ebeling of Hanover, Germany
Erika Schmutzler of Geretsried, Germany

PROLOGUE: AFTER THE BEGINNING

MY FATHER'S MEMOIRS had lain unread in the back of the closet for over a decade. His sudden death in 1981 left the family grief stricken, but I also came away burdened with guilt for knowing so little about his early life. Sure, he had left some memoirs, but hadn't he said they were incomplete and parts had been lost? Not until a family crisis ten years later, did I realize how quickly the years were collapsing one upon the other and if I didn't get more facts from my mother and old friends, all would be lost.

I opened the closet door, pushing aside colorful old scarves and an assortment of handbags, and pulled out a tattered brown envelope. I popped open the flap and rippled through the stack of handwritten pages that held the story of one person's journey through a historical decade that was significant, not only in Canadian and American history, but pivotal and profound in European history as well.

Although my father's life had no consequential effects on history itself, for he was but one of thousands and thousands of Europeans who had immigrated to the North American continent, he nevertheless left his mark in the decade of the Hungry Thirties, the Depression years, the Dirty Thirties, whatever you want to call them, by creating his own minuscule pieces of patchwork in the wilderness landscape of British Columbia.

He started out alone and penniless in that wilderness, but it didn't take long for him to make friends, some short lived, some that lasted a lifetime. My mother, known as Margaret, and whom he called Grete in the early years, became one of those lifetime friends. During the sixties, when they became grandparents to nine grandchildren, we began to call them Oma and Opa, which is German for grandmother and grandfather. Actually, the story of my mother is no less remarkable than my father's. Imagine saying good-bye to your family knowing you may never see them again. "Go West, young man" was a common enough theme in the old days, but it was far less common for a woman to just pack up and go.

She was, and still is, an independent soul. When family and friends gathered to celebrate her eightieth birthday on November 23, 1991, her self-reliance and independent spirit still shone from her soft, blue eyes. "Quit complaining and get on with life. It's the only one you have," always was her motto. But this isn't her story, although she becomes very much part of the tapestry.

So I sat down and made myself comfortable. On top of the manuscript lay a white envelope. I opened it and unfolded two single-spaced sheets of typewritten paper.

Suddenly I was propelled back ten years, a day still vivid in my mind, a day that none of us in the family could quite grasp because of the suddenness of grief, the imposition of death, the painfulness of mourning. Yet as I read the eulogy, I could feel my lips break into a smile, and though my eyes began to blur and tear, they were happy tears, for his eulogy was open and true to his spirit.

November 12, 1981
Port Alberni, B.C.
Dear Friends:
The family is a unique and vital part of Creation. It is in the family that we experience joy and tears, pain and thanksgiving, and discover that these events serve as a time of sharing and growing. It is in the family that we can really share precious memories, reflect on events and draw meaning and strength from them. It is in the family that we trace our roots, uncover our origin and see our future.

We have gathered as a family and as friends and neighbours to lay away Paul Hertel. We shared many events and experiences, some as fresh as last week, others that go back a lifetime. These memories are happy, sad and serious. Paul left his mark on our lives. But now there is pain and a great emptiness because someone we love is no longer with us. This mixture of deep feeling and pain must be acknowledged.

Paul loved life and he loved people. He was a free spirit. He lived life with zest and a flare that marked him among his peers. To me it always seemed fitting that I should meet Paul at a wedding. I was at the door of the reception hall gazing over a sea of faces trying to find a seat when I heard Paul call out, "Come over Reverend, there's a seat over here. I'm a Lutheran Atheist, but that's all right. You sit with me." That was for me the beginning of a precious friendship. So he lived with humour and friendship, touching life around him. And all our lives are richer and fuller because he lived.

Some people dream of leaving home to seek fame and fortune. Paul left his homeland of Germany as a young man and cut a heritage out of the wilderness in a new land. He was a gracious friend, a good neighbour, a loving husband and a proud father. And in time of need he was generous to a fault.

Some people talk of dying with their "boots on." Paul did his day's work, came home and went to his rest. Now he is removed from our midst, but he is not lost to us. Though we may leave here in tears, we do not leave in despair, but rather with that deep feeling of thanksgiving that he lived among us and shared and mingled his life with ours.

Amen.

Rev. T. Fenske

I folded up the eulogy and set it aside, thinking he didn't quite die with his "boots on" like his Western heroes, but he went so quickly as a result of a heart attack that it may as well have been with the crack of a gun. I placed the stack of handwritten notes in front of me and spent the rest of the afternoon reading. When I finished, infused by then with nostalgia and emotion, I knew I had to write my father's story. But it wasn't so simple. The pages he had written were riddled with gaps even my mother couldn't fill, and quite frankly, I needed his help. There was so much I didn't know. So I wrote him a letter. Now that may seem strange to you, but I really felt confident that I could recreate his spirit so we could work together.

December, 1991

Dear Opa,

Do you have any idea how much we've missed you all these years? And now I'm writing to you, writing you this very unusual letter. But maybe it's not so unusual. Many people, after all, write to their loved ones after they have passed away to help them soothe their grief, or their conscience. I have to be honest with you and say my grief has long ago eased. And we never had any unsettled grievances, did we? I'm just writing to ask your help in solving the riddle of your memoirs.

I went back to visit you on your tenth anniversary, do you know? You're out there somewhere beneath that tall sweeping redwood you planted. The day was the same as ten years ago, everything yellow and brown and dripping wet, mottled leaves lying still and scattered on the soaked ground. The Monkey Puzzle tree, your prized possession, is gone, but the goldfish ponds are still there, the lily pads, the rhododendrons you planted. I still remember that day so clearly, how the pain of it washed through me like gritted sand. But now I can only smile when I think of you.

Remember when George and Tommy and I were kids and you used to tell us those stories about the North? We would roll our eyes toward the ceiling and say, "Oh, no, not again." I wish we had listened harder and asked more questions. I guess when you get older and history begins to weigh heavy on your shoulders, the past looms up close like looking through a telephoto lens and you want to know more about it. But when I was a kid in the Fifties, the Thirties seemed like a thousand light-years away.

As I said, I wish we had listened more carefully to your stories, but I guess I thought you would be around forever. I wish we could start right from the beginning before you left Germany in 1929. I wish I could ask you all those questions about the Thirties that didn't seem important to me as a kid, or even as a young mother, for that matter. Perhaps I know more than I realize, since I didn't entirely close off my ears when you talked so much we couldn't stand to hear another word. But your adventures into the wilderness of B.C. never seemed that overwhelming or important, yet from today's point of view, they're extraordinary.

Yeah, you were a free spirit all right, just like your friend Reverend Fenske said. But when you bought that old turn-of-the-century house in the Port Alberni Valley at the end of Bland Road in 1941, I think your wings had finally been clipped short enough. What was it you paid for the old place? Three thousand dollars with 350 acres to boot? The house was covered with pink wild roses just like in the German fairy-tale "Briar Rose." Remember? You had to hack your way through those brambles, but unwittingly you rescued yourself from your wilderness fever and finally established a real home. Oma's been in that old place for over half a century now. We're all glad you stayed there, but the credit for that clearly belongs to Oma. Had she not put "her foot down," you surely would have pulled up roots again and again. At least we were given a true sense of home.

I know I'm talking to you as if you're still alive, but the truth is, I feel that you are. You're living for all of us, and I'm giving you this chance to go on living. I'll help you. I promise we'll listen now. We want to hear your voice, your story, just one more time. How about it, old man? You know you could never resist a listening ear. Thanks, Pop . . . I love you too,

Rosie

1. The Golden Sun

WELL, IF THAT ISN'T THE DARNDEST THING, hearing from you. I know you got tired of listening to my stories, but I kept on talking anyway, figuring that some of them would eventually soak in. I don't know if I can recall things exactly as they were, but you know there's nothing I would like to do more, and I don't mind giving it a shot.

You say it would give me a chance to go on living. I think I had my chance, made plenty of mistakes, too. But one thing I can tell you is that the years during the Thirties were one long adventure, and more than anything, I wanted to find out what real living was all about.

When I left Germany in '29, and I'll tell you later about the circumstances that led up to that moment, I had no idea what was in store for me. It was a heck of a thing to do, looking back on it, one day packing up and leaving for Canada, but at the same time it was an easy and logical step to take because I had always been fascinated by America. As a boy I grew up reading Karl May's books about the American frontier, and his books were so realistic you thought you were right there in the middle of the prairie even though he had never been there himself. I dreamed of the Wild West he described in *Old Surehand*, but never for a moment did I think by age nineteen that dream would become a reality. You see, I was the only son and it went without saying I would take over our family business, which included our *Gasthof* or inn, a butcher shop, and over one hundred acres of farm land. But because my sisters had grown up in the business and were very competent, I couldn't see that leaving home would be a hardship on my family.

As things turned out, my mother was darn glad to see me go, and I had convinced my parents that I wouldn't be gone for more than a year or two.

Plenty of people packed up and left the Old Country during the Twenties. The Germans were still recovering from the First World War and were hungry, especially in the cities where they were squeezed together like sardines with no jobs and little food. With inflation rampant, in 1923 four trillion marks weren't worth more than a one dollar bill, and you needed a wheelbarrow full of money just to buy a loaf of bread. Later that same year, you could exchange a trillion old marks for one new rentenmark.

Before I get on with my story, though, I want to tell you a little about the town in Germany where I grew up. We lived about a hundred kilometers north of Nuremberg, close to the Czech border, in the small town of Rehau. Surrounded by forests of fir and spruce, it lies nestled among fields and rolling hills, all part of the Fichtelgebirge, a range of low-lying mountains in the heart of Europe. In winter, bitter cold winds blast across the *Erzgebirge* from the East and the summers can bring stretches of long, sweltering days. When I grew up there, the roads that led in and out of town were lined with ash trees. As a kid I'd pedal my bike along the dirt road and click my tongue with every tree I passed trying to count them, but an oncoming wagon or coach, sometimes even a car, always sidetracked me.

Rehau was well known as a town where livestock was traded. It was also known for its foaming beer, its leather work, and fine porcelain. That whole area manufactures porcelain. Rosenthal and Hutschenreuther porcelain is manufactured only a few kilometers southeast of Rehau in the town of Selb; and Meissen and Dresden, the cities in Germany most famous for porcelain, are less than an hour's drive northeast of Rehau.

There's an interesting story about Meissen china. My grandfather, Johann Paulus, who had an interest in the Zeh Scherzer porcelain factory in Rehau, told it to me when I was a kid. He had these big ears that looked like blinders on a horse and wiggled when he talked, so when he began to tell me about the history of porcelain, I kept looking out the window to stop myself from laughing. But I sat up straight and listened all right when he yanked my ear good and hard and pushed out his chin saying, "Sit still you little bugger, someone's got to tell you."

Now, you don't have to listen to this next part, just as I didn't want to hear it, but it's actually quite an interesting story. You see, it was the Chinese who first discovered how to manufacture hard porcelain way back in the 7th Century, but they kept their secret in Asia with the threat that anyone with a loose tongue would lose it with the chop of a sword. So it wasn't until the early 1700s that the key to producing hard porcelain was finally unearthed in Germany. August the Strong, who was King of Poland at the time and ruler of Saxony, had thrown this guy named Boettger, an alchemist, into jail in the old Albrechtburg in Meissen, a castle built about a thousand years ago. August needed money to pay off war debts and ordered Boettger to make gold for him. Well, Boettger couldn't spin any gold, but he discovered kaolin, a white clay, which lay in heavy deposits all around Dresden. This discovery lead to the manufacture of porcelain, which turned out for August to be better than gold.

So in 1710, the first fine china factory in Europe was founded in Meissen right in the Albrechtsburg, close to my hometown. I know the French will argue this, but their stuff was too soft to be called good china. The Meissen china was so hard that it could be cut only with a diamond.

In 1945, the Americans and English bombed the hell out of Dresden, but Meissen was untouched and the old Albrechtburg is still standing today right up there on the hill. So the porcelain industry became very prominent in our neck of the woods. In fact, one of the porcelain factories in Rehau, founded in 1906, was under the name Hertel, Jacob & Co. They've long gone out of business and I don't even recall which branch of the Hertel family it belonged to.

Our town wasn't touched by the Second World War, at least not by bombs, but it burned to the ground three times over the centuries. If you went over there today, you would find the family Inn, *Die Goldene Sonne*, which means The Golden Sun, still standing on the corner of *Ascherstrasse* and *Ludwigstrasse*, just down from the main square. Hertels have lived on Ascherstrasse for the last one hundred and fifty years, and have been in Rehau since the 1500s, almost since the year the town was founded in 1427.

My father was a *Metzgermeister* or master butcher who prepared all the sausage for the business. I apprenticed as a sausage maker in Berlin, went there in 1924 when I was only fourteen. Naturally, my father expected I would eventually run the business, but things didn't turn out that way. And I have to say that had my mother not meddled in my affairs, my whole life would have turned out far different.

As a property owner with an old, established business in town, she had great expectations for her children, wanting them to marry someone from a family that also had a substantial amount of wealth and property.

She was a tall, broad-shouldered woman with black almond-shaped eyes that grew round and threatening if you tried to cross her. She always wore a black dress that hung down to her ankles and sometimes her black stockings would gather around the tops of her heavy black shoes like wrinkled sausage skins. One thing I have to say is that she was a hard worker and kept the business running during the First World War, or Great War, as it was known then, when my father was away at the Front. My sister Gusti was born the last day of the year in 1914, just after the outbreak of the war and she didn't get to know her father until he came home over three years later.

My father was easy to get along with and, by nature, a quiet man. Although he stood several inches shorter than my mother, he never paid much attention when she yelled at him for passing out drinks on the house or handing out a free meal to someone. "*Du alt's Rindviech*," she'd shout, waving her fist in the air. "You fool." He always took it with a gleam in his eye and a shrug of his shoulders.

My two sisters, Gusti and Jette, and myself, kept up our sense of humour. We spent a lot of time in the *Sonne* where there was an atmosphere of warmth and *Gemuetlichkeit*. That was our home. That's where we grew up, and the *Stammgaeste*, or regular customers, were part of our family. Although we always had hired help,

Hertel family, Rehau, Germany, 1929. Left to right: Anna, Paul's mother; Jette, Paul's older sister; Gusti, Paul's younger sister; Paul, and George, Paul's father.

we kids were expected to pull our load around the place. I started helping out behind the bar when I was only ten or eleven. I stood on a wooden box, to see over the counter and be able to reach the beer mugs and glasses. The *Stammgaeste* had their own mugs, which came in various pot-bellied shapes with pewter lids, and when a regular customer came through the door I would have his beer poured and warmed for him by the time he sat down. Some of them liked their beer warmed, especially in the winter. We had a heated coil that we would stick into the beer to take off the chill.

The *Stammgaeste* dropped by every night. Some would play cards, others would sit and smoke and discuss the weather, the crops, or the inflation that was rampant at the time, or the subject would turn to the stories about the Great War. One had an eye missing, another a leg, but I never paid much attention to what they said.

When your mother was only six years old, her father, Anton Wendler, was killed in that war in France in 1917. They were holed up in a deserted farm house and had retreated to the cellar when the artillery fire began to get heavy. By dusk things had quieted down and her father—wanting to calm his nerves, I suppose—crept upstairs to get his pipe and tobacco. A minute later, he came stumbling down the stairs and fell dead at the bottom from a gunshot wound. A stone mason, he had grown up in Pilgrimsreuth, a village near Rehau. His brother survived the war, but lost a leg.

I can still remember when the war ended in November, 1918. We all gathered at the *Marktplatz*, the main square of the town. People jammed together around city hall, shouting and cheering and listening to speeches. Times were hard after that, but we weren't affected as much by rationing since we were in the meat business and could always trade with the local farmers.

The *Sonne* was a busy place where you could always count on a good meal. My mother would cook a huge pot of pork hocks and sauerkraut for the guests and serve them with plenty of boiled potatoes. A big crock of tamped kraut always stood in the corner of the kitchen. For special occasions she would make *Sauerbraten* or beef roulades with red cabbage and *kloese*, the dumplings you used to call "glue balls." Friday and Saturday nights people would crowd around the tables and swing and sway to the music, and by the time my sister Gusti was ten, she played the accordion and sang right along with everybody. She loved music and had no idea what the word shy meant. She had a smile that spread from ear to ear, and teeth as white as a plate. That's what I would remember most about her in later years when I'd get homesick for the Old Country. She would toss back her head and come out with this loud, rolling laughter.

When Gusti was older, she had a deep, lusty, melancholy voice. "*Ach, du Pauli, komm sing,*" she would say to me. Her black eyes glistened and she'd throw her arm across my shoulder. One of her favourite songs was "*Du, du liegst mir im Herzen, du, du liegst mir im Sinn,*" which means "You're in my heart, you're in my mind," but it's just not the same in English. We all loved listening to her sing. I can remember my father sitting at the *Stammtisch*, that's the head table, and he'd shake his head and run his hand across his polished dome. Tears welled up in his eyes as a slow smile spread out from under his dark brown mustache. Then he would call out to Jette and me. "Sing, come and sing." I was no real singer, and Jette, a couple of years older than me and much quieter, preferred to play the piano.

My mother was also very musical and played the zither well, so we were all expected to master an instrument. Gusti was a natural musician, and Jette went on to study piano at the Conservatory in Weimar, but I had too many things on my mind to practice. Five minutes on the violin was enough for me. I was probably about twelve years old then and kept pigeons and owls up on the roof. My mother knew she could always find me there.

"You get down to your room and practice, you hear, you *Taugenichts, du!*"

One Saturday morning, after listening to myself screech back and forth on the strings for five minutes, I threw the violin down and went up to the roof to feed my pigeons.

"Paul," she hollered up the stairwell in her deep voice a few minutes later. "You come down here!"

Reluctantly I made my way down the dark narrow steps. She stood in my bedroom holding the violin. Streams of sunlight picked up the particles of dust swirling around her ankles and she stood there straight as a ramrod with her chin in the air.

"So, you don't want to practice," she said with a scowl. Her eyes were hard and she shook the violin at me. "Come here. I'll show you."

Before I had a chance to duck, she raised her arm and cracked the thing right over my head. My arms flew up, and the strings snapped and twanged around my wrists. "That's the end of the violin," I thought with glee. But when I glanced up, the glare on her face was black as coal. I didn't hesitate a second and turned and leaped down the stone steps which led outside.

"You good for nothing, you," she yelled after me.

I knew I'd have to pay later, but I didn't stop running until I got out into the fields. So my violin lessons came to an end. A teacher came to the house every week to give Jette piano lessons and I was always grateful that my mother hadn't insisted I learn piano. Nevertheless, the bit of music I had must have made some impact, because years later I was able to sit down at the piano and play by ear.

After I finished my apprenticeship in Berlin and returned home in 1928, things didn't improve between my mother and me. She thought she could still tell me what to do, but I had grown up while I was away those four years.

While in Berlin I lived with my Aunt Gretel, an easygoing, cheerful woman, but she nevertheless kept a sharp eye on me, and for good reason.

Berlin was in its heyday then. The *Kurfuerstendamm* overflowed with all kinds of people, especially in the summertime. Peasant women in black dresses and brightly colored kerchiefs sold cabbages and carrots from their baskets and wagons. Beggars, crippled from the First World War, sat in the street, holding out pencils and cigarette papers, begging for handouts. Well-dressed gentlemen in bow ties and ladies in short dresses and high heels sat at sidewalk cafes drinking coffee and smoking cigarettes. In the long twilight of the evenings and late into the night, jazz music floated through the air along with the mingling city smells of smoke and streetcar exhaust, grilled bratwurst and sweet perfume. Even prostitutes in their heavy makeup mingled with the crowds and you could always find a man along the sidewalk winding his barrel organ and the monkey groping for pennies. Bars were on every street corner, and at every doorway stood a man selling "tssigarettes." You could buy tickets to hear Richard Tauber, the famous tenor, or you could take a tour of Al Capone's hangouts, the Chicago gangster known as Scarface Al.

Storm-troopers in their brown shirts were also part of the scene by then. They were the young, unemployed men who had been hired by the struggling Nazi Party with promises of a bed to sleep in and boots to march in. You would see them goose-step down the street in their brown shirts, carrying bright red flags with the black swastika sign, or you could find them on a street corner passing out leaflets.

When I was nearly eighteen and finishing up my apprenticeship, a group of us went to the Wintergarten, a cabaret along a broad street sparkling with lights and blaring with music. For 60 pfennige we saw jugglers and acrobats and a Maharaja lie down on a bed of nails. Then this comedian dressed like Hitler came on stage. In those days Hitler was just an upstart and nobody paid much attention to him. Well, this guy wore a brush for a mustache and perfectly imitated Hitler's shrill-pitched voice, and you should have seen the audience go wild when he started crowing like a rooster. He cracked all kinds of jokes about Hitler, one on top of the other, and people pulled out their handkerchiefs left and right to wipe away the tears. But when the comedian turned around and lifted his jacket to expose the swastika on his backside, the house came down.

But getting back to my mother and how she tried to run my life. I had turned nineteen and been home from Berlin for over a year. It was the spring of 1929, and that's when the real trouble began.

2. Carnival Time

"**T**OMORROW WE'RE GOING TO VISIT the Hermann family in Wurlitz," my mother said to me that Saturday afternoon when she marched into the sausage kitchen. Max Troger, a tall, well-muscled young guy with hair the color of beeswax, who was apprenticing with us, had finished his work and gone home. I was alone and stuffing the last of the bratwurst.

"I want you to meet their daughter. She's a young lady in her early twenties and they've invited us over for *Kaffee und Kuchen*."

My hand clamped down on the sausage and meat squished slowly out of the end. I hardly knew who she was, but her relatives owned a big gravel quarry business in Wurlitz, a village just a few kilometers east of Rehau. They owned a lot of property, and besides running the quarry, also manufactured tombstones and shipped them all over Germany. Naturally, my mother was interested in marrying me off to someone with property or money, or the possibility of it. I scraped the sausage off the board with a knife, and without looking at my mother, continued to stuff the sausage.

"She's too old for me," I finally said, "and I don't even know her."

"*Ach, quatsch*, she's twenty-two. What do you know?"

She may as well have been thirty as far as I was concerned, and besides, my heart was already set on a girl I'd met the year before. I stopped work and turned to my mother, wiping my hands on my apron. "*Mutter*, I'm not interested."

"*Horch auf*," she said, shaking her finger at me. "You listen to me." Her black eyes glittered, and her mouth turned downward. Strands of black, kinky hair had come undone from the roll around her head and hung down the side of her face. "I want you to stop seeing that Wendler girl," she threatened. My heart began to pound, and I could feel my mouth tighten. "She's nothing, you hear me?" she continued. "A seamstress, huh. You won't marry a seamstress."

Heat flamed up in my face. I pushed myself back from the counter and lifted my chin. "You can't tell me who to marry."

"You have nothing to say, just remember that," she said, pushing her hair out of her face. "I warn you."

She gave me one of her black looks and turned to leave the room. Her black skirt swished around her ankles and almost caught in the door as she slammed it shut behind her.

My jaw clamped together, and I picked up a steel and began to sharpen the butcher knife. The vigorous, slashing movement of the steel and the piercing clang of the blade helped me let off some steam. I had no interest whatsoever in that Wurlitzer girl. I had a girl, and a real pearl of a girl, too. I ran my thumb across the blade, testing it for sharpness and set the knife down. I knew I was in trouble and that my mother wasn't going to let me continue to see Grete without a fight.

I had met Grete the year before at a *Faschingsball*. We always celebrated carnival time in Rehau. It was the end of February and the last big masquerade dance of the season, the weekend before Ash Wednesday. The dance was in the *Turnhalle* where we held our gymnastics meets. I had recently returned from my four years in Berlin and just celebrated my eighteenth birthday, so Grete would have been about sixteen and a half. I didn't know some of the young people at the dance, especially the girls, because I had attended an all-boys' school until age fourteen.

I decided to dress up as Charlie Chaplin, the tramp. I had seen Chaplin's silent movie, *The Gold Rush* a few times in Berlin. It was the funniest movie I had ever seen. I got to know his character well and had his kick-in-the-pants and shuffling walk down pat. The movie was about his prospecting trip to Alaska and how he had become a millionaire. I never dreamed then that I would find myself in a similar cold wilderness, and later on, when I was in British Columbia nearly starving to death, I thought back on that movie many times and wished I'd have had some good soft shoe leather to eat like Chaplin had cooked up for himself.

So I dug out my old black Confirmation suit and put on the jacket which was by then a couple of sizes too small for me. I borrowed a pair of my old man's baggy pants and tied a piece of rope around my waist to hold them up. I found some old shoes and a bowler, put on a mustache, white gloves, and picked up a cane on the way out the door.

I arrived late at the dance because a *Fasching's* celebration was also going on at the *Sonne* and my parents were short handed that night. The smell of cigarette smoke, beer and perfume hit my nostrils as I pushed my way through the crowd of merrymakers. Balloons and streamers hung from the ceiling.

Max Troger, Arno Michael, Adam John, and some of my other friends were sitting at a long table with large foaming glasses of beer in front of them. The three were dressed as pirates, but with red kerchiefs covering their heads, a patch over their eyes and thick handlebar mustaches drooping over their lips, I could hardly recognize them. Max was nearly a head taller than Arno and Adam. Of course, they laughed like heck when they saw me, shoving a glass of beer in front of me when I sat down. The room was blue with smoke and a band was playing some pretty jazzy tunes. People blew noisy whistles and tossed colourful streamers across the room. Some drunken masqueraders were dancing on a couple of table tops by then, singing loudly and swinging liters of beer.

I looked across the dance floor and fixed my eyes on a beautiful girl dancing with a guy wearing a phony Mozart suit. Her arms and shoulders moved with ease, and she kicked up her slim, shapely legs to the rhythm of the music. Butterfly wings were attached to the back of her short, puffy blue dress. I bumped Arno with my elbow. "Who's she, the one with the wings?"

He winked at me and flashed his square white teeth. "Oh, that's Margarete Wendler, but we all call her Grete. She lives on Regnitzlosauerstrasse above the tracks."

I picked up my mug of beer and took a long draft. Her hair was short and dark with heavy waves, and even from the distance I caught a sparkle in her eyes. The clatter of the castanets, the banging of the drums, and her white swinging arms nearly hypnotized me.

When the music stopped, I stood up, pulling and tugging at my jacket. Her partner led her back to her table while I eased my way between chairs and streamers and people, never losing sight of her. Then the drums banged and the band began to play "Five Foot Two, Eyes of Blue." I adjusted my mustache and gripped the lapels of my jacket. Suddenly I was staring down at the beautiful Georgia right out of Charlie Chaplin's *Gold Rush*. Startled blue eyes looked up at me, and my ears began to buzz. I felt like the real tramp and thought if I took one more step my pants would fall down or somebody might trip me.

I stood there frozen in place for what seemed like minutes before I stepped back and made a quick bow.

"May I have the next dance, please, Mademoiselle?"

She looked sideways to her friends and then back to me, a soft, full smile on her lips. She stood up, barely reaching my nose. I put my hand on her warm back, careful not to disturb the floating wings, and guided her onto the floor. We began to dance the Charleston. My legs moved like pistons, and my throat felt as if a vise had gripped it.

Grete looked up at me and smiled. Her cheeks were fresh as ripened apples. "I saw the Charlie Chaplin movie, *The Kid*. You look just like him," she laughed, not missing a step. "You're Paul Hertel," she said, raising her voice above the music.

I nodded, knitting my eyebrows together and feeling my face go hot. "And you're Grete Wendler?"

"Everybody knows everything in this town," she said, fanning her hands and tilting her shoulders. "I even know when you came back from Berlin. Somebody mentioned it one night at the coffee house. Was it exciting to live there?"

I leaned in a little closer. "Well, I worked mostly, but yes, it was. It's a city that never sleeps."

"And the nightclubs never close?"

I nodded my head and smiled down at her. "But the city is beautiful with lots of parks and lakes."

"I can't hear you . . . " she laughed.

I leaned closer and her hair brushed my cheeks. She turned away from me, kicking up her feet in perfect rhythm. I took a deep breath, and when she turned back to me I tried again. "On Sunday afternoons . . . "

Her hand went up to her ear and she shook her head. Finally the music stopped with the clang of the cymbals.

"What about Sundays?" she asked.

I tucked her hand under my arm. "We would walk along the shore of the Wannsee . . . my aunt and I. Her name's Gretel, like yours. She would buy pickled cucumbers from the Spreewald. Sometimes we rented a rowboat on the Wannsee. From out there on the water you could see all the old mansions along the shore."

"Lots of rich people must live there."

I nodded. "I loved Berlin, but too many people. My aunt was good to me, though. Once she took me to the theater to see Anna Pavlova, the Russian ballerina."

"I've never seen a ballet. It must have been beautiful."

The band began to play a slow waltz, and I slipped my arm around her waist. Grete told me she was apprenticing as a dress-maker and belonged to the *Turnverein*, or gymnasts club. Suddenly the evening was over and we were the last two on the dance floor. My friends were nowhere to be seen, but it didn't matter . . . by then my heart belonged to Grete.

We walked out into the crisp, night air. Several young men and girls she knew from school accompanied us. They were laughing and singing and had their arms around each other. I wanted to take Grete's hand, but hardly dared. When we arrived at the three-story house where she lived with her family on the ground floor, her friends said goodnight, and we stood there in silence with our heads turned toward the echoing sound of the cobblestones.

I thought of Charlie Chaplin holding Georgia's creamy-white hand on New Year's Eve, and finally I turned to Grete. She tucked her hands under her brown fur collar, lifting it up around her ears. White puffs of air melted in her face, which glowed soft and golden in the street light. I nervously took her hand and slipped off her glove, feeling the warmth of her soft skin flow into my icy fingers. Her glowing strawberry-red lips curved into a smile, but before I could say a word she pulled her hand away.

"I must go now. Mother's waiting," she said quietly.

"Can I come by tomorrow?" I asked, brushing her face with my fingertips.

"No, not tomorrow, but our gymnasts club meets at Cafe Horn on Wednesday evenings." She politely shook my hand and disappeared through the doorway into a dark hallway.

My face burned all the way home, and I felt like I was walking in high speed like in the silent movies. Golden light spilled onto the street from the windows of the *Sonne* where the *Fasching's* celebration was still in full swing. Noisy laughter and singing rung in my ears as I snuck up the back steps into my room. I undressed and crawled under the cold, damp feather quilt and kicked aside the unheated brick. Long after, when the music from downstairs had finally died away, I still lay awake thinking of Grete and planning when I would get together with her again.

The first thing I did was join the gymnasts club. Even though we practiced on different days from the girls, it was a good way to get to know Grete. I had belonged to a club in Berlin and competed in tournaments there, so it was the natural thing for me to do, and gymnastics was one of the most popular sports in Germany in those days.

The club was very organized, and many weekends we would travel to other towns to compete in tournaments, or outside teams would come to our town. When there wasn't a tournament we would all get together on Sunday afternoons and walk through the forest, or pack ourselves a lunch and hike up the Kornberg, a local lookout point in the Fichtelgebirge. Although Grete and I met at the Saturday night dances or at the local coffee house during the week, we actually spent very little time alone together.

One Sunday afternoon we all decided to go back to the *Sonne* for some beer, even though I was a little leery that my mother might object to my keeping company with Grete. My mother had made her position perfectly clear when Jette, my older sister, started making eyes at a young man who worked as a porcelain painter at the Zeh Scherzer factory. I was in Berlin at the time, but Gusti had told me all about it.

Paul Hertel,
Confirmation 1924.
Age 14.

This young fellow began to stop by the *Sonne* after work for a glass of beer to talk with Jette. It didn't take long for my mother to figure out what was cooking, and she told him in so many words that a porcelain painter wasn't welcome around the place. That was the end of the relationship. Jette would never have dared to defy my mother. Sadder still, a couple of years later Jette met a young man my mother actually approved of. His family was well off; he even owned a motorcycle, which was not too common in those days. Then one afternoon he came roaring down the Ascherstrasse, and just as he was about to turn into Ludwigstrasse, right there in front of the *Sonne*, a car turned up the street and crashed head-on into his motorcycle, killing him instantly. Jette took a long time to recover, but she eventually found someone else my mother apparently found acceptable, though he wasn't too well off financially.

Anyway, on this afternoon we had just raised our glasses for a toast when a silence fell over the table. I turned, and there stood my mother, her hands on her hips and her black eyes focused on Grete. Her face was like cardboard, except for a muscle twitching

Grete Wendler,
Confirmation 1926.
Age 14.

in her jaw. I stood up to introduce Grete and my other friends to her, but before I could open my mouth she turned and left the room. Grete's face flushed and she pushed back her chair.

"Don't go," I said. "Finish your drink. She's just in a bad mood today."

Grete didn't say another word about it. But over thirty years passed before she finally set foot inside the *Sonne* again.

When I later asked my mother why she had walked out on my friends, she shrugged her shoulders. "I don't have to answer that," she said.

As the months passed she continued with her threats. "You're not going to marry a nobody." And if I came home late, she'd be waiting for me at the top of the stairs in the half dark. "You've been with her again," she'd say, grabbing my arm.

But she didn't scare me and I just ignored her. And so it was about a year after I'd met Grete, not too long after my mother insisted I meet the Wurlitzer girl, that the whole affair came to a showdown.

3. Fall Harvest in Canada

A N ORDER OF SAUSAGE WAS WAITING to be delivered to a farmer about a mile out of town, so I harnessed our two Great Danes to the wagon and we left at a good clip. They were beautiful animals and their tan coats glistened in the sun.

I tied up the dogs and knocked on the door of the farmhouse. In the yard an old hen with her chicks pecked and scratched at some grain.

"*Ach, der Hertel's Paul,*" Frau Bauer said, wiping her hands across her apron front. "Come in, come in, Paul. You can set the sausage on the counter here. Ralph," she called. "Come, see how handsome the boy is. Here, let me take your jacket. I've some fresh crumb cake warm out of the oven."

"Thank you," I said, squinting my eyes in the dark, low-ceilinged room. "It smells good."

Her husband shook my hand. "Exactly like his mother," he said grinning. "Same wavy black hair, same black Gypsy eyes." Then he laughed. "You just as stubborn?"

"*Ach*, for heaven's sake, Ralph," his wife said, spreading a white linen cloth on the heavy, wooden table. "Now, just give me a minute to grind some coffee beans."

We sat down, and Herr Bauer leaned back in his chair and crossed his arms. "Say, what's all this I hear about the Wendlers' daughter," he asked. "Your mother isn't too happy about that, heh?"

I ran my hands across the smooth cloth. "Where did you hear that?"

"Ralph!" Frau Bauer said, setting a piece of cake in front of me. "*Um Himmels willen*! Let him be."

He slowly rubbed his hands together and shrugged his shoulders. "Talk . . . it's only talk."

I took a deep breath and drummed my fingers on the table. "Grete's a beautiful girl, you know," I said, staring him in the eye, "and one of the smartest in school."

Frau Bauer poured me a cup of coffee. "Never mind, Paul," she said, patting me on the shoulder. "Eat up."

"My mother still has some old fashioned ideas," I continued, stirring some thick cream into my coffee, "and I wouldn't put much stock in what you hear around town."

I finished my cake and coffee and made my excuses to leave, backing out the door under Frau Bauer's protests.

I unhooked the dogs and headed them toward home. The air was damp, and the smell of rotting manure drifted across the fields. Thinking about what old man Bauer had said made me wonder how far my mother's venom had spread. With her ideas about marriage, she was as flexible as an iron rod when it came to Grete. The funny thing was that I had never mentioned marriage to Grete. We had never even said how we felt about each other, though I knew it was understood.

I released the barking danes in the courtyard and left on a run to Grete's house. When she opened the door and saw me standing there, a troubled look spread across her face.

"What is it?" she asked.

"Can you come for a walk?"

She squinted her eyes in the late afternoon light and hesitated only a moment. "I'll get my coat."

I tucked her hand under my arm and we walked up the street past walled stucco houses towards the fields where apple trees were in bloom. A slight wind had come up and blossoms floated in the air. My stomach muscles were cramped and tight, and when I tried to get the right words out of my mouth, my heart jumped and tumbled around in my chest like a yo-yo on a string.

"Grete," I finally blurted out. "Has anyone ever said anything to you about us?"

An uneasy look crossed her eyes.

"You know . . . " I said, clearing my throat. "You know how my mother doesn't want me to see you."

Her cheeks flushed red and still she didn't say anything. I kicked at some stones. Fog had settled in the low-lying fields, and the mingling smells of new grass, manure and blossoms clung to our clothes in the damp air.

She pulled her hand free and walked over to the side of the road, staring out across the greening fields toward the dark forest.

"What is it, Grete?" I asked in a low voice, following her and laying my arm across her shoulders. "Please, if there's something wrong, tell me."

She shrugged and put her hands into her coat pockets. "Everything is wrong, Paul." She glanced up at me, then lowered her eyes. "We shouldn't even be here. The truth is, I don't think we should see each other any more."

I dropped my arm and kicked a stone off the road. "It is my mother, isn't it," I prodded.

She pulled her coat together and bit her lips.

"Did you hear something then?" I asked.

Grete turned and began to walk slowly along the side of the road. "I don't . . . I don't even know how to tell you, but yes, it was something your mother said. She warned me . . . "

My face began to burn, and I pushed my hands into my pockets.

"Mathilde and I were on our way to the movie house," she continued. "I didn't even *see* her. Suddenly she was right in front of me. 'You stay away from my son, you hear!' she yelled at me. She shook her fist in the air and said it a second time, even louder, 'you stay away from him!' Everybody in the marketplace heard her, I just know it!"

I didn't know what to say, feeling at once embarrassed and furious with my mother for confronting Grete in public. "She gets her ire up sometimes. That's how she is. I wouldn't pay any attention to what she said. She's always telling everybody what to do so I wouldn't worry about it. It's going to be all right."

"How can it be all right after what she said?" Grete asked, lifting her chin. "You know I could never stand up against her." She pulled her coat together and turned towards home.

"Grete," I pleaded, reaching for her hand and pulling her toward me. "Grete, don't you know I want to marry you?" Her eyes opened wide and she leaned back, pulling her hand away.

" . . . you can't listen to what my mother said," I uttered.

She slowly shook her head. "No, your mother would always come between us, and I'm too young to think about marriage anyway. And imagine what she'll do if she finds out you want to marry me."

"But we wouldn't be getting married tomorrow."

"It doesn't matter. This town is too small for us, and I know my mother wouldn't be happy about it either."

"We could move away—to Berlin."

In that moment I really liked the idea of Berlin. My aunt lived there, and with her connections she could easily help me find a job.

"Berlin!" Grete said with a laugh. "But you're expected to take over the family business! And didn't you say you could never live in that city with so many people roaming the streets day and night?"

"All right," I said, putting my arm around her waist. "I'll forget about Berlin, but I'm going to talk to my mother. I know if she just has the chance to really get to know you . . . "

"Oh, no," Grete said with a firm shake of her head. "I think I know your mother better than you. She'll never give me that chance. She knows me well enough already."

After I left Grete at her front door, I turned home with heavy footsteps, not believing that my mother had gone so far as to scorn Grete in public. It almost made me laugh, but in a small town it wasn't laughable. Although I was certain I could win Grete over in good time, I had no idea how to deal with my inflexible mother.

I turned up the Ascherstrasse. The deep afternoon haze had turned the walls of The Golden Sun the color of autumn straw. I pushed open the side door, not knowing whether to confront my mother then and there, or just go upstairs and think things over. Gusti was leaning over the stove in the sausage kitchen. Links of knackwurst were looped around in her hands. She turned toward me with a harsh look on her face.

"What are you looking so black about?" she asked, her voice echoing the sharp tone of my mother. "It's time you're back."

"What's it to you?" I said, unbuttoning my jacket.

"Nothing to me, but *Mutter* is hotter'n a poker. You were supposed to come straight home to help out here. The place is full. Annie is sick today. Beer glasses need to be washed." Then she paused a second. "You met with her, didn't you." Her black, kinky hair looked wild and she glared at me.

A singeing heat ran through my body. "I thought you liked Grete. Why are you being so ornery?"

She shifted her weight and turned towards the pot of simmering water, carefully sliding in the handfuls of knackwurst. "*Mutter* is hopping mad, that's what she is." She put the lid on the pot and turned to me. "She yells at me, at *Vater*, at Jette, at everybody because of you!" She picked up four baskets filled with black bread. "Please, can you open the door for me?"

"Wait a minute. What did *Mutter* say?"

"She's going to throw you out. She said as much."

Suddenly the door swung open, and my mother barged through, pushing Gusti aside.

She raised her fist and spit out at me. "So, you've been with her again . . . with that hussy! You're supposed to be here working!"

My body tensed. She leveled her fist and walked right up to me. "Where have you been?" she spit out in a whisper. I sucked in air and pulled myself up to my full height. She shook her fist and leaned in close to me. "I've told you to stay away from her. You can find someone better, like the Wurlitzer girl."

I gritted my teeth and crossed my arms not budging an inch. "I'm going to marry Grete," I said, easy and controlled, looking directly into her eyes. My heart knocked inside my neck. "And nobody is going to stop me."

Her eyes grew round and black. "You're what?"

"Marry her," I said in defiance.

"*Du Taugenichts, du,*" she yelled, and the next thing I knew her fist landed on my ear.

My hands flew to my head and I stumbled backwards. Gusti's eyes caught mine and I saw the gleam of fear in them. I took one look at my mother and turned and walked out into the fading light of the day. I didn't know which direction to take, and began to think that maybe Berlin would be the best place to go, at least until the old lady simmered down.

I rubbed my pounding ear and ran up the street towards the fields. White, hot anger burned inside me. The cool air soothed my face, but my heart felt like every bit of feeling was being squeezed right out of it. I didn't know which way to turn or what to do. Grete had made it pretty clear that she had no intention of marrying me, not yet anyway, and I knew there never would be peace in our family if I didn't give her up. But giving up my sweetheart was out of the question for me.

As it turned out, not long after, my life changed with the blink of an eye. I was reading the local newspaper, the *Rehauer Tagblatt*, when an advertisement flashed in front of my eyes.

"Farm Help Needed in Western Canada." I put my finger on the ad and read on.

"Norddeutscher Lloyd— Direct Service to Canada. Free information through our agency in Oberkotzau."

My hand began to shake. I had only dreamed of going to America, but now the possibility was real. America! Canada! what did I care? Canada was good enough for me.

I didn't waste any time and hopped on the next train to Oberkotzau, a neighboring town. The shipping agent explained to me that the Canadian Pacific Railway was offering special excursion fares to Europeans to help bring in the fall harvest in Canada and that a boat would be departing from Hamburg on August 2nd. He gave me instructions where to go in Hof, a town ten kilometers to the north, to make arrangements for a passport, which would take a few weeks to process.

As soon as I got back to Rehau, I went straight to see Grete. I had to tell somebody, even though the thought of leaving her already lay heavy on my heart.

"Canada? But you don't know anyone in Canada," she exclaimed. "And isn't it just a wild, empty country filled with ice and snow?"

It was a warm May evening, and we were walking along the Perlenbach, a stream that winds through the middle of Rehau. "It can't be much different from America," I said.

"But how can you just leave?"

"A job will be waiting for me. And I'll be back by next summer, you'll see." I had to convince her that it was the right thing for me to do, for both of us. "We're still young, we have plenty of time. And it'll give my mother a chance to cool off. You know I've always talked about America, and Canada can't be much different."

I took her soft hand and touched it to my lips. "I'm going to miss you like crazy."

She looked up at me and nodded her head. "Maybe it is for the best that you go . . . and I'll miss you too," she said quietly.

"I haven't told the family yet."

Grete stopped and grabbed my arm. "You mean you don't even know for sure you're leaving?"

"Oh, I'm leaving all right. That I know for sure. I've already reserved passage. I have to get the money though, but when I tell my old folks I think they might even like the idea."

My parents were stunned. My mother walked back and forth in front of the upstairs living room window.

"If you want to go away, why not Nuremberg, or Bayreuth? Go back to Berlin. Why so far away?"

And my old man clearly didn't like the idea.

"*Bist du doof*?" he asked, pointing his finger to his head and raising his voice. "You're a fool! We need you here." He shoved his hands into his pockets. "What do you want in some wild country filled with bears and Indians? *Menschens'kind!* We need you here." He began to pace the floor and ran his hands across his shiny, bald head.

I raised my hands. "You did okay without me when I was in Berlin, and I would only be gone for a year at the most."

"But you know the business now," he persisted.

"Maybe it's just what Paul needs," my mother broke in, sitting down at the table and looking at my father. "He needs a change." She looked back at me. Her black eyes softened and she patted my hand. "I think it will do you good to get away from this town for awhile. Canada must be just as rich a country as America. You will earn good money there. And we can help you out with the fare over."

My father stood in front of the window, fixating his eyes on the street below. The room was quiet except for the ticking of the grandfather clock. Then he turned to me.

"You'll be back in a year then?"

I nodded and began to grin. "I don't see why not. I've got the best of both worlds. A job's waiting for me in Canada and as soon as I fill my pocketbook I'll sail back home and get to work here."

"The business is yours, you know," my father said shaking his hand. "There's no other Hertel in our branch of the family. You know you're to take over the business—inherit the property."

"*Jawohl*," I said grinning. "When I come back I promise I'll settle down, run the place, anything you say. And don't you worry about my return fare, *Mutter.* I'll make it back on my own steam."

4. AUF WIEDERSEHEN, REHAU

SO I LEFT REHAU AT the end of July in 1929. As I walked with my family alongside the loaded wagon on the way to the train station, the sheen of gleaming windows, the echo of the horse's hoofs on the cobblestones, the smell in the air of freshly baked bread, impressed upon me that I would be gone for a long time. My arm brushed against my father's jacket, and as I glanced at his quiet, somber face, an uneasy feeling of guilt ran through me. He had always been fair to me, and I knew he had come to depend on me more and more to help him in the business.

He cleared his throat and turned to me. "We'll take care of things here, Paul, don't worry about us. Just see to it that you make it back home next year." Then he leaned in closer and said to me in a whisper. "What about Grete? She coming to see you off?"

"No," I said, shaking my head. "You know how that would have upset *Mutter*." I patted him on the arm. "I want you to know how I appreciate that you never said anything against Grete. I'll never give her up, you know."

Grete and I had spent the previous day walking along the edge of the forest where the air was sweet with the smell of freshly mowed hay. I promised her I'd be back home in a year.

"We'll write to each other," I said. "And when I come back we can get married. My mother will have forgotten everything by then. You wait and see."

She stopped and looked out across the rolling fields, pushing back her shining reddish-brown hair that was blowing across her face. I turned her chin towards me. Tears glittered on her eyelashes.

"Why even talk about marriage?" she said looking down. "It'll never work out, not as long as we live in this town."

"Just promise you'll wait for me," I begged. "Things will be different when I get back." I put my hands on her shoulders and gently blew the hair out of her pale, sad face. "When I return and my mother realizes how serious we are, she'll change her mind, she'll have to. And don't forget my father has said nothing against you."

"But that doesn't mean she couldn't make life miserable for me . . . for us."

The dark forest of spruce lay silent behind us. We sat down in the warm sun, and she rested her head on my shoulder. "Promise you'll wait?" I asked again, pulling at some stalks of grass.

She lifted her head and reached into her pocket. "I have something for you," she said, looking up at me with her soft, tear-filled blue eyes. Then she took my hand and dropped a silver engraved pocket watch into it. On the front was a deer leaping across a meadow. The story has it that someone named our town Rehau when they saw a *Reh*, which means deer, jump across an *Aue*, which means meadow. Engraved on the back in fancy letters were my initials *PJH*. "You'll need it to tell time in Canada," she said blushing.

I squeezed her hand. Yes, she would wait for me, I thought. Then she handed me a photo and with a quick laugh told me it wasn't a very good one.

"You're the best looking girl in the world," I said, smoothing my fingers across the silent, sepia-toned face. Her heavy waves glistened and her eyes looked dark and mysterious. I slipped the picture into my breast pocket. "Don't worry about a thing." I hugged her close to me and felt her soft hair against my cheek. "A year will go fast."

"*Paul, hast gehoert?*" My father nudged my shoulder, drawing me out of my thoughts. "When does the train leave?"

I pulled out my pocket watch. "In fifteen minutes."

My friends, Max, Adam, Arno, and other family friends and relatives had joined us. They were dressed up in their best suits and hats and pushed cake and fruit and sausage into my arms to eat on the trip. When the train pulled in right on time, I shook hands all around, hugged and kissed my family and climbed aboard. I pushed the window down and hung my arms outside. Tears had welled up in my father's eyes and his mouth was pencil straight. My mother looked stern, and her eyes were dark and sad and glistening with tears.

"Wish me luck, *Mutter*. I'll bring you back a fur."

Gusti's porcelain white teeth sparkled and she shouted, "*Denk an mich, Pauli.* Think of me often and write."

"Don't forget us," Jette waved. "And good luck."

As the train pulled out of the station, I looked toward Grete's house hoping she might be waiting for the train to leave so she could wave to me.

Then Gusti began to sing *"Das Wandern ist des Mueller's Lust, das Wandern ist des Mueller's Lust, das Wand-e-r-n!"* She grabbed Jette's and Arno's arms and then everyone began to sing and sway back and forth. It was a big event that someone from our town was leaving for Canada.

"*Aufwiedersehen,*" they all shouted. "Until next year, Pauli, and don't forget to write to us." Their voices were dimmed by the whistle of the train and the heavy chug of the engine and they were quickly left behind in a din of black smoke.

I arrived in Hamburg the next morning with my suitcase and trunk, which was filled with winter clothes, my feather bed, some knives and three guns. I had packed the guns because I figured I might be roughing it somewhere in Northern Canada, though at that point I wasn't even sure where the North was, except that it would be cold and I might have to protect myself against wild animals. I took a taxi from the train station down to the pier, and when I saw the huge harbour and ships and had my first whiff of salt air, a real sense of adventure grabbed hold of me.

The black, murky water lapped and rocked the *S.S. Seidlitz*, a ship that looked like a bathtub, compared to other ships in the harbor. I walked up the gangplank and found a spot at the railing where I could watch the crowds of immigrants milling around the dock. I scanned the crowd watching and hoping for a familiar face, and suddenly a wave of fear and homesickness came over me and

I wondered what I was doing all alone on a ship going off to a land I knew nothing about. Young couples with children were on board, and I couldn't help but wonder what it would have been like to have Grete along on that trip. My feet turned cold, and I felt like walking right back down the gangplank, but I clung firm to the rails knowing full well I couldn't turn back to make a laughing stock of myself. Besides, I was pretty confident I would be able to earn enough money in Canada from the fall harvest and get back home by Christmas to surprise everybody.

There were about six hundred people on board from all over Europe, all of them heading for different destination points in Canada. I probably was the only guy who didn't know for sure where I was headed. Down in steerage we were working class people—butchers and bakers, miners and masons, carpenters, factory workers, blacksmiths, and even a chimney sweep. The first couple of days out I tried to talk to so many different people that my throat went hoarse, even though I did most of the talking with my hands. I even talked to some Germans whose dialect was so different from my own that I had trouble understanding them.

By nightfall of the second day, the last point of land disappeared and I could hardly believe the huge waves that just kept on rolling, one after the other, hour after hour. Our little two-ton Tessie bobbed up and down on those waves like a cork. By the next morning I was so seasick I didn't care about anything anymore.

But twelve days later and ten pounds lighter, when I finally set foot in Halifax, Nova Scotia, I felt truly free for the first time in my life. My misgivings about leaving home had vanished, and I knew I had taken the best road. But I also knew that every move I made from there on out would be of my own accord, and if things went cockeyed, I'd have to take all the blame. In one way, I felt like I had been cut out of the herd and freed up to do what I wanted to do, yet I didn't even know where I was headed. It was an uneasy feeling, and I wished I would've had a relative or known somebody I could visit, or at least have had some destination in mind.

We were pushed here and pushed there and we all looked pretty tired and bedraggled standing in line waiting to get through Immigration. Kids were crying and porters were yelling in a language I couldn't understand. I kept checking that I had my passport and the special papers that would allow me to work. Finally my passport was stamped, my papers were checked and I was asked questions I couldn't answer. Then I was hustled onto a Canadian Pacific train along with a mix of other immigrants and shipped off to Winnipeg.

Somebody had pointed Winnipeg out to me on a map hanging on the wall of the Immigration building, and when my hand spanned from Nova Scotia to Manitoba, which was about fifteen hundred miles to the West, I didn't think it could be too far. I knew that Canada was about three thousand miles from coast to coast, but growing up in a small country like Germany, where I got around mostly on foot or bicycle, made it tough for me to visualize what real space and distance were.

So, there I was on my way to a city I'd never heard of, in a new country I knew nothing about, but my feet were itchy and I was ready to face the unknown.

5. APPLE PICKING IN THE OKANAGAN

WE WERE ON THAT TRAIN for four days, chugging forever through wild-looking forests and around quiet, desolate lakes, bypassing all the major cities. I guess the authorities didn't want immigrants melting into the streets and alleys of Montreal or Toronto as they had more than enough foreigners to contend with. We stopped at a few small towns, but one place that stood out in my mind was a flag-station, a small building beside the tracks way out in nowhere about half a day out of Winnipeg.

Some guys were standing around in high-heeled boots and leather chaps with cowboy hats pushed back on their heads. They were leaning against the building. Some were rolling smokes. I was on my feet and pushed the window down because here were some real cowboys right in front of my eyes. But something didn't seem right. They had black eyes, dark skin and long, black hair. Then I realized they were Indians. I was a little confused that Indians could be cowboys, because that's not the way it was in the stories I had read. I guess there were a few things Karl May didn't know, including the fact that the first cowboys actually had been Indians.

When we finally arrived in Winnipeg, everybody was herded out of the train like cattle. There were several fellows on board who had connections to go to British Columbia on the next train leaving several hours later, including my new friend Freddie Gerdes who was going to live with his aunt and uncle in Winfield, a small settlement in the Okanagan Valley. Freddie was a tall, lanky young man about eighteen with an easy smile and a thick crop of wavy, blond hair. Those of us without connections were handed a ticket to move on to different farms around Winnipeg to help with the harvesting. Well, I stood there feeling like I'd been transplanted to the backside of the moon. A quagmire of tracks went every which direction. A hot wind blustered up swirls of dust, and the sun burned into my face like an iron.

I made up my mind right then and there that I wasn't going to stick around Winnipeg, harvesting or not, and I was prepared to catch the first boat back to Europe from the Pacific Coast, provided I could get that far. The only way an immigrant could get beyond Winnipeg and to the coast, however, was to have some connection for a job, or better yet, relatives, though I didn't know that at the time. All I knew was that I had to do some fast talking if I wanted to get on the next train out of there.

I took my stamped papers and ticket back to the authorities and shook my head pointing to the train and the westerly direction, saying, "No, no, *nicht bleiben. West, nach Westen gehen.*" At first they couldn't understand me, but I finally got across to them what I wanted to do. One of them could speak a little broken German. He shook his head and waved his hairy arms. "You have relatives in the West? *Ein Onkel* or *Tante* maybe? *Brauche* relative. You understand?" His fleshy face dripped with sweat.

Fortunately for me, I had a connection—my friend Freddie. "*Ja, mein Onkel in British Columbia,*" I burst out.

"If you have an uncle in B.C., then show me a letter of proof. *Brief, verstehen Sie? Ich brauche Brief.*"

It didn't take me a second to figure out what they needed. "*Moment*, please." I found Freddie and asked him if he had a letter from his uncle that I could borrow. His eyes lit up and he pulled a crinkled piece of paper out of his pocket. "*Jawohl*," he said grinning. "Lots of luck."

Nobody could read German at Immigration, so when I gave them the letter and told them it was from my uncle in Winfield, they just nodded and stamped my papers, saying it would cost $18.75 for the train fare, which was a reduced rate for immigrants. When we pulled out of the station, I had seven dollars left in my pocket, but that didn't worry me at all because money had never meant much to me and ran through my fingers like sand anyway. Freddie and I had become pretty good friends by then and were darn glad for each other's company on the train. As it was, he didn't have a nickel to rub between his fingers either. But we could eat fairly cheap. A bowl of soup cost two bits and we could get scrambled eggs and toast or a stack of hotcakes for fifty cents with all the coffee we wanted to drink.

As we crossed the miles and miles of wheat fields and burnt prairie grass, the rhythmic clicking of the train wheels lulled me to sleep. When I awoke half a day later, the landscape was unchanged. Strange names like Swift Current, Medicine Hat, Moose Jaw flew past my eyes. The days of endless prairie and rolling swells of dry hills and gullies began to worry me. I was beginning to find out how big a country Canada really was, but there wasn't much in it. I kept looking for trees and mountains, but the only things that punctuated the landscape were tall grain elevators. The endless swirling dust, shimmering heat, and flat sky bigger than the ocean made me think that maybe I should have stayed in Winnipeg, but Freddie assured me that his uncle had told him all about B.C. and that it would be different. When the train finally pulled out of Lethbridge, Alberta, and we could see the black line of the foothills of the Rocky Mountains, my spirits began to rise.

The flatland soon became brown grassy hills. The higher we climbed, the more enthusiastic I felt. Suddenly the Rockies were in front of us, stretching north and south at the edge of the plains, a line of deep purple cloud-scratching peaks still tipped with snow.

As we wound our way through the Crows Nest Pass and plunged downward into the green and golden valleys of British Columbia, I think that was about as close as I ever came to riding a roller coaster. It was a different world from the prairie. Turquoise rivers swirled through black canyons and lakes looked like uncut jewels. Forests vanished into a sea of green and black. Practically around every bend we saw bighorn sheep, and high up in the alpine world of cliffs and rocks we spotted Rocky Mountain goats. Before we reached the Okanagan Valley, we had seen bear, moose, deer and elk. We were both overwhelmed by the scenery and I couldn't have dreamed it would be that spectacular.

But once we got into the Interior of B.C., the landscape changed from lush dark-green forests to straw-colored, rolling hills spotted with pine. Dry shrubs and yellowed grass grew in patches in the bare landscape, and when we got off in Winfield, four days after we left Winnipeg, I again wondered about the trade-off I had made. There we stood in front of a deserted station house. A dry, dusty road led off into the brown hills and the only sound we heard was the chirping of crickets. The air smelled thick and pungent, and the hot sun beat down on our heads. We couldn't go very far with our trunks, so we took off our shirts and found a shady spot beside the building. There wasn't much we could do but hope that someone would come along so we could ask directions and maybe get a ride.

"*Scheisse, ist es aber warm, und kein Wasser,*" Freddie said, wiping the back of his hand across his bloodshot eyes.

"This heat is worse than Winnipeg," I said. "There must be water somewhere and I'm so hungry I could eat a horse."

Finally, after what seemed like hours, a Model-T Ford came chugging along in a cloud of dust. We quickly put on our shirts and ran over to the road. An old Englishman in a broad-brimmed hat hollered something to us over the roar of the motor.

"We no speak English," I said, shaking my head.

He climbed down, leaving the motor running. His face was darkly tanned and cracked into wrinkles when he grinned and introduced himself. He checked the tags on Freddie's baggage, and nodding his head, jerked his thumb toward the rumble seat. We loaded up and climbed aboard.

He drove us to Munson's Sawmill, which was about five miles from the flag-station. Freddie's aunt and uncle, the Knolls, lived in a shack close by. It was exciting for them to have a nephew arrive from Germany, and though I was unexpected, they welcomed me as part of the family. Mrs. Knoll sat us down at the table and gave us some good stew and biscuits without even asking if we were hungry. Their place had only two rooms, so they put me up with the Klinkes, their daughter and son-in-law. Both families had been in the country about three years, and as work was only seasonal, nobody had enough money for anything but the bare necessities. They used apple boxes for furniture, and had put some old bedsprings on blocks of wood. Their way of life was quite a novelty for me, but they were warm, generous people and made us feel right at home.

Mr. Knoll found Freddie a job at the sawmill which paid thirty-five cents an hour and I managed to find work falling timber with an Indian by the name of Tobee. Things weren't quite like I'd expected, and though I had no idea what was in store for me, in my wildest dreams I would never have imagined sawing down trees with an Indian. I never figured that an Indian and a white man could work together, or that Indians even did that kind of work. Tobee was tall and wiry, and had sharp, black eyes; but every time I talked to him, his face lit up in a wide, slow grin. We couldn't understand a darn thing we said to each other so we talked in sign language.

He taught me a few things about birds and animals. He'd hear a harsh, low pitched cry and flex his muscles. "Blue jay. Him powerful bird." Or if he'd hear a whistled wheeooo, he'd cock his head and say, "Gray jay." Occasionally, we'd spot a yellow-bellied sapsucker and hear its distinctive tap, tap, tap. When I first spotted a golden eagle, I couldn't believe its six-foot wingspan. I only learned later that Indians believe that birds and animals have spiritual powers, that blue jays are heroes to the Interior tribes and the eagle is a messenger who can fly back and forth from the spirit world.

One day, Tobee showed me some huge footprints on a trail after it had rained. "Cougar," he said. "Big cat." He spread his arms out wide. I bent down and stretched my hand across the muddy imprint, feeling the hair raise on my arms. I learned about the coyote from Tobee, too. When I first heard their yapping, ending in a long, wailing high-pitched howl, shivers went down my spine.

"Good and bad animal," he gestured with his big hands, making first a happy face, then a mean one. "Coyote great power." He told me about the Indian coyote myths, but all I could understand was that the coyote was darned clever. Sometimes he'd change people into animals and punish them, other times he'd save people and help them, at least that's how I saw it.

I no longer thought about catching the next boat home, mainly because my pockets were empty, but I did begin to think about other options the country might have to offer. Falling trees wasn't exactly the sort of work I'd been looking for, though it did put food on the table for me. I was fairly confident I could always find work in a butcher shop, but I was looking for something more challenging and adventuresome.

As soon as I found time, I wrote home to my family and told them about my new friends, what a beautiful country Canada was, and that I was making some good money falling trees. And naturally I wrote to my sweetheart. Every night I would pull Grete's picture out of my shirt pocket and set it in front of me. Gazing at her beautiful eyes would put me in such a melancholy, woeful mood, that sometimes I felt sorry I ever left the Old Country. I always tempered my letters to her, not wanting to embarrass her about my feelings for her, though I always wrote that I missed her twenty-four hours of every single day. In that first letter I wrote to her I told her all about my new experiences, but I didn't want to admit I was earning peanuts and couldn't see any way of making enough money for a return fare in the near future.

I worked with Tobee for about a month, but one day our cross-cut saw broke, which gave me a good opportunity to move on. All my wages were used up for room and board and a pair of shoes. With empty pockets and no job in sight, what possibility did I have to save a few dollars?

But the apple picking season was in full swing in the Okanagan Valley, and I soon found work with the same Englishman who had picked us up that first day in Winfield. He owned a big fruit farm, in the area and my job was to move apple boxes under the trees for the pickers. Rows of apple trees stretched out across the field as far as I could see. They were hung full with ripe-red fruit. The orchard had well over a thousand apple trees of different varieties, and thousands of boxes were picked and trucked to packing houses and exported all over the world. The pickers were mostly women and girls from neighbouring towns, and got paid seven cents a box. If you were fast, you could make about five bucks a day. I was paid hourly at thirty-five cents. Conditions for fruit farming were perfect in the Okanagan Valley with cold winters and hot summers and plenty of water for irrigation from lakes and streams in the surrounding mountains.

The foreman explained to me what I was supposed to do. He pointed, kicked at the boxes, lifted his chin, raised his eyebrows. I nodded and couldn't understand too much of what he said, but shook his hand and got a head start early the next morning before the pickers arrived.

The job was easy enough. All I had to do was put apple boxes under those trees that were to be picked in the next couple of days. Around noon, the old Englishman strutted up to me, his long legs like stove pipes, and yanked off his hat. He began to yell, sending spit in every direction. He shook his head, flung out his arms, repeating the words apple boxes and trees, until he finally got through to me that I had moved hundreds of boxes under the wrong trees. It took me the rest of the day to move the boxes where they belonged.

I think he felt sorry that he had flown off the handle like that because the next day he came up to me with a couple of ears of corn, all buttered and salted. At first I thought he was making a joke, taking me for a fool, because in the Old Country we only fed corn to pigs. I pointed to myself and raised my eyebrows. He nodded and bit into one of the ears himself. Not wanting to insult him, I bit into the terrible, sweet butter-yellow kernels. My jaw went slack, but I grinned at him and picked at my teeth and the next chance I had I tossed the cob into the bushes.

What really tasted like a million bucks, though, were the fresh apple pies the Englishman's missus baked. The Germans make a good apple cake and a delicious strudle, but her pies were special.

The apple picking season was short, so my job lasted less than a month, but Mr. Knoll found work for me at the Circle J Ranch in Westwold, which was a small settlement north of Winfield that lay between Vernon and Kamloops. Of course, when he told me I'd be working on a ranch I was pretty excited as it sounded more like the sort of adventure I was seeking and meant I'd be getting into the heart of the real Wild West. The pay was only $15 a month with room and board, but I think I would've worked for free just to have an opportunity to experience that kind of a life.

6. CIRCLE J RANCH

THE SMALL FARMING COMMUNITY of Westwold lay in a fertile valley, which had a good source of irrigation from the Salmon River. I arrived on foot at the Circle J Ranch, looking like the greenhorn I was, with a suitcase in my hand. My trunk with guns and feather bed was back at the station. The place looked deserted, but just as I was about to go up to the main house, Mr. Bulman, the owner of the ranch, came driving up in a dilapidated old car with the top folded down and two big collies sitting in the back. He was a big man with a cigar sticking out of his mouth, and when he stepped down he gave me a hearty welcome.

He had immigrated from England at age eighteen in the late 1800s, and arrived in the Okanagan Valley flat broke. He started out as a cowhand and when he later became a successful rancher he never hesitated in helping out immigrants or drifters who needed work or a good meal. His ranch land covered about 45,000 acres, which included a grass-run outfit called the Willow Ranch closer to Kamloops. The headquarters in Westwold produced mostly hay and was used as winter quarters for their cattle. He was also a horse trader, buying bunches of young unbroken horses to match up into teams. He gave me a job as a ranch hand, cutting firewood, fixing fences, hauling water, and helping an Irishman look after the piggery.

The foreman put me up in a log bunkhouse with the Irishman and four cowpunchers who were staying on over the winter. The room was large and drafty, and the double-decked bunks, fastened to the wall, were made of rough boards with straw mattresses thrown on top. A bench stood next to the door with a water bucket and a wash basin. A wood stove stood in the center of the room, and above it hung a wooden rack that we used for drying clothes. When we sat around of long winter evenings, the smell of drying socks, sweat, and cigarette smoke made the air so thick it could gag a horse.

By late October the thermometer dropped way below freezing and when the snow began to fly, the cowhands would ride out before daylight and sometimes be gone for days checking on the cattle to make sure they had enough hay when they could no longer rustle their feed.

When the mercury hit forty below and there was a sharp wind blowing, the place got so cold and drafty that we took turns throwing cordwood into the stove all night long. In the morning we would have to break the ice in the water bucket. It was cold all right, but my thick feather bed kept me good and warm. When the weather was clear and the air nice and dry, I'd hang it on a nail on the outside wall of the bunkhouse to give it a good airing, just like my mother used to do when she would hang the quilts out the windows. That's about as close to a good cleaning as it ever got.

Even though life on the ranch was different from anything I had ever experienced, and I was kept busy from morning to night with all the chores around the place, there were times I felt so homesick I could hardly eat. My thoughts would turn to the warm *Sonne* and I'd picture Gusti playing her accordion, singing in her deep, mellow voice. My mouth watered at the thought of freshly grilled bratwurst tucked inside a crispy roll, or potato dumplings and red cabbage soaked in thick, brown gravy. But I sure couldn't complain about our food as there was enough of it. We had plenty of hotcakes, fried potatoes, bacon, beans, sow belly, prunes and biscuits. A good-natured Chinese cook kept the stove in the cookhouse burning day and night and had the meals on the table like clockwork.

During that time I really began to pick up on my English. I made use of the long evenings, reading whatever material was on hand, straining my eyes under the light of the coal oil lamp which hung from the ceiling. Mouse-eaten *Field & Stream* magazines, *Star Weeklys*, and battered westerns were always available, but I started out simple by reading the funnies and the *Eaton's Catalogue*. The men played poker every night and were good company, and someone was always telling jokes or some story about mad bulls or man-eating pigs. I laughed right along with them, never quite understanding everything they said.

One night this one guy was rolling some cigarettes, and the fellow next to him bumped him on the shoulder. "Hey, you know there was camels right here in Westwold?"

The guy licked the cigarette paper and without looking up said, "Quit bullshittin' me, Mac."

"I'm not bullshittin' you. I tell you there was camels here when the place was known as Grand Prairie. You can ask my old man. He grew up here."

He finished rolling his cigarette. "Well, if you ask me, I prefer Chesterfields myself."

All the guys started to laugh except for Mac and me. "It ain't bullshit. They was used as pack animals durin' the gold rush days."

Of course, I was a pretty good target for jokes, and they'd try to pull my leg whenever they could. One time one of the guys offered me some snuff. "Here, try some, Paul." I dipped my fingers into the little round can, gave the snoose a smell, popped it into my mouth and swallowed it. Well, you could have heard them laugh all the way to the North Pole. I got sick as a dog, and you better believe that was the last time I ever tried the stuff.

Then they would go on about Grete. They had seen the picture of her, and when they saw what a beautiful girl she was they never quit with the questions.

"What's she like, Paul? When's she comin'? You dream about her at night, Paul? Does she have a sister?"

As time passed, I had no trouble understanding them, but my vocabulary still wasn't too good, and the worst of it was that I couldn't speak well enough to tell my own stories, and you know how I liked to gab. I would have liked to tell them more about the Old Country and some of the pranks I pulled as a kid, but I knew I'd never get the stories straight. As kids we used to make all kinds of trouble, especially for the Catholic priest in our town. One time we found him asleep and tied his shoelaces together; another time we exchanged the holy water for unholy water. Harmless pranks, on the whole, but if you got caught, you got the beating of your life with a stick.

It was the beginning of November when we first heard about the stock market crash. Remember, that was 1929. At first, because I knew that stock meant cattle, I thought it had something to do with the ranch, but when I saw the newspaper headlines and the guys explained to me about Wall Street collapsing, and even though that didn't make sense to me either, I finally figured out the seriousness of the picture. I didn't know anything about the stock market or pay much attention to politics, and at the time it didn't seem to matter to us anyway because we had nothing to lose, living from day to day as it was, but the Hungry Thirties that were to follow would affect all of us in one way or another. The good times of the Twenties for Canada were over, and by the spring of 1930, the cattle market would go to hell as well, which had a massive impact on Joe Bulman's ranch. It also meant, of course, that any prosperity that Germany had begun to experience would also come to a halt because it meant the end of foreign capital.

Around the end of November a letter arrived for me, forwarded from Winfield. My heart jumped right into my throat, but when I didn't recognize the handwriting, I felt a real let down. Grete had a beautiful, graceful writing style, and my parents wrote in the old German, but the letter wasn't from either of them. Then I saw it was from Arno, my old friend in Rehau, and I tore open the letter. Any mail you got being so far away from home meant a heck of a lot to a guy. Arno naturally wanted to know all about Canada, so I wrote to him right away and told him about the conditions, the different jobs I had since arriving in B.C., how cold it was, and about life on the ranch in general.

By Christmas time, all of us were a little homesick. I wasn't the only one. We sat around the stove stoking the fire, playing cards, exchanging Christmas stories. One of the guys just sat and played one Christmas carol after another on his mouth organ. I think by then I must have worn out the initials on my pocket watch because I would rub it between my fingers until they burned, or pull it out of my pocket and spin it around on the chain. If one of the guys received a card or letter he would pass it around with a grin on his face, feeling pretty happy that he wasn't forgotten. On mail day, which was twice weekly, I'd always look for a letter, the one thing that kept me going. Although I was living out my dream, it didn't mean I was happy all the time, but I never expected to feel as lonely as I sometimes did. Finally, just the week before Christmas, a card and parcel arrived from my family. My mother, much to my surprise, had sent me a warm, plaid shirt and some long, woollen underwear. But my excitement didn't last for long, and when the days passed and I didn't hear from my girl, I felt so miserable I began to think about heading for the Coast and catching a freighter back to Europe. Even the guys didn't tease me anymore about Grete. We tried to make the best of it on Christmas. We had hung some pine boughs on the wall and drank whiskey to keep ourselves warm. But all I could think about was home and Grete. I could remember in perfect detail the long walk she and I had taken the winter before across the snow-covered fields the day after Christmas. We didn't have a care in the world and had no idea what the future held.

We had come to the edge of the forest where tracks of birds and small animals zigzagged back and forth. Tufts of brown grass poked up through the snow, and the early afternoon sun hung low on the horizon. Grete squinted her eyes toward the yellow winter glow on the distant mountains.

"It's so peaceful here," she said, tugging at the ends of a blue knitted scarf. "The farmers have a good life living out here in the country away from the noise and dirty, slushy snow of the town." Her cheeks and nose were red from the cold.

"I don't know. They work hard and winter is the only time they can rest a little," I said. "Would you ever want to live somewhere else? Leave Rehau?"

She shrugged her shoulders and stepped over to a tree heavy with snow. She poked at the frosty crystals. "I don't know about leaving, but I'd like to see Berlin someday. Mathilde and I have talked about it. I would never live there, though. You've said yourself it's a big, noisy city. And someday I'd like to go to Italy ... where it's warm. Ride on one of those gondolas in Venice.

Wouldn't you?" Her eyes flashed and her skin glowed golden from the sun. "At least I could leave if I really wanted to."

She grabbed the snow-weighted branch and began to laugh. "You're the one that's stuck here," and with a yank, a heavy sheet of snow piled down on both of us.

I caught hold of her, but she broke free and ran through the icy shade of the trees, I not far behind. Her laughter rang out in the crisp, clear air like the song of a nightingale. Suddenly she stopped and turned toward me. A white mist formed around her face.

"You look like a snow princess," I said catching my breath, wanting to tell her she was the only girl for me, but the words wouldn't come. I stroked some snow from her cheek and touched a red-brown curl that hung loosely on her forehead. She smiled and bit her lips.

"I'll race you to the lookout," she suddenly exclaimed, and gave my shoulder a push. She was gone like quicksilver.

But back to that first lonely Christmas in Canada. On Christmas Eve, after we were relaxed from a few warm swigs of whiskey and talk was easy, I began to tell them in my broken English how we celebrated Christmas back in the Old Country, how special a celebration it was.

I told them how my parents made us stay in our rooms on Christmas Eve while they prepared the tree. It was never set up before then. After what seemed like hours, my father called us into the living room. We crept down the cold, dark hallway and he would be waiting outside the living room doorway, which was draped with a heavy curtain to keep out the draft.

"Close your eyes and don't forget to make a wish," he'd say with a smile, and with a sweep of his arm would draw the curtain aside. The first thing I saw was the round glow of the flickering candles that lit up the Christmas tree. The room was warm and filled with the scent of fresh spruce. We rushed to the tree to find fluted decorations overflowing with nuts and candy.

When it came time to open presents, we had to recite a poem for each gift we opened. My sisters always got dolls and I would get a hand-carved train or a knitted sweater. Then Jette would sit down at the piano and play "O Come Little Children," "Silent Night," or "O Tannenbaum," all our favourite songs. On Christmas day friends and relatives came to visit. The table was set with salami from our sausage kitchen, cheese and rolls, cookies and plenty of *Stollen*, the German Christmas cake that is a sweet bread filled with almonds, raisins and marzipan. And we always had *Lebkuchen*, spice cookies from Nuremberg, even oranges from Italy. Christmas was always special. My mother would lean back in her chair and sing along with us, tapping her fingers on the armrest. The rooms would be filled with the smell of a roasting goose.

"When we were kids we ne'er 'ad enough to eat," the dark-haired Irishman said in his accent that was always hard for me to understand. "Christmas came and we were lucky to get knitted socks. My family was 'appy when I left for Canada . . . meant one less mouth to feed."

Christmas Day at the ranch was quite a feast, with all the roast pork, heaps of mashed potatoes and gravy, and all the apple pie we could eat. We actually didn't have much time to celebrate, though, because on the ranch one day was like the next. Firewood had to be chopped and the livestock taken care of.

Finally in January the first letter from Grete arrived. It wasn't a mushy kind of love letter, if that's what you might have expected. That wasn't her nature, but I read between every line.

November 1, 1929
My dear Paul,

Your letter didn't reach me until late October. I didn't know mail from Canada takes so long, but how happy I was to hear you had safely arrived and that you are well. I thought Canada was all ice and snow and you wouldn't have hot, dry weather. And then you write you are chopping down trees with an Indian! Can that really be true? You are so far away. Your life seems so primitive.

Mathilde and I still go to Cafe Horn every week. Most everyone from the club meets there and ask about you. They talk about the

Socialists and the Marxists and how they hate each other and how the Nazis are beginning to make headway in the elections. I don't understand any of it. When you hear Hitler on the radio he raves and shouts like a maniac.

Carnival time will soon be here and you'll miss all the Fasching balls, but I don't think it will be as much fun this year. No one can dance the Charleston like you. Do you go to dances? Mathilde and I are going to the Kristkindle market in Nuremberg next month. I'm going to buy Lebkuchen and a music box for my mother.

I see your friend Arno sometimes. He goes to Hof quite often to visit his girlfriend. He said he wrote to you. Got the address from your parents. You are so far away from this drab, gray world. It's already icy cold and we've had our first dusting of snow. Mother hoards the coal like gold. She never lets me forget about the Great War and how we never had enough to eat. I was so young when my father was shot. All I can remember is that he had a mustache and was so tall I could walk between his legs. One time we walked down the street and for only a second he let go of my hand, but oh how I cried. I thought I had lost him.

If I put my nose to the window I can see the apple trees behind the house in the orchard. Except for a few mottled red leaves they are otherwise bare. I know you won't be back in time to see the branches white with snowy blossoms, but maybe when the apples have turned red? Or the Harvest Ball? That's a long year away.

  Much love,
  Your Grete

That letter really lifted my spirits, and when I went about my work whistling, the crew knew exactly why.

"C'mon, Paul, what'd she write? Did she say she dreams about you?"

When I wrote to Grete, I didn't beat around the bush about telling her I thought of her every second of the day. And it was true. She was always on my mind, always floating around inside my head. But when I told her a year would pass quickly, and I would be dancing with her at the Harvest Ball, even I doubted my words.

Sure, I knew my old man would have sent money in a minute, but I wanted to prove to my parents that I could earn my own way home, not owe them anything. And in my heart, as much as I missed my girl, I wanted to see more of the country and discover some real wilderness.

My twentieth birthday on the 25th of February passed without fanfare and I barely noticed how one day ran into the next.

Not long after, Mr. Bulman came into the bunkhouse one night with a cigar in his mouth and hat in his hand. He grabbed a chair, spun it around and straddled it backwards.

"Weather's been damned rough this winter," he said in his English accent. "We been losing a few too many 'ead."

"We been out every day, boss," one of the cowhands said. "Can't be helped when cattle go missing and tracks are covered with snow."

Mr. Bulman turned his old felt hat round and round in his hand. "Yeah, I know 'ow it is. Maybe it doesn't matter much. Maybe better than giving the meat away. I guess I don't 'ave to tell you fellows what's been 'appenin' to the price of beef. How the market's down. And nothin' can be done about it."

He took his cigar out of his mouth and tapped it on the back of the chair. Then he looked at me.

"A neighbor of mine talked to me today, Paul. Asked if I could spare a hand to 'elp him out over the lambing season. He'll pay you $15 a month and board. You can start right away."

There wasn't much I could say, so I found myself living on a farm a few miles away, all alone in a drafty, cold bunkhouse. Sometimes I had to sit up all night to keep the heater going, and while my back almost froze, my front would get scorched. When lambing started I was awake all night keeping careful watch over the ewes for fear if any lambs were born they would freeze to death. I had to take the newborns into the bunkhouse and lay them down beside the heater to keep them warm until they dried. Once they were dry, I could return them to their mothers. Aside from looking after the sheep, I chopped firewood everyday and hauled water to the house.

Then about the end of March, I had the surprise of my life. I was chopping wood and the farmer hollered over to me. "Hey, Paul. Some bohunks lookin' for you."

I figured my friend Freddie had come up from Winfield looking for work. I swung the axe into a block of wood and went over to the main house. Well, I couldn't believe my eyes. The blood drained from my face, and for a few seconds I wasn't sure of my bearings, thinking for a moment I was back in a dream I had just a couple of nights before.

I was sitting in the Sonne with my old friends drinking beer. Gusti was singing and playing the accordion and my mother went from guest to guest talking and laughing. Her eyes were shining and her black hair was neatly tucked into a roll around her head. The door opened and in walked Grete. Her blue eyes lit up when my mother walked over to her and took her by the arm. "Ja Madla, komm rein," she said softly. "Come in and make yourself comfortable." Grete sat down beside me and I couldn't believe the change in my mother. When my friends and I pounded our mugs of beer on the table and shouted "Zum Wohl," I was jarred out of my dream with the banging of the wind on the barn door.

So when I came to my senses and saw that my friends really were in front of me, I was speechless. There stood Arno Michael with his big, flashing white teeth and long horseshoe face. Behind him was Max Troger, the big blond guy with the crooked nose who had apprenticed with us back home, and Max Hopperdietzel, a short, heavy-jawed, skinny young guy who had gone to school with Grete, though I never knew him from back home.

I let out one long yahoo and all hell broke loose. We threw our arms around each other, and I could feel the tears run hot down my cheeks. Then Hopperdietzel's Max handed me a letter from my girl and I felt like a whole person again.

But after the initial euphoria faded, I had to seriously think about finding jobs for my friends. Since I was the only one who could speak a workable English, I put myself in charge of finding work for them. Fortunately, spring was just around the corner. The snow had begun to melt and from one day to the next you could see tufts of green filling in the patches of gray-brown hills. I found work for Big and Little Max on a local farm, where they actually ended up staying for several years. They never got paid much, but always earned their keep. We nicknamed Max Troger Big Max because he was a head taller than the rest of us. Max Hopper-dietzel—he later dropped the Dietzel—was my height and skinny as a matchstick, so we named him Little Max, solving the problem of the two Maxes. I didn't think much at the time about how young Little Max was, but he was only seventeen then, even younger than Grete. He couldn't even grow a beard yet.

I probably could have stayed on at the farm, but it was too darned lonely for me working there by myself, especially after my friends had arrived. I knew the Circle J would probably need extra hands come haying time, but that was three or four months down the road, and I had no intention of waiting around that long with no guarantees. Besides, Arno and I were looking for a little more excitement. When I heard there might be jobs at a sawmill up around Shuswap Lake, which was somewhere north of us, we figured we had nothing to lose. So we packed our bedding and left one morning for what we hoped would be greener pastures.

7. 1924 HUDSON

WE HITCHED A RIDE UP TO the junction of Monte Creek and set out on foot to Shuswap Lake, hoping to pick up another ride along the way. Train tracks ran along the side of the road, but there was no train and no other traffic, and after walking about fifteen miles, Arno's feet began to get sore and blistered.

"*Nur ein paar Kilometer?*" he asked. His thick, black eyebrows looked like they were about to slide right off his face. "Only a few miles you said? Where's this Schuschwap anyway?"

I stopped and set down my heavy pack, wiping the sweat off my forehead with my sleeve. I pulled a dog-eared map out of my pack and unfolded it. "The lake's not far," I said to Arno. "Take a look for yourself."

"Looking at the map isn't going to help my shredded feet," he said, throwing down his pack.

"Heh, take it easy. We'll spend the night right here, if you want. Don't worry, you'll toughen up soon enough."

Arno lay down rested his head on his pack without another word. About ten minutes later a train came rumbling down the tracks. It was chugging north in a cloud of smoke, and about twenty men were sitting on top of the boxcars. We waved and hollered, and it was just our luck that a few hundred yards down the tracks the train pulled up to a siding. Arno and I swung our packs on our backs and started running.

When the train pulled out fifteen minutes later, we were sitting on top of the car with the rest of the guys. At first we kept a good firm grip on the metal rods, but once we got into the rhythm of the swaying boxcars we slumped into a comfortable position and pushed our faces into the cool wind. Nobody seemed to worry around that neck of the woods when guys hitched rides on the freight, but as the Depression deepened, and as I was later to learn, the railroad police, or yard bulls, closely guarded the freight yards and division points, and you had to become clever at catching a freight and avoiding pot-shots and billy clubs.

We got off at Chase, a village on Little Shuswap Lake, and asked at the local sawmill if they could use a couple of strong men, but there was nothing for us. We soon found out, however, that the swarms of mosquitoes were so thick that if you tried to talk you had them for a meal. They stuck to your face, were in your ears and down your shirt so, we were just as glad to get out of there.

A couple of days later back, in Westwold, I was in the general store making inquiries about jobs when in walked my friend Freddie and his uncle, Mr. Knoll. It was good to see them again. The whole family had moved north since there wasn't any more work for them around Winfield. The men had just started working at the Ponderosa Pine, a sawmill at Monte Lake a few miles northwest of Westwold.

"We have plenty to do," Freddie said, "and I think they could use extra help."

Arno and I hightailed it over there and got hired on right away. We were offered $2.50 a day and had to work ten hours a day, six days a week, and that didn't include room and board. We were put up in a bunk house and started work first thing the next morning.

To supplement our diets, we did a lot of fishing in the lake and went hunting up in the hills around the area. Meat was expensive and we had big appetites.

One Sunday morning Freddie, Tom Klinke, who was Mr. Knoll's son-in-law, and myself left before daylight to see if we could scare up a nice buck. It was my first serious hunting trip. We climbed a ridge and were heading down into a gully through a grove of jackpine when I noticed a movement out of the corner of my eye. I turned my head and saw what looked like an overturned stump with roots dangling in the air. I nudged Tom and whispered.

"Over there. What's that look like to you? You think it could be a mule deer?"

He turned his head and snickered. "If that's a mule deer, I'm a jackass."

I wasn't any sureshot Annie Oakley, and if it was a buck, I didn't want to chance missing it.

"I saw it move," I said, eyeing Tom. "C'mon, you said you're a good shot."

He tightened his lips and shook his head, but slowly lifted his rifle and fired. The stump went straight up in the air and hightailed it through the trees. We took off after it, following the sound of cracking twigs and rustling leaves. Then all went quiet. Not too many steps further along we found the deer lying on its side, a deer almost as big as a moose with a pair of horns wider than my outstretched arms. It was a beautiful animal with brownish-gray fur and I couldn't believe the size of it.

"I told you it wasn't no mule deer. That's an elk," Tom said proudly.

It dressed out at about four hundred pounds which gave us plenty of good roasts and steaks for a couple of weeks.

The summer of '30 wore on and we had built up a lot of strength in our backs and arms from pulling lumber off the green chain. Arno and I saved our money and talked about buying a car. We didn't need one, and the thought of owning a car in those days was a pretty far-fetched idea, but we kept talking about it.

By then I was quite certain I wouldn't return home in the fall, and for that matter, probably not for another year. My friends had no intention of returning to the Old Country any too soon either, and I have to say that since they had arrived I no longer suffered the loneliness and homesickness I felt those first few months away. I still longed for my girl, and that was one dull ache in my heart I learned to live with, but at least I didn't miss my family or life in the *Sonne* as much by then. Being with my friends and working six days a week just didn't leave any time to get lonely.

I got to know one of the fellows at the mill pretty good and when he found out I was game for adventure, he told me about fur trapping up north. The more he talked the more I listened. He described the Babine and Stuart Lakes where the Indians trapped and fished, where fur was prime and where plenty of land was still available for pre-empting.

"But it's wild country," he said. "The Babine can be a bugger when the wind gets blowing and the temperature drops to twenty below in the daytime, just like that," and he gave his fingers a snap.

That was all the fuel I needed. I located the area on the map and was quite excited to see how far north the Babine Lake was situated. I only had to convince Arno to come with me as I wasn't too eager to head into unknown country on my own.

"We get free land," I said to Arno, "just think about that. And there are plenty of trees to build a log cabin right where you stake the claim. All we have to do is file some papers and we get 160 acres each. It'll be ours," I told him.

"What's the hitch? Nothing's for free," he said, lifting his heavy eyebrows.

"Like I said. We build a cabin on it. The only hitch is that we'd have to live on the land for a couple of years or so and make a few improvements."

"And that's it? The land would be ours?"

"That's it," I said, throwing up my hands.

"But aren't you planning to go back home in a year?"

"Who knows what's going to happen in a year, but to get back home I'll need money, and if I can earn it trapping, it's worth a shot. One thing for sure, I want to earn my own way home. I don't want to owe my parents anything, especially my mother."

"So how do we get where we're going with all our gear?"

I grinned and gave Arno a wink. "Well, I suppose we could travel light and hop a freight, but if we pool our money we can buy that car we've been talking about."

Arno folded his arms and ran his tongue across his lips.

"So what do you think?" I asked.

A grin finally crossed his face. "You know, that's the best idea you've had in a long time."

So we hopped a freight to Vernon and bought ourselves a sleek, black 1924 Hudson for $125. Next we went to the courthouse to pay the two dollars for a driver's licence.

"What if they want us to drive for them?" Arno asked. "*Donnerwetter*, we've never had a steering wheel between our hands."

"Don't worry, I'll handle it."

I went up to the window trying to figure out what I would say if we were asked to drive.

"Just sign here please, gentlemen," the man said, passing us a slip of paper. We scratched out our names and stood there expecting to at least answer some questions.

"That does it," he said, sticking a pencil behind his ear. "Keep your hands on the wheel and your eyes on the road and you'll do just fine."

When we got back to the car lot feeling darned smug, the salesman showed us how to crank up the Hudson and demonstrated how to use the gearshift and its various pedals.

"You do the driving," Arno said, jumping in.

I rubbed my hands together, sitting myself down behind the steering wheel. The salesman reached in and pushed the gearshift into low.

"Now as you press down on the pedal, just remember to let the clutch out nice and easy, eh," he said. "And when you get a little speed up don't forget to shift into the next gear, like I told you. You'll figure it out."

At first I didn't try to shift any gears. Keeping the car on the road was challenge enough, but once we were out of town and after some chugging and grinding, we found high gear and cruised along about twenty miles an hour on our way back to Monte Lake, feeling like a couple of millionaires.

The next weekend we drove down to the farm in Westwold to visit Big and Little Max and show off our fancy buggy. They were quite impressed, and Big Max wanted to drive it in the worst way. After we showed him how to operate the car, he put his rough, square hands on the wheel, pressed his foot down on the clutch, and after a few good solid jerks got the car rolling. He managed to grind it into second okay, but when he tried to shift into third, he kept looking down to figure out what he was doing wrong. Suddenly he was off the road and heading straight for the ditch. I grabbed the steering wheel, hollering at him to let go, but he was so strong and had such a firm grip that the car went out of control and rammed into a solid fence post.

Arno jumped out and began to yell. "*Was a bloede Sau.* Look what you've done now . . . broken the front wheel!" I thought he would collar Max and drag him right out of the car. "I hope you know you're going to pay for this!"

Big Max jumped out of the car and threw up his arms. His face was burning red and with his crooked nose he looked mad as a bull. "The bloody fence got in the way."

"Bloody fence, my eye," shouted Arno. "*So ein derber Hund.*"

It took some doing to cool them down, and we ended up sharing the repair costs, but Arno and I agreed we would never let anyone else drive it again.

By the end of August, we had saved a few more dollars and decided it was high time to leave for the North to get a head start on winter. Big and Little Max weren't at all interested in joining us. They preferred to stay on at the farm where they had a roof over their heads and could at least work over the winter for their room and board.

I wrote to Grete and told her of our change in plans but assured her that the following year, in the fall of '31, we would be picking apples together, and I would be back home and spinning her around the dance floor before she could say Jack Robinson.

I didn't exactly put it in those words, but I wanted her to know she was my girl and that I wouldn't let her down. How could I exactly explain to her that the prospect of homesteading and heading into an unknown wilderness was like a slow burning fever in my system, and once I returned to the Old Country my days of adventure would be over and I would have to get serious about running the business with my father.

We loaded up the car with our bedding, my guns and knives, extra Stanfields, a tent, and a few cooking utensils. My feet were itching and we were raring to go. We said so long to the boys and told them to send along any mail that came for us when we had a forwarding address.

8. North to Burns Lake

OUR FIRST STOP WAS KAMLOOPS, a fair-sized town with clean, wide streets and old, established buildings. We decided to stock up on more staples and camping supplies, not knowing what lay ahead of us. A light rain was falling and dust rolled off the black hood of the car in beads. The sharp, pungent smell of wild sage hung in the air. We went into the general store where a broad-shouldered fellow in a plaid shirt greeted us. A wad of snuff was tucked in his cheek.

When we told him our plans, he raised his eyebrows and said in a deep, raspy voice, "Homesteading, eh. Well, you've come to the right place." He pushed aside some tools and gave the counter a swipe with his hand. "We've got about everything you need right here."

I glanced around at the shelves of canned goods, bolts of cloth, jars of candy, guns, axes, barrels of beans and rice, and traps of all sizes.

"How about a sack of rolled oats to start with," I said, "and we need a couple of those packboards you have hanging there." I always did the talking for Arno and me because he still had trouble with his English.

"Anything you want," he said, heaving a sack of oats on the counter. "Gold miners, fur traders, ranchers, you name 'em, been comin' through here for a hundred years now." Then he unhooked the packboards.

"These are the best in the business. How about a good sharp axe for you, too," he said, laying a single-bitted axe on the counter. He slid his thumb across the blade. "Sharp, always keep it nice'n sharp, eh, or it's useless. And you need a hatchet?" He turned back to the wall. "Indians used to call this place Cumloops. Means meetin' o' the waters. Right here's where the North and South Thompson got married."

I picked up the axe and tested the blade.

"You'll take the axe then? And you'll be needin' a shovel too—to dig a hole for the outhouse," and he let out a booming laugh.

Arno looked at me and I quickly translated. We followed the big man's large round eyes from one end of the store to the other with a grin on our faces.

"You'll wanna take along one of these here knock-down sheet-iron stoves," he continued, and began to set it up for us. "Here, she works like this. You'll have trouble finding one farther north." He dismantled it again and snapped his suspenders. "Oh, and you'll want to take a chim'ey pipe too. You got a tea kettle and a frying pan, I hope?"

Then he grabbed a coil of rope and a roll of wire and threw them on the counter. "Haywire's pure gold to the homesteader," he said, smacking his lips, " . . . and some first aid stuff." He pulled a flat round tin off the shelf, spun it into the air and banged it down on the counter. "Some good salve always comes in handy."

"One other thing we'll be needing is candles and an extra supply of matches," I said.

He put a handful of candles on the counter, rolling them into some newspaper. "Be sure you wax the matches to keep 'em watertight. By the way, you need guns and knives? And a whetstone?"

"Nope, we've got all that," I said, shaking my head. Then I pointed to some snowshoes hanging on the wall. "You think we'll be needing them?" I asked.

"Damn rights," he said, taking down two pair and laying them on the counter. He picked one up and fingered the webbing. "You'll want to keep the rawhide well greased, eh. I'll even throw you in some good bear grease for old times' sake. Good for your boots, too, or frying up some fresh bannock."

"Gee whiz, thanks. That should about do it," I said.

"Say, how about traps? I have the best supply in the country right here."

"We'd better wait and see about traps." I didn't know anything about trapping and began to get worried about the precious few dollars we had left.

The proprietor arranged the goods on the counter and tallied everything up. "Oh, by the way, I've got some good warm mackinaws, nice plaid ones just come in. They're extra warm."

I held up my hands and shook my head, pulling some dollars out of my pocket. "Thanks, but that should about cover everything we need."

We loaded all our provisions into the back of the car and Arno got behind the wheel.

"Next place is Cache Creek," I said, spreading the map across my legs. "Just follow the road."

The roads in the Interior were just gravel and potholes in those days. The sun was out again and dark rain clouds hung over the golden brown of the hills. Shadows from the clouds slipped and drifted across the wide open spaces. I had taken a real liking to the long, dry days of summer and the clean, sharp air. Even the winters, cold as they were, had more than enough days of bright sunlight. I leaned back into the seat and pulled Grete's picture out of my pocket.

"You think she'd come to Canada?" Arno asked, jerking his head towards the picture.

"Just keep your eye on the road, Shorty."

"You still going to marry her?"

"Darn rights I am. If I can swing it, I should be back home by next year."

"You don't think she would ever come over here?"

I shook my head, smoothing out the ragged edges of the picture. "Don't think she'd like it much. The country is pretty rough, and I doubt she's ever had dirt under her fingernails. Her mother does everything for her, you know, and she can't even cook."

"So what kind of a wife is she going to make if she can't cook?" Arno asked.

"She'll learn, just like we did. You know, hunger makes the best cook. And she's a master seamstress. I suppose Marga's the best cook in the world." That was Arno's girl in Hof, back in the Old Country.

"She *is* a good cook," Arno said, giving me a flash of his teeth, "and she's got the most beautiful legs in the world too."

I smoothed my hand across the picture, smiling to myself.

"Marga's some dancer," Arno continued, "but I couldn't see her dancing around in this country either. No, she wouldn't like it here and she'd never leave her family."

I focused on the black and white photo, on Grete's soft, warm eyes with their glints of white. "I wonder what Grete will think when she finds out we bought a car."

Arno pounded his hand on the steering wheel and laughed. "That we're rich, that we've struck a gold mine."

I thought of Charlie Chaplin's movie, *The Gold Rush*. The gold rush days were over, and even the heyday of fur trapping was past, but at least there was still a market for furs out there. I put the picture away and was thinking about Charlie Chaplin's crazy pranks, Grete's dancing legs, when all of a sudden I began to bounce around in my seat as if I were on a runaway train.

"*Donnerwetter*," I shouted, jerking myself up straight. "What the heck's going on?"

Arno's arms looked like pinwheels flying around trying to get a grip on the spinning steering wheel. Fence posts, barbed wire, tall grass flew past my head. Every time the car bumped into another post it lurched and bounced, and my head banged on the ceiling.

"Gas . . . take your foot off the gas, *du Sau Bayer, du*," I shouted.

When the car finally jolted to a stop, we both sat for a minute in a stupor. My door was jammed so Arno pulled me out on his side. I held my aching head wondering what our next move would be when I looked up and saw a farmer running toward us across the field hollering and cursing with a pitchfork in his hand.

"Crank her up, Arno. Fast!"

I jumped into the driver's seat and rattled the choke. The old Hudson turned over like a charm. I slammed the car into reverse,

Arno jumped onto the running board, and we pulled out of there hell bent for leather. Arno started to laugh. His black hair hung down in his eyes and he shouted in through the window.

"Bloody fence posts got in the way."

But several hundred yards down the road we had a blowout and I was forced to pull over to the side.

"He's still coming after us," shouted Arno.

I turned around and the farmer was gaining on us fast, shaking his pitch fork up and down. I jumped out of the car and put my hands up.

"You goddamn sons of bums," he puffed and yelled, poking the pitchfork at us. "Don't think you're gonna get away this!"

We spent the next day fixing his fence, but by then he had cooled off and showed us how to repair our flat tire and bang some of the dents out of the fender and the side of the car. When we were ready to leave he brought us a package.

"Now I appreciate you stayin' and fixin' that fence, eh, but keep that fandangled rattletrap on the road and look out for yourselves. And, ah, here's a couple of loaves of bread and some fresh-churned butter from my missus. Now, you two get going."

This time I got behind the wheel. "I don't want anymore detours," I said to Arno.

We drove through dry, parched countryside that looked as barren as an Arizona landscape, though in those days I didn't know anything about Arizona. Cactus, tumbleweed and sagebrush grew out of the rocky, red and yellow-coloured cliffs and hills. When we got to Cache Creek we stopped to cool off the radiator. The town wasn't more than a dot on the map with the Bonaparte River running through the center of it, but it was suitably named. Some robbers who had held up a pack train carrying gold, hid their "cache" right there along the creek where they were hiding out so they could make a clean getaway. But they all died in a shoot-out and the gold's still there waiting to be found. That's how the story was told to us.

From there we turned north onto the Cariboo Highway which had been the old wagon trail for the Cariboo-bound gold miners in the late 1800s. Long stretches of road were still under construction in those days and the curves were only single lane. Our old buggy rattled and danced over that washboard of a road until we thought our teeth would jar loose. The further north we drove, the more we learned about how that part of the country had been overrun by gold miners just a half century before. We drove through 70 Mile House, 93 Mile House, and when we finally got to 100 Mile House, which had a huge barn and a cafe on one side of the road and an inn on the other, we set up our tent for the night.

Early the next morning, we went into the cafe and filled up on coffee and hotcakes. The woman who ran the cafe wore pants and cowboy boots. She was tall with an angular face, and had thick, wiry gray hair. She filled us in with a little history, and how the roadhouses had been built up for travellers on their way to Barkerville and the lure of gold.

"You remember the gold rush?" I asked her.

"Sure do," she nodded, pouring us more coffee. "I was just knee high to a grasshopper then, but miners used to come through here in their wagons, headed for Barkerville. Not much there now—never been there myself. But my Mum always told me Barkerville was as classy as San Francisco with its hurdy-gurdy dancing girls. And gold nuggets as big as your fist, the miners found."

I'd always known about the gold strikes in Alaska and the Yukon, had even heard of the gold rush days in California, but really had no idea that the gold rush fever had made such a mark in B.C.

I checked the map and our next destination was Williams Lake. I guess we weren't much past Lac la Hache, a beautiful turquoise-green lake dotted with white caps, when the hood of the car began to rattle and steam. We stopped at the next creek and I grabbed a pot and poured water into the radiator. Before we could ask any questions the radiator practically blew itself sky high with water pouring out like a geyser. We let it cool and then I told Arno to get into the car to try to start it. I wound the crank. "Choke it easy," I yelled.

The car coughed and sputtered and I heaved and cranked, but it wouldn't turn over. It looked like we were stuck so we pitched our tent off the side of the road. The next morning I hitched a ride up to Williams Lake, the next big town, which was about seventy miles north. It was a major shipping point for cattle and it looked like a cow town, too, with its false store fronts and board sidewalks.

"Sounds like you cracked the head all right," the mechanic said after I explained to him what happened. "The parts will take a couple of weeks. Have to ship to Vancouver for 'em."

I hitchhiked back to the car and Arno, and we didn't mind at all that we had to wait for the parts. The leaves of the poplar and aspen had turned to yellow and gold and the days were still quite warm. We camped by a small lake and spent our time fishing and hiking around in the hills. We shot ducks and bush chickens and roasted them over an open fire and always made up a batch of bannock with our meals, which was a mixture of flour, salt and water fried in lots of grease. At night the coyotes yipped and wailed in the distance and I was reminded of Tobee, my Indian friend who had taught me so much about the different birds and animals. Whiskey jacks hung around the camp looking out for scraps with their sharp, beady eyes, and we never tired of watching the fish hawks circle round and round above the lake. Suddenly one would drop like a stone and in a spray of water lift off with a fish between his talons.

Two weeks later I again headed north to Williams Lake. The mechanic drove me back to repair the car which left Arno and me with only eighteen dollars. By the time we rolled out of there, black clouds had moved in and the rain was coming down in sheets. In places the ruts became so deep we nearly sunk out of sight in mud. Fortunately, cars were built with a high clearance in those days, so at least we didn't lose our oil pan. The country on the way to Quesnel was fairly open and rolling, and the settlement itself, set on the Fraser, had served as a jumping-off point for gold-rush traffic to Barkerville. But further north toward Prince George dense forest of fir and spruce, poplars and alders took over the landscape.

Prince George is situated on the junction of the Nechako and Fraser River, down on flatlands, and at one time had been a major fur-trading post. Probably not more than a thousand people lived there when we went through.

From there we turned west to Burns Lake, another one hundred and fifty miles, where we planned to find out about setting up a homestead. We camped out every night except when the rain was so heavy we slept in the car. The going was slow, but our good old Hudson finally pulled us through.

Burns Lake was a friendly little village with no more than two hundred fifty people. It lay nestled between the lake and rolling wooded hills and was a supply point for homesteaders, trappers and prospectors. We drove along the crooked, dog-legged street and pulled up in front of the Omineca Hotel for a bite to eat.

We ordered stew and biscuits, carefully counting out our money. We got to talking to Barney Mulvaney, a short, stocky Irishman in his early fifties, who was one of the original settlers in the village. I asked him if he knew anything about homesteading on Babine Lake where we could do some trapping.

He looked us up and down and began to grin. "I know a bit about it," he said. "Did some trappin' myself in days past. But why don't you think about settlin' right here? I dabble in real estate and know of some choice land." Then he turned his head and lifted his finger. "Hey, George, bring these thirsty young men a beer. "

"We don't have any cash to spare," I said. "We're after some government land. Heard there might be some available around Babine Lake."

"So, you want to be homesteaders," he said, pulling a pencil out of his shirt pocket. "Down at the eastern tip o' the Babine you'll find some land that's already been staked out." He drew a map on a napkin. "Some nice flat country down there. Beaver Creek's on the north side."

Then he gave us a sharp look. "You had any experience a'tall out in the wilderness?"

I nodded. "Oh, yeah, I've had a little."

He pointed to the Taltapin Lake. "That's where you'll wanna head for. You can follow an old wagon road . . . pick it up on the other side of town," and he gave his head a jerk. "Mind you, now, that's rough country, especially o'er the winter. There's a few small Indian settlements down 'round the end of the lake, but the Indians won't bother you. When you get started with trappin' they can show you a few tricks, knowing the habits of the animals like they do. There's a good bounty on wolves, too. Enough of 'em around down there."

Arno's eyes got wide as saucers when he heard the mention of wolves and Indians. Those two words were nearly the same in German.

"You sure you know what we're getting ourselves in for?" he asked me in German in a low voice.

"How many wolves?" I asked Mr. Mulvaney.

"Hard to say. Sometimes they run in packs of ten, sometimes thirty. But you don't 'ave to worry. They're afraid of humans and stick to themselves. Now if you're gonna trap, and you'll be able to lay out lines perfectly legal on your homestead, be sure to talk to the Indians about it. And a fur buyer comes through here regular o'er the winter, so you can bring in furs anytime."

"What do furs go for?" I asked.

"Oh, not for what they used to. Maybe you'll get a buck or two for muskrat, and a good mink pelt might bring you in twenty dollars, same with marten. Ten years back fur buyers from New York was bidding seventy-five dollars a pelt for marten. We had fifty thousand bucks worth hangin' from the ceiling right here in the hotel in the Snake Room. I owned the hotel back then—that's when my wife was still alive—God rest her soul. She ran the place single-handed and could she belt out a song." He leaned back in his chair and crossed his arms.

I took a drink of beer and wiped my mouth. "My parents run a hotel and restaurant back in Germany," I said to him with some pride.

"Oh, yeah? Then you know all about the business."

I nodded. "If we make enough money on furs over the winter, I'm going home next year to take the place over."

"I thought you had in mind to homestead for a couple of years."

"Yeah, well, that's what we have in mind, but you see I have a girl in the Old Country . . . and right now there's not much work around that pays a decent wage, so we want to try our hand at trapping, see what it's like."

"Well, you'll need a little luck o' the Irish to earn a decent wage from trappin' these days. During the war years a prime silver fox pelt paid up to five hundred dollars, a black fox a thousand. But they been trapped out." He stretched out his legs and crossed his ankles. "Just like the beaver. Game Department's prohibited trappin' of 'em in most of the province, eh. Marten are rare too and sneaky little sons-a-guns." He ran his fingers through his red hair streaked with gray and crinkled his eyes.

"By the way, it would be a good idea to take along some extra tobacco for trade with the Indians. They make the best moccasins in the country, and if you take my word for it, that's about the best thing to wear for snowshoein' and to keep your feet warm."

We thanked Mr. Mulvaney for all his advice and headed over to Brunells' General Store.

"We'll get a real taste of wilderness if that Irishman knows what he's talking about," I said to Arno on our way up the street. "Sounds just like what we're looking for."

"I'm not sure we know *what* we're looking for," Arno said, throwing me a dark look.

We pushed open the door and a middle-aged man with a long, stubbly face was warming his hands over a pot-bellied stove. "Well, some new folk in town," he said, rubbing his hands together. "What can I do for you young fellers?"

I told him our plans, looking around the well-stocked store. "Mr. Mulvaney down at the hotel told us to pick up some tobacco along for trade with the Indians."

"You'll need a darn sight more than tobacco. What are you plannin' to live on?"

"We're stocked up pretty good, but I guess we could use a slab of bacon and a sack of rice yet."

"That's all you'll be needin?"

"And the tobacco. We don't have much money left."

"Your word is as good as cash around here. I can always extend you a little credit if you're staying the winter."

I thanked him for his offer and was surprised that he'd give us credit just like that. He put our supplies on the counter. "Look here," he said. "The Indian women always like these here red kerchiefs."

I took the lid off a candy jar and reached in for a handful of jellybeans. "Say, are there many wolves around that area?" I asked, tossing a candy into my mouth.

"Sure, there are some, some winters more than others," he said, lifting a few kerchiefs off the peg. "Their bark's worse'n their bite, but if you're on a trappin' run or out overnight I'd keep a fire going to keep 'em at bay, which you'll have to do anyways to keep from freezin' to death."

A shiver ran down my spine, and I mentally checked through our belongings to make sure we had extra socks and extra thick, woollen Stanfields.

"But everybody's got his own opinion on the matter of wolves," he continued. "No hunger equals that of a wolf, it's said. You plannin' to hike in?"

"We got a car. Down the street there," I said, pointing out the window.

He hitched up his overalls and craned his neck. "You aimin' to head out in that gas-eating wagon? How far you expect to get?" He shook his head and began to count up the goods, muttering to himself. "That'll be $6.35."

I counted out the money from the few dollars we had left.

"No country out there for some darned jalopy that'll just freeze up on you," Mr. Brunell continued. "That's a rough road into Taltapin. Ruts, that's all. Ain't no country for motor cars, I tell you. Useless in winter."

I shrugged my shoulders. "We'll see how far we can get. Any white men out there by the way?" I asked.

"Yep. Old George Nelson. Comes in regular for supplies. He's got a few head of cattle and a team of Clydes. He'll always be able to give you some good advice if you're needin' it. And there's an old miner at Taltapin. He's still there as far as I know but gets out before winter really sets in." Then he looked us over from head to foot and gave us a smirk. "Might be a good idea to drain the radiator when you get as far as you're goin', eh."

I thanked him for his help, relieved to hear we wouldn't be the only white men at the lake. We left for the post office where Arno and I wrote a few lines to our girl friends and family, letting them know they could write to us c/o General Delivery, Burns Lake. We also let Big and Little Max know where they could get in touch with us. The next morning we turned right onto the old wagon road, the last leg of our trip.

9. HOMESTEADING ON BABINE LAKE

TOWERING MINARETS OF PERFECTLY formed spruce and lodgepole pine crowded the side of the narrow dirt road. We bounced along the well-worn ruts for about ten miles till our old Hudson began to cough and sputter. The stink of gasoline flooded the car as I worked the choke, trying to keep the motor running. Arno jumped out to give it an extra push, but after a short stretch the car shuddered and sagged into a stall.

"Try cranking it," I yelled to him, sticking my head out the window. I pulled the choke, but the motor wouldn't turn over and the stink of gasoline only got worse. We lifted the hood and acted like we knew something about cars, wiggling this wire and lifting that hose.

"Maybe if we let the engine cool." I suggested.

Twenty minutes later we tried again, but the old buggy still wouldn't cooperate.

"What are we going to do?" Arno asked. "We can't just leave it on the side of the road to rot. We put all our money into that car."

"If you ask me, I don't think it's worth putting another cent into, especially when our pockets are empty."

We lifted the hood of the car again and poked around in the motor.

"We'll give it another try," I said to Arno.

Nothing worked, so we decided to push the car off the road, leaving the stove and heavier supplies behind to pick up later. We drained the radiator and packed up everything we could carry.

We were really loaded down, and I can tell you that we sure were plenty relieved when we finally arrived at the miner's shack at Taltapin some twenty miles later. The sweat was pouring off our faces and when I dropped my heavy pack to the ground, I felt like I was floating.

A big man in overalls with a full beard ducked out from under the door frame. "Holy mackerel, a couple of krauts," he said, when he heard our introduction. "Come in, come on right in."

The cabin was dark and smoky inside, but when the smell of rabbit stew hit our nostrils, the old miner didn't have to tell us twice to sit down and make ourselves at home. I told him about our plans for pre-empting land down at the end of Babine Lake.

"You know your way 'round the bush?" he asked, dishing up the stew. "All that's down there is Indians and a white man."

"We're willing to tough it out," I said, dipping a piece of hot bannock into the stew.

"One thing you'll wanna know goin' in," he warned, tugging at his beard and shaking his head, "there's no room for mistakes up here. The Babine is one helluva big lake, over a hundred miles long. Storms whip up mighty fast and six foot waves come outta nowhere. And you got any idea how cold it can get?"

"If it's like the southern Interior," I said, rubbing my hands together, "it'll get cold enough to numb the toes a little."

"Try forty below on the turn of a dime," he chuckled. "It can be a real bugger at times."

Arno and I weren't strangers to cold, so I didn't let that worry me any. He put us up for the night on the extra bunks in his cabin, and after a breakfast of our first real sourdough hotcakes, we packed up and made our way another few miles to the lake and headed east along the shore. Our heavy tramping spooked flocks of ducks, and with a loud quacking and a whirring of wings they'd be airborne. We stopped at the edge of the lake for a drink of cold, refreshing water. The blue-gray lake was a good two miles wide at that point, and a low mountain, about a thousand feet in elevation, rose out of the opposite shore like a sleeping giant. Patches of red and yellow poplars and birch stood out like flags against the rocky bluffs and dark virgin forest. Thick gray-trunked cottonwoods, willows and alders grew in abundance along the edge of the lake. We were about to load up again when a strange wail, a haunting sound, almost like the cry of a woman, echoed across the water.

"You hear that?" Arno asked. "Sounds like a kid crying or a sick animal?"

"It's loons, I think." I cupped my hands over my mouth imitating a hooee-ooo in a long shivering cry. "Tobee, the Indian I worked with down in Winfield told me about 'em." An answering call came floating back across the water.

About noon an Indian came along in a flat-bottomed boat with an outboard motor. We began to get a little leery when he cut the engine and eased the boat to shore, but we quickly relaxed when he waved to us and grinned, showing straight yellowed teeth with a gap on one side.

"*Hadi, Hadi,*" he said, jumping out of the boat and pulling it up onto the gravel. He was about thirty years old and had pitch black eyes and shoulder-length black hair. He wore a thick, plaid flannel shirt and heavy woollen pants

We shook hands and introduced ourselves. His name was Joe Hansen and he spoke in a low, clipped voice. "You go to end of lake?"

I was happy that he spoke English, and when I explained to him our intentions, he told us to throw our packs into the boat and he would take us. Arno and I couldn't believe how lucky we were to get a ride on a power boat. When Joe revved up his engine and sped across the rough, black water, we tightened our jackets and pulled our woollen toques down over our ears. The chilly wind blew Joe's long black hair around his angular, copper-coloured face.

The end of the lake was squared off like a bathtub, and as we came into the shallow bay, Joe pointed to some bluffs.

"My cabin over there," he said. A thin wisp of blue smoke came out of the roof pipe. Several other cabins were set back from the lake up on a knoll, and according to Joe about ten Indian families lived there around the lake.

He cut the motor and tipped it up, poling in the last fifty feet to a narrow, wooden wharf. A gray, weathered dugout was tied to the side and bobbed up and down in the water. It was the first time I had seen one.

"That canoe from one tree?" I asked Joe.

He nodded and climbed out of the boat, picking up the end of the rope. "Cottonwood," he said, securing the boat to a post.

"Dugout make goot solid boat, eh, but much work to chop and hollow out tree."

Arno and I heaved our heavy packs onto the wharf and jumped out of the boat. "But how do you get it so wide in the middle?" I asked, spreading my arms.

"Oh," he said grinning. "We put heavy rocks in bottom of hollow boat. Pour boiling water over them. Then wood soft, eh, and easy to shape. Goot boat, but this boat more better. Go faster."

We picked up our packs and walked up a grassy knoll to Joe's log cabin. A huge set of moose horns hung above the door. He lived there with his wife and three kids and they slept right on the floor on deer hides. His wife greeted us with a shy, dark-faced smile and his young children clung to her dress.

The smell of burning wood and thick, sweet smoke drifted up the slope toward us. Several long, open sheds with shake roofs stood next to the lake.

"We dry salmon in sheds," Joe said. "Come, I show you."

The Indians used the sheds year after year. Several were repairing nets, and they greeted us with friendly "Hadis." Skinny dogs ran around barking and snarling, but Joe just raised his finger and gave them a mean look, sending them away with their tails between their legs.

Fish hung from horizontal poles under the roof, and even though a smudge burned underneath, swarms of blowflies had laid their eggs right on the drying fish. Joe pulled out his sheath knife and brushed the flies off a slab of blackened, oily salmon.

"Soon my people come from Stuart Lake to net *stumpahn*," he said, slicing off a chunk of the fish. "Last run of the season."

It was our first taste of raw, smoked salmon and I nodded to Joe as I bit off a piece. My fingers smelled of smoke and grease. Arno took a small bite and rolled his eyes at me.

"Best smoked fish I ever ate," I said to Joe, swallowing hard and licking my fingers

"Salmon goot to us. Feed us all winter when run goot." He tucked his knife away and motioned to us. "Come. We go up there on rocks where you see much land."

We climbed up on a high bluff behind Joe's cabin and looked out over the flats. Slough grass and willows covered the marsh about two miles across the end of the lake. A soft breeze rippled the patches of golden grass and a warmth radiated from the black craggy cliffs behind us.

"George Nelson live way over there," Joe said, pointing to the other side of the flats. "Him only white man down here. Has mebbe twenty head of cattle. We go visit. I take you tomorrow."

I looked west across the shimmering lake. Rays of the afternoon sun broke through luminous pink clouds and danced across the water like torch lights.

"It's like living right next to heaven," I said to Joe, wondering if their notion of heaven was the same as that of the white man.

"*Ah-ah*, yes ... *Loozoo*, very good," He picked up a stick and poked the ground with it. "We on this earth short time, eh," he said, "This most beautiful place to prepare for journey to next life. When weather good ... *whudinzoo.* Life good here."

When Arno and I rolled into our feather beds that night I wasn't in the least tired. An easy wind blew through the trees and I could hear the soft hooting of a night owl.

"Well, Shorty, we've made it, and tomorrow we'll stake us some land. No one back home would believe we can get 160 acres for next to nothing. That's almost more than my old man owns."

"Only if you live in this place for the next three or four years, or whatever it takes. Don't forget that. And then you still have to pay a dollar an acre."

"Well, we're not losing anything by applying, and at least we'll get trapping rights."

Arno rolled over and went to sleep, but I lay there for a long time, thinking over what Joe had said about preparing for the next life and their ideas about Mother and Father Earth. It all made sense to me. I had finally found exactly what I was looking for. I had always loved being out in the woods, but to actually come upon the opportunity to explore the real wilderness, to live like the Indians and among the Indians, was more than I had ever hoped to experience. My life had taken quite a turn and I have to admit that it felt darn peculiar to have come from a civilized Europe to a part of the world still largely untouched by civilization.

I missed my homeland, but I was almost grateful to my mother for the road I had reluctantly taken. I still would have been in the Old Country dreaming about the Wild West if it hadn't been for my troubles back home. My parents had lived in Rehau their whole lives, except for my father when he had served in the First World War, and here I was on the other side of the world.

It would be early morning back home, everyone crawling out of bed. I wondered how my old man was handling the business and if Gusti still ran across the street in her nightgown with a coat thrown over her shoulders to pick up fresh rolls for breakfast. And did Jette still play Beethoven? I pulled out the pocket watch Grete had given me and rubbed my fingers across the smooth face. I squinted in the deep twilight. She'd be on her way to work, walking down the old *Bahnhofstrasse*. She started work punctually at seven every morning and put in a twelve-hour day, six days a week. It was no kind of life, I thought, compared to the freedom we had.

Off in the distance I heard a long, deep howl. I held my breath and leaned on my elbow. Was it wolves or just Indian dogs? The hair began to crawl on my arms and I gave Arno a poke. "You hear that?"

"Huh, huh?" he said, yanking his quilt over his ears. I settled back down and listened with a cocked ear to the night sounds, the distant melodic whistles, the whir of crickets. The smell of grass and earth filled the tent. There I was in the kind of wild country I had been searching for, and it was everything I had expected, no doubt about that, but a vague feeling of homesickness began to gnaw at my insides. I knew it would pass, and it wasn't as if I hadn't spent any time at all in the bush, but lying there in that dark tent, listening to strange sounds with the wind moaning through the trees, made me begin to wonder if we could really stick it out. I had to reassure myself that it was a chance in a million and we could leave anytime. Every day would be an adventure for us. I gave my feather bed one last tuck, and the next thing I knew it was morning and the wind was flapping around our tent.

Joe came by and took us over to George Nelson's cabin. A mix of poplars and pine, dark-pointed fir and blue-green spruce grew up the low ridge along the back edge of the flats. The dried smell of autumn was in the air, and the sound of chirping crickets clicked on and off as we wound our way through thickets of willow, tangled peavine, and fireweed. Flocks of blackbirds skimmed overhead and a hawk floated lazily in the air. We broke out into a clearing and a big German shepherd came charging toward us.

"Quiet down," George yelled, stepping out of the cabin. He was a short, thickset man of about fifty with sharp, blue eyes. "*Hadi*, Joe. Good to see you," he said. "Brought some company along, eh." He looked us over and then his face broke open to a weathered grin. "Well, come on in, fellows. Make yourselves at home."

We pulled out some stools and sat down while George stoked the fire in the stove and added water to the coffee pot. His cabin, about ten by twelve, was surprisingly roomy and comfortably warm. Two small windows faced east and west, and on a corner shelf stood a variety of knickknacks. Yellowed wallpaper with red flowers covered the wall behind his bed, and a striped Hudson's Bay blanket was tucked neatly under the mattress.

"So what brings two Germans to this part of the world?" George asked, unhooking three tin cups from the wall.

"We're looking to make a little money trapping."

George cinched his eyebrows together. "You ever done any?" he asked, pushing aside a can of dried grasses and wildflowers. "Fur prices are rock bottom from what I hear, and it's a tough way to make a living, even with experience." He poured thin, steaming coffee into the cups and sat down.

"Arno and I are willing to learn."

"We give you hand at it," Joe offered.

"Yeah, we'll be needing it since we don't know a thing about traps or animals," I said, sipping my coffee. "I hear you have a few head of cattle, George."

"Yeah, sure do, but I don't like what's happening to the price of beef either. Nothing's worth a damn since the Crash. But we got in a good supply of hay for the winter anyways, didn't we, Joe," and he slapped him on the shoulder. "Him and his brother always helps me with the haying."

"You know anything about homestead land?" I asked.

"Sure, I can show you some plots," he said, spreading some thick jam onto his biscuit. "C'mon, help yourselves. Yeah, you'll get to know this country real good if you stick around. You'll learn you gotta work hard and run fast just to stay in one place." He laughed and stuffed the whole biscuit into his mouth. "But it's a good place to live nonetheless," he said with bulging cheeks. "C'mon, when you finish your coffee we'll head on out."

We crossed the flats and Joe returned to his cabin.

"You can trust Joe, all right," George said. "He's a good man, but I'll warn you young fellers right now. If you're gonna stick around here and don't want no trouble, no foolin' around with their squaws, and don't give the Indians no whiskey. And there's one more thing. Don't try to pull no wool over their eyes."

"Wool over their eyes?" I asked. There still was a lot of English jargon I didn't understand.

"You know, don't try to cheat 'em, eh."

The land that was suitable for settlement had been surveyed into 160 acre plots before the turn of the century. Iron pegs had been driven into the ground at each corner of a plot, and on top of the pegs were spruce posts with the lot numbers carved into them. Most of the posts had rotted away, but we had a compass along and were able to distinguish which lot was which.

Arno and I located our plots along Beaver Creek and then searched around for a good building site, having been reassured by George that we wouldn't have a problem with the homestead applications. We chose a sheltered spot about half a mile from the lake where a natural meadow sloped down to the creek. Plenty of lodgepole pine grew in the area, which was perfect for building a cabin, as the trees were about ten inches in diameter and grew straight up like a needle.

We didn't know much about construction, but with George's tools and his advice, we got right to work. Maybe the best advice he gave us was to get busy and dig a deep hole for an outhouse before the ground froze too hard. That done, we measured a twelve-by-fourteen-foot area and dug down a couple of feet after George told us it would keep the cabin warmer. Then we axed down the trees and limbed and debarked them with an adze, a tool like an axe with its arched blade turned perpendicular to the handle. It didn't take us more than a couple of days to fell enough logs and cut them to size.

After we rolled the first logs into place, George showed us how to notch the corners by cutting a deep square into the ends of the logs. "Then all you do is saddle a log over the cuts and up you go, one after the other," he said, swinging his axe. "Logs're a little green, but they'll hafta do. And no use makin' the walls too high either. Less space to heat and you fellers ain't none too tall anyways."

In two days we had the walls up and a window cut out. George suggested thick cellophane for a window instead of glass, which we could buy in Burns Lake our next trip out. Next we cut poles for rafters and split spruce shakes for the roof. When we nailed on the last shake, we filled gunnysacks with moss and dragged them back to the cabin, chinking the damp moss between the logs, under the rafters and around the door frame to make the inside of the cabin as airtight as possible. To keep the moss from falling out after it dried, we cut and peeled thin willow poles and nailed them over the moss between the logs. All we needed was our stove and chimney pipe and the rest of our supplies.

George was getting ready to drive some cattle to town to ship them to market, so we said we'd help him out and at the same time mail our homestead applications to Prince Rupert and apply for our trapping licences.

Before we left I asked Joe about trapping and what we might need for the winter. He also ran a line, but he knew of an old Indian who he thought might be willing to help us out. He took us across the lake to talk to Sam who lived in a small cabin with his family. His hair was thick and yellow-white and hung to his shoulders. A wad of tobacco was stuck in his brown cheek.

"You mebbe buy *chaco*, buy trap for muskrat and mink. No need trap for lynx or fox," he said, shaking his head and looking up at us from his stooped position. "Use snare, eh. Mebbe you want use my line. It run right 'long Sutherland down there end of lake. We can mek deal. My bones get old, eh," he said, pushing the tobacco under his lower lip.

We didn't know a darn thing about trapping, and after Arno and I talked it over, we figured if the old Indian was willing to let us use his line on a percentage basis that was jim-dandy with us. "Sure, we'll make a deal. And you can show us the trapline?"

"Goot deal, goot deal," he said, grinning.

So in Burns Lake we stocked up on traps, and bought a few extra supplies, taking advantage of credit because we didn't have so much as a wooden nickel left to our name by then.

George didn't fare too well with his cattle. "Woulda been better off givin' the meat to the Indians," he complained. "I don't know—if the market don't turn around by next summer who's tellin' what's gonna happen."

When we got back to the homestead we finished up the inside of the cabin. We nailed together a couple of rough bunks made of poles and filled sacks with dried marsh grass which we used for mattresses. A few slabs of wood became the door, hinged with old harness straps. We made a table from shakes, used stumps of wood for stools, and set up our sheet-iron stove. A few nails driven into the logs for hanging up clothes and pots and pans and we were done. The cellophane stretched across the window opening was clear as glass.

We felt damned proud of ourselves, considering it was the first log cabin we had ever built. To celebrate, we invited George over for a meal of roast duck. Babine Lake was a flyway for migrating birds, so we had no trouble picking off as many ducks as we needed. After our meal we had some hot rum to settle our stomachs.

"I took my homestead over from Charlie McDonald," George told us, taking a finger-full of tobacco out of his shirt pocket. "He broke his back so couldn't run the place no more."

"Never been married?" I asked him.

He shook his head, carefully sprinkling the tobacco onto the thin cigarette paper. "Nope. Never found me a decent woman. They was always scarce. Any decent woman there was got herself hitched right away." He licked the edge of the paper, spitting out bits of tobacco. "There was a woman once," he said quietly. "She was thin as a willow and sang like a swallow. A school teacher lady. Yep, I thought we about had it all tied up."

Grete's face came into my mind. She would have made a fine school teacher, I thought. But who had a choice in those days to do what you really wanted. You did what your parents decided for you to do. She had been a good student and the teacher's pet, though she never bragged about it. But she did go so far as to say she had never been hit across the fingers with a stick for talking in class, even though the other kids got whacked.

"And then what happened?" I asked.

George struck a match across the bottom of his boot and lit his cigarette. Tobacco smoke drifted up to the ceiling.

"I worked in the bush down on the Coast then, eh, outside of Vancouver. You guys don't smoke a'tall, do you? Well, there was this one weekend. I come to town expecting to take my girl dancin' and she tells me she's getting married. Just like that. Never saw her again. Maybe it was all in my head she was interested in me. I left the Coast after that. Eventually found my way up here."

He puffed on his cigarette, leaning back in the chair. "This is the most peaceful place you'll find in the world. No one to bother you none here."

"And you never worry about getting sick?"

He ran his hand through his thinning, blond hair and laughed. "Huh, only civilization makes you sick."

When he finished his cigarette, he butted it out on the dirt floor. "Well, thanks for the grub boys," he said, standing up and reaching for his jacket. "I'll be on my way now. Holler if you need something."

"What did he say about the school teacher?" Arno asked in German after George left the cabin. Arno still had a hard time understanding English.

"Oh, I think he just took it for granted she'd marry him, but one day when he came to town it was too late."

We didn't have any time to waste because winter was just around the corner, and George warned us to get in a good supply of wood, not to mention meat, if we didn't want to freeze or starve to death. Windfalls were a good source of dry wood, so we hauled them up to the cabin and sawed them into firewood length. We sawed and chopped and stacked until we had several rows of wood several feet high and ten feet long on each side of the cabin, hoping it would hold us until spring. Fish, ducks and bush chickens were plentiful so we didn't have to worry about our next meal, at least not then.

By the third week of September, the band of about forty Indians from Stuart Lake arrived and set up camp. They came every fall when the last of the *stumpahn*, or salmon, were running. Each family set up a tent, and they slept right on the ground on hides of deer or bear. It was quite a feeling to be right there among people who had been living like that for probably thousands of years.

Their brown faces and slanting black eyes gave them a wild look, but they were very friendly and didn't mind at all that Arno and I hung around and watched what they were doing. The rancid smell of smoke and grease and sweat was pretty strong, but it didn't take long for us to get used to it.

The men wore grease-stained deerskin jackets or plaid mackinaws and parkas. Some had shoulder-length hair and beards. Some wore toques and others old cowboy hats. The women had thick, black braids that hung down their backs. They wore heavy skirts, or a couple of layers of old dresses. A few of the women carried babies on their backs. And most of the Indians wore ankle-high moosehide moccasins.

The Babine Indians were known for their moccasins, and when Arno and I wanted to do some trading with them, the first thing they asked for was tobacco. "*Daka*? You have *daka*?"

They netted the salmon right from the shore of the lake close to where the fish went up Beaver Creek to spawn. They set the nets out at night and hauled them in first thing in the morning. A rock was tied to one end of the net and a floater on the other, and the nets would float about fifty feet out into the water. The men hauled in the fish and the women prepared them for drying. It was a real spectacle to see all those fish flopping around, mangy dogs yapping like crazy and fighting over the scraps, and the Indians going about their business, talking in their native tongue, which had a clipped, sing-song sound to it.

The women slit the fish down the middle, gutted them, and then poked short willow sticks crosswise into the bright pink flesh to hold them open for drying. Then they hung the fish up on the racks in the drying sheds where they had a smudge burning. With all those fish, the place swarmed with blowflies, and like I'd mentioned earlier, the fly eggs dried up right along with the fish. Each family had to dry about five hundred salmon, which seemed like a lot of fish, but that was part of their winter diet. I guess we could have done the same, but we figured we knew better since salmon wasn't our favourite food, and we thought there would be plenty of game around to keep us going.

A fisheries officer was stationed on the lake for the season, and came around every few days to check that the Indians didn't set their nets too close to the entrance of the creek so that enough salmon could go upstream to spawn. I didn't know anything about spawning and asked the officer what it was all about. He explained how the fish went upstream to lay their eggs, and we were told there would be black bears or grizzlies up the creek feeding on the rotting fish.

"They're on a feedin' frenzy, fattening themselves up for winter hibernation," the officer said. "Up near the headwaters you'll find plenty."

Arno and I gave each other one look and were on our way, following a well trodden bear trail, not knowing what to expect. We each had a gun for protection and hiked in about six miles along Beaver Creek. There was plenty of evidence that bears were around because fish, with chunks bitten out of them, littered the trail along the banks of the creek. Trunks of alder and birch had been scratched by their claws and their tracks sunk deep into the mud.

We didn't even know the difference between black bears and grizzlies. Bears were bears to us. Every now and then we heard a snort or a huff, which stopped us dead in our tracks, but I guess we were too noisy because they were long gone before we got anywhere near them, not to mention they would have picked up our scent.

Even before we got close to the headwaters of the creek, the stench of dying fish hung in the air. The creek was choked with hundreds of salmon digging in the gravel with their torn tails, spawning in water so shallow they could barely swim. Their bodies had turned a deep red and many of the fish lay among the rocks struggling for their last gasps of oxygen. It was hard for us to comprehend such a phenomenon of nature.

By then thousands of birds were heading south. Long, ragged V's of honking Canada geese and dark clouds of quacking ducks filled the sky. It really was a sight to see and the greatest kind of symphony you would ever want to hear. Sometimes a skimming whistle of wings would alert you and you'd look up to see a black line of ducks disappearing over the treeline.

The daytime temperature was close to freezing by then, so it was time for us to lay in a good supply of deer meat as it would be easy to store. The first time we went out hunting and had no luck, we didn't think much of it, but after a couple of weeks without seeing hide nor hair of any deer, we began to get worried.

"They go far away and winter in other valley," Joe said. "We not see much moose either this fall."

If there weren't many moose or deer around that fall, we finally had our chance to see some bears, even if they weren't live ones. You see, the Indians trapped bears, drying the meat for the winter and tanning the hides. So when a couple of Indians invited Arno and me along on one of their trips we felt quite privileged and excited. They used a wire snare line, which they rubbed with brush and spruce needles to kill the human scent, and set it up right along the bear trail. They attached the snare to a heavy spring pole which was weighted down with stones or lashed to a tree. The device was quite complicated and had to be set just right. When the bear came along sniffing the ground, his head would get caught in the noose and immediately lift him partially off the ground, choking him instantly. The Indians set eight traps and when we went back the next morning five black bears had been caught. I was amazed how the whole tribe turned out to help dress the animals and cut up every last bit of meat and carry it back to camp where the women cut the meat into strips and hung it up to dry.

Early in October Old Sam came by and said it was time to prospect the trapping line before the snow got deep. White hair poked out from under his toque and a straggly beard hung from his chin. His trapline ran along Sutherland Creek, and was a forty-mile round trip. At the end of the line was Teakettle Camp where trappers from Fort St. James and Fraser Lake could also spend the night. We made that first trip in just two days because there was no snow to speak of and you could make good time. Sam walked a little bandy-legged but we had to move along pretty good to keep up with him. Sometimes we'd come across fresh wolf tracks or see where a couple of coyotes had crossed in front of us. He showed Arno and me signs of muskrat runways and pointed out their tracks, which crisscrossed back and forth with their dragging tails. He showed us where they built their dens—some in overhanging banks of streams and others in swampy marshlands that were dome-shaped huts of mud, sticks and grass. He set up several traps so he could catch a few and show us how to skin them and stretch the hides.

"But no trap muskrat in fall," he said, shaking his head. "Fur more better in winter, late in winter."

We came across some old beaver cuttings among a grove of poplars. "No good beaver," Sam said, sticking a wad of tobacco under his tongue. "All trap out. Mebbe come back slow."

He picked up mink tracks through thickets of brush, along streams and under roots of trees, sometimes pulling off bits of hair stuck on a root. "Mink, him travel many miles. Like best to eat muskrat." Sam grinned, showing stumps of yellow teeth He spit out a stream of tobacco. "Good mink bring mebbe fifteen dollar."

He moved silently along the creek in his stooped posture then stopped and crouched down, pointing to some fresh tracks. "*Ah-ah Wassay.* Lynx cross here." He pulled some snare twine out of his pack. "You rub good with leaves, eh," he said. "Kill smell." Alongside the trail he quickly pulled together a small shelter of twigs and leaves and tied the catch loop to a spring pole at the opening of the shelter. "Lynx . . . him like look inside. But better you wait for winter," he said, sticking the snare line back into his pack. "Fur thick . . . bring more better price."

On our return trip we had three trapped muskrats. A few precise cuts and Sam peeled off the fur, turning the skin inside out. He hung it up to dry a little before.

What we didn't expect was roasted muskrat for lunch. Sam dropped the crisp, dripping muskrat onto a tin plate.

"Don't cut too deep," he explained jutting out his lip and shaking his head. "Shit inside."

By the end of October the Indians packed up their camp with all the salmon and dried meat and moved back to their main village on Stuart Lake. The bears had gone into hibernation, the birds had flown south, even the chipmunks had vanished. A soft dusting of snow covered the low lying brush and meadows and the nights dipped well below freezing.

About a week later we got an unexpected visitor. It was late in the afternoon when Arno and I decided to try some fishing at the mouth of the Sutherland. The sun had dipped low behind the mountains, setting the lake in deep shadow. Across the flats a black figure approached us. We thought it was one of the Indians from across the lake. When he came closer, he dropped his pack, pulled off his cap and started to wave and shout.

"*Donnerwetter!*" I hollered. "It's Little Max."

Arno pulled off his toque and let it fly into the air. We both took off on a run. Were we ever happy to see him.

"*Menschens'kind*, am I glad to find you guys here," Max exclaimed, sticking out his heavy jaw and shaking his head. "Just took a chance. I've come all the way from Burns Lake today."

"You're nuts. That's over forty miles," I said.

"You must have left way before daylight," Arno added. "You can't make that trip in a day."

"If you start in the moonlight you can make it," Max said. "I've got legs like a packhorse."

"Cripes almighty, but it's good to see you," I said, reaching for his pack. "Come on, you gotta see our fancy place. What the heck brought you up here?"

"No work around the southern Interior until spring, and I guess curiosity got the best of me."

"And where's Big Max? Why didn't he come?"

"Oh, he decided to stay on the farm. Gets his room and board. By the way, what the heck happened to your Hudson? Damn near scared the hell out of me when I saw it there off the side of the road. Was almost afraid to look inside."

Arno and I both laughed. "It conked out on us," I said. "We should have left the heap in Burns Lake or sold it."

So Max settled in with us. Aside from some basic grub, he brought us chocolate bars, whiskey, strawberry jam and had even stopped by the post office in Burns Lake to check the mail for us. He had the approved applications for the homestead and our trapping licences, and there was a letter for Arno and one for me from my sister Gusti, which Max had carried along from Westwold.

As I expected, Gusti wondered when I was coming home and everyone was expecting me by Christmas for sure. Arno quietly read his letter and tucked it into his shirt pocket.

"What's the news from Marga?" I asked.

"Oh, she didn't write much," he said, drumming his fingers on the table. "Her mother's been sick and she's had to do all the extra cooking and shopping. Now her brother is out of work since summer. Plenty of people unemployed back home, too."

I shook my head, feeling pretty let down there was no mail from Grete, and what could I expect, moving around the way we did. But there wasn't much time to mope because we were into trapping season.

Old Sam came around again to take us out on the trapline. We gave him a supply of chewing tobacco which he gladly accepted. Arno and I loaded up our traps, bedding and provisions and followed along behind Sam. There was about a foot of soft, dry snow on the ground and the mercury had settled somewhere just below zero. We set traps along the creek beneath overhanging banks, and when we came to a marsh, Sam pointed out where the muskrats had pushed up mounds of weeds and twigs above the ice.

"Him climb inside from water and eat," he said, testing the crackling ice and easing his way to a mound. He brushed aside the snow and pulled back some twigs, dropping the baited trap into the house. Then he carefully covered the top and marked it with a stick. He pointed out mink tracks and we set some No. 2 traps along their feeding trails in sheltered places under trees, behind windfalls and large roots, blending the traps carefully into the underbrush.

Finally about three o'clock Sam looked up in the sky. The sun had disappeared and a fine frost sifted in the air. "We mek camp now," he said rubbing his hands. "Dark soon."

We found a well protected area among some spruce trees where we could bed down for the night. The snow was dry and soft and had drifted in under the trees. We first collected a good supply of dry windfalls for firewood, enough to last the long night, and some pitch shavings and small twigs to get a good fire started. It always amazed me how quickly the wood burned, but the cold, dry weather sucked every bit of moisture out of it up there in the North.

Sam took his hatchet and chopped a pile of fresh spruce branches. He lay the spines of the boughs against the snow and arranged them like feathers. "Good bett, eh, soft and dry. You sleep goot," he said, throwing his moose hide on top. He handed me the hatchet. "Now you mek bett."

So we chopped and arranged a thick pile of boughs and threw down our feather beds, which we topped with a canvas tarp. We melted down snow for tea water and heated up beans to eat along with our smoked salmon and bannock. Sam really wasn't much of a talker, but as we sat there on a log, thick quilts around our backs, I kept prying him with questions

"Wait," he said, smacking his lips. "I tell you story about my people. They live long time here, eh." He paused and took a drink of hot tea. "Long time before white man come."

"Where did your people come from, Sam?" I asked.

He looked at us and wrinkled his forehead. "Babine people . . . *ah-ah*," he said nodding his head and pulling his jacket tight together. "From loon, mebbe. But I hear mebbe Mosquito Flats. There people see squirrel cross bridge where salmon run. Everyone afraid when squirrel do that. They think great sickness come from sky god. Then many people run away to Babine."

"How long ago was that?"

"Oh, long, long time, eh. But long time before that . . . long time before white man come, we have no moon, no sun." He scanned our faces with his black eyes and lifted his eyebrows. "But one Old Man. He only man that have fire and light and water. Rest of people get water only from dew. It gather on moosehides, eh. People from loon not too wise, mebbe. Don't know how to get light and fire and water." He drank the rest of his tea and wadded some chewing tobacco into his cheek. "People ask *khunai* for help, ask wolf and fox and coyote. Animals go to Old Man and say, '*Yulkat.* We want light.'

"Old Man shake head. '*Saholkas!*' he say. 'No light for you. It stay dark.' But animals keep crying. Soon him tire of animal cry and let daylight come.

"Then people ask animals to help with fire. Old Man no let them have fire. Fox say to friends, 'Put melted pitch on my tail. We sing and dance round house of Old Man.' They sing and dance and fox leap into fire of Old Man and his tail burn. Whooooosh."

Sam raised his hands and laughed. Firelight glanced and flickered across his face. "Fox run away. Set fire to everything. Forests burn. My people get fire.

"Then they want water. All animals, all birds, they try. No get water. Then spirit come. Spirit say, 'I get water.' One day daughter of Old Man come and put water in basket. She dip up spruce needle and swallow by mistake. Next day she have baby boy. In one moon boy big and can run. Old Man happy. But boy cry and say he want to play with water. Old Man give him ball of water and boy play with ball in house. Soon boy strong and run away with ball. Old Man run after him. Boy run away fast. Drops of water fall over land and mek cricks and lakes. When ball nearly empty, boy throw it down. It bounce and rest of water mek Stuart Lek and Babine Lek." Sam pushed the tobacco around in his cheek. "That story of Babine people. Goot, eh?"

Our eyes were heavy and our heads had begun to nod.

"*Ahah*, that's quite a story, Sam," I said, standing up and holding my bedding in front of the fire. "Maybe it's not so different from white man's story."

He grinned and threw a couple of logs on the crackling flames. "We tell many stories, eh. You sleep now. I watch fire so him no go out."

Arno and I rolled ourselves into our warm quilts. Off in the distance I could hear the wail of wolves. My heart began to pump and I pulled my feather bed tight over my ears. All night long Arno and I turned like a spits, trying to stave off frostbite on the side away from the fire. By morning, snow had drifted across everything and we had to shake ourselves out of our beds like animals. It was bitter cold and snow swirled in every direction, but the fire was crackling and sizzling and hot tea was ready.

Later on in the morning we found the bloody remains of a rabbit and some lynx tracks. "Lynx eat much rabbit," Sam said, handing us the snare twine. "This good year for rabbit."

I clumsily began to build the lynx trap, a shelter of twigs, while Arno rubbed the twine with spruce. Sam watched us and nodded his head.

"You careful you no catch yourself in trap, eh," he said laughing.

We spent that night in the cabin at Teakettle Camp and next day covered the twenty miles back home, hoping we knew enough about trapping to get us started.

A few days later Max and I went out on the trapline on our own. You had to go over the line at least once a week. There had been another snowfall and we had to strap on snowshoes over our moccasins. The going was pretty slow for us and on top of that it was hard to find the traps. We had blazed a good trail, but with heavy snow everything looked different. And I guess I had expected a rat in every trap, and a lynx or fox in every snare, but most of the traps we found were unsprung and the snares untouched. We had better luck shooting ptarmigan and rabbits, and even they were difficult to spot because they turned white in winter.

Out there on our own it wasn't as easy as I thought it would be. You had to be constantly on the alert, always ready for the unknown, and careful you didn't get lost, misstep, or get too cold. And most important was to keep the fire going all night long, which meant you had to take turns keeping watch or train yourself to wake up before the fire died, or it meant you would die. We finally ended up taking home a half dozen muskrats and a mink. At least a mink pelt was good money, but muskrat hardly brought in a dollar a skin.

After a few runs on the trapline, we started to get a good feel for it and the business became second nature. We took turns at it and I even enjoyed going out by myself.

The trapline was another challenging and free way of life for me. The weather was always a factor. It could quickly turn from mild to sub-zero, with wind-chill bringing it well down to forty below or colder. However, I found that when you worked hard and built up a good sweat, you scarcely noticed the cold. You just had to learn to adapt to the environment and deal with it on its own terms. By then my muscles were as tough and sinewy as a wolf's and I could glide across the snow on my snowshoes as efficiently as any Indian. I began to love the beauty of the cold North more and more. Some days the frozen, crusty snowdrifts shimmered like diamonds and the sky was like a deep sapphire blue lake.

The northern lights were a common occurrence up there in the North, especially on clear nights when the temperatures plummeted. Flickering jolts of blue and green and pink filled the night sky, and shafts of rainbow colors would ripple across the horizon and fill the air with crisp, crackling sounds. On nights like that I missed Grete the most. I wanted to share the grandeur of the northern wilderness with her and wished she could be with me. Then an idea hit me like extreme frost snapping a tree in half.

Why couldn't Grete immigrate? We'd get married, maybe try our hand at homesteading, if she was willing. If she didn't like the country we could always go back to Germany after a year or two. My father was still plenty young enough to handle the business, I thought, and if I stayed in Canada two or three years longer it wouldn't make much difference. The least I could do was check with Immigration to find out what the procedure was to sponsor someone from the Old Country.

When I got back from that run on the trapline, I told the guys about my idea of applying to Immigration to find out if Grete might be able to come to Canada.

"Huh, what would a woman want in this cold country?" Arno laughed. "We're living about as primitive as you can get and you want to bring a woman into the picture?" He poured a shot of whiskey into his tea. "There's no way Marga would ever consider it, that's for sure, and I don't think Grete's much different . . . "

"What do you mean by much different?" I asked, getting my ire up.

"Woman like comfort, you have to figure that much," Arno said throwing up his hands. "I'm beginning to doubt whether I'll make it through another winter here myself, let alone this winter. Look at the lousy few skins we're getting. You think we can live off that?"

"A woman would go crazy in the bush," Max added. "It's so damn lonely out here with nothing and nobody around and fighting all the time just to stay alive."

"You guys aren't giving things a chance," I said. "It takes a little while to learn the ropes. And in case you don't know," I said, poking Arno on his shoulder, "Grete's not Marga. She's a strong woman. Has lots of common sense. She told me herself she likes adventure and being away from city life." Grete had never mentioned adventure to me, but now that the idea of her immigrating to Canada had hatched in my head, I thought it was a pretty good one.

"It's too bad common sense isn't more common, if that's what you think," Arno quipped, leaning forward and shaking his heavily bearded face.

"Well, I'm going to write to Immigration and see what they say."

"It's not what they say, it'll be up to what Grete says, and up to now, you don't even have yes for an answer."

That's how we passed the evenings, arguing and discussing our plans. But Arno was right about one thing. We wouldn't get rich from trapping. We used the dried fish for bait, set the snares and traps like Sam had showed us, but somehow the animals seemed to evade us. A few muskrat and mink here and there would barely be enough to bring us through the winter.

In those days there was a bounty on wolves and coyotes, so we figured we would try to make a few dollars that way. We needed some bait, and as it turned out, some Indians had an old cayuse they didn't want to feed over the winter. We traded a few skins for it and took the poor old nag out into the bush and shot it for wolf bait. Believe me, it was on its last legs. We didn't go near it so there wouldn't be any human scent. After a few days we noticed a few wolf tracks around the dead horse, but it was left untouched. We even climbed into some trees and waited in the bitter cold with our guns, hoping they would come by to inspect the horse again, but no luck. A week later we checked again, but the horse still lay there untouched.

By mid December we had enough skins to make a trip into Burns Lake worthwhile. Max had twisted his foot so needed to give it a couple of days rest. "Don't worry about me," Max said. "I'll keep the cabin warm for when you get back."

Arno and I piled the stretched hides together and loaded them onto our packboards. We also took a bail of skins along to sell for some Indians. They let us use their dugout canoe to get us the ten miles down the lake to the wagon road. From there we had to pack everything out to Burns Lake. We had stashed the dugout and weren't too far from the lake when we met several Indians who told us they had seen wolves about forty strong further up the lake and that they were heading south. Wolves could easily cover fifty miles in a day, but we weren't too concerned because we were headed in a different direction.

The trip was miserable. We had to break through three feet of heavy snow all the way. A warm Chinook had blown in from the Pacific and softened the snow. In some wet conditions, snowshoes don't help as the snow sticks to the bottom of the shoes like glue. Few words were exchanged as we sludged along, white steam puffing from our mouths. Suddenly we both stopped. We lifted our heads. A low blood-curdling wail somewhere off to the right of us echoed through the forest. We looked at each other, shifted our packs, and moved on. By then a few howling wolves no longer scared us, knowing darn well they would never outright attack, but it's a sound that always makes you feel a little uneasy, especially if you know there might be more than just a few around. It started to get dark, but the night was clear and a moon hung low in the sky, lighting our way. We wanted to spend the night at the old miner's cabin. Then the howling really started, and it came from different directions. The hair rose on the back of my neck.

"They must smell the skins," I said to Arno. We were pretty exhausted by then, but we pushed ahead with extra vigour. Every time they howled there seemed to be more of them. First on our left they howled, then to our right they howled, then behind us.

"They're following us," Arno said nervously.

I looked at him and nodded, pushing my exhausted body forward. "Yeah, mebbe you're right."

When we finally arrived at the cabin and slammed that door behind us, I don't ever remember feeling more relieved to have four walls around me. The next morning when we went outside to replenish the wood supply, that was one of the rules of the North, the snow was packed down with wolf tracks and their markings were all around.

We left the cabin and continued to push our way toward Burns Lake. Along the way we passed our old jalopy, disguised under soft blue-white mounds of snow.

"Yeah, had we listened to the guy in the general store we'd still have a decent car," Arno said, puffing hard.

"Had we listened to every bit of advice we'd still be back in the Old Country."

"You know, my father used to say that it's the smart man who learns from other's mistakes."

"Well, then, it's time you start learning."

Arno threw a look at me and yanked up his pack. "I'm learning all right. Learning that I'm a fool to be out here and struggling to make a living."

"We're not here to make a living, haven't you figured that out yet? We're here to learn about living."

Several miles later we came upon some old truck tracks which made our trip a little easier, but after twenty miles of putting our feet down one in front of the other, we didn't think they'd ever operate again.

We sold our skins for fifty dollars, but the Indians had three hundred dollars worth. The following summer I got into real hot water for selling their furs, but what did I know in those days.

The next stop was the post office where we mailed a few letters home and I sent an inquiry off to Immigration. There also was mail for us, which made the whole trip worthwhile. We headed for the beer parlour in the hotel. Arno and I sat down with our backs next to the old pot-bellied stove and tore open our letters. The beautiful handwriting jumped off the page as I quickly scanned the lines. An old timer was sitting next to me puffing on a cigarette. He kept looking my way.

"It's a letter from Germany," I said to him grinning. I fumbled around in my shirt pocket and pulled out Grete's picture and handed it to him. He raised his eyebrows and nodded his head.

"I guess she didn't get my last two letters," I said to Arno, but he was already deep into his mail. So I settled back and reread it.

September 28, 1930
My dear Paul,

It was no surprise to me when you wrote you wouldn't be home this fall. When Arno and both Maxes left last winter, I knew you would stay longer. Maybe I would do the same if I had the chance. Life seems boring when I hear about your adventures.

It's just as well you're not here to pick apples. They are full of worms this year. The weather has been cold and rainy and it's only September, but it was a good year for wild mushrooms and we got bucketfuls. Do you ever go mushroom picking? Mother puts them up in jars and dries some too. We had a hot, dry August and took full advantage of it, hiking up to the Kornberg every weekend with our packsacks. We could see for a hundred miles. In two weeks is the Harvest Ball. I have sewn a lovely new dress for it. You never did tell me if you go to dances.

Elections are coming up in another week. Hitler is full of promises—bread and work—everything for the glory of Germany. You said so many people are unemployed in Canada. It keeps getting worse here, too.

Too soon the cold winter will be here again and Mathilde and I will be rereading the books at the library. There's not much else to do on long winter nights except read and knit and crochet doilies. I found one book about a woman who left England for Canada with her husband about fifty years ago. She wrote to her mother describing the hardships and loneliness of her life and how cold and raw the country is, but insisted she loved it anyway. I guess some people can survive the wilderness with nothing but a teaspoon of honey. You said you are leaving for the North. I thought you were in the North. Who knows where you'll be by the time you get this letter.

I expect I will hear from you soon. That always happens, you know—our letters cross. Wherever you are, I wish you well. Maybe you'll be home by summer? I send you all my love . . .

  Your Grete

The old-timer was still watching me. "She your girl?" he asked.

I carefully folded the letter and slipped it into my pocket. "Darn rights she's my girl," I said, swallowing down the feeling of sadness and homesickness.

"You're a long way from home and she's a beautiful lady," he said, handing me back the picture. He opened the top of the stove and stuck in a rolled up piece of newspaper to light another cigarette. "Hope she waits for you."

"We're getting married," I said, standing up and walking over to the window. Icicles hung silently from the roof, and mounds of snow lay piled along the side of the road. The distant hills were colourless and gray and to the west the last streaks of yellow light were fading from the sky. A young woman in a hooded parka walked past the window pulling a little boy on a sled. I knew Grete wouldn't wait forever, but she had my word, and if I couldn't get home within the year, there still was the possibility she could emigrate. I looked down and touched the silent, glossy face that hinted of a smile. She had turned nineteen the month before and had never lived away from home. I looked over to the old-timer.

"She might come to Canada," I said. "I've already applied to Immigration." I knew it was probably pointless to think she would leave, and even if she wanted to, her mother wouldn't just let her pack up and go. I sat down and took a long drink of beer. "You get a letter from Marga?" I asked Arno, wiping the foam from my mouth.

"Nope," he said. "My mother wrote. The usual complaints, you know . . . too little money and never enough meat."

"By the way," interrupted the old guy. "In case you young fellers is interested, the C.N.R.'s awardin' a contract of 500 railroad ties to each homesteader to help out the employment situation. If you're homesteaders all you hafta do is send away for a contract."

"Ties? What are ties?" I asked him.

"You know what ties are," he said nodding and chewing on his lip. "Them crossbeams that holds the tracks together."

We never turned down a chance to make a few bucks, so we took his advice and before we left town sent away for three contracts. If we could make money cutting railroad ties, we sure wanted to give it a try.

With the money from furs, we paid off some of our credit and picked up more supplies. After a day in town enjoying a few relaxing beers and a good hot bath—whether we needed it or not—we headed out early the next morning.

We each had about eighty pounds on our packboards and began the long tramp back through the silent, white wilderness, unaware that come nightfall we would encounter one of the most harrowing experiences of our lives.

10. Moonlight on the Babine

BY THE TIME WE REACHED BABINE LAKE, a hazy half moon had risen above the mountain to the east. Beads of light rippled and glanced off the rolling, pitching waves, and long black shadows of clouds streaked the sky. We were eager to get back to our cabin, and even though there was an icy, sharp wind blowing across the water from the north, I didn't expect there would be a problem paddling those last ten miles down the lake. The temperature was well below freezing, but when you've been walking and working your body hard, you don't notice the cold.

Arno put his mittened hands up to his eyes. "Looks a little rough out there. Maybe we should camp here overnight."

The thought of setting up a shelter on the windblown, freezing beach and poking around for some firewood in the dark wasn't exactly up my alley. I dropped my pack, relishing the prickly feeling of relief that ran across my back and through my arms. Telescoping my hands around my eyes, I peered across the lake, which couldn't have been more than two miles wide at that spot.

"If we head across to the other shore, the water'll be calmer," I said. "Wind's just piling up the waves on this side a little and there's no whitecaps. Let's just get the boat and give it a whirl."

We dragged the dugout to the edge of the water where the waves rolled and grated the gravel back and forth along the beach. Arno pulled his toque down over his ears and began to shake his head.

"I don't know," he said puffing. "What's our hurry anyway. We can lean the dugout against those logs for a windbreak. We'll get a good fire going. Some good hot tea . . . "

"You want to scratch around in the snow looking for some dry windfalls? If we stay here we'll be frozen carp by morning," I said, throwing up my hands. "We got plenty of moonlight, and the wind always dies back. We'll keep warm enough paddling. Since when are you worried about the cold?"

Arno looked at me and pointed his finger to his head.

I turned away and walked over to the packs. Arno always was the more cautious of the two of us and had to turn everything over ten times. I pulled out a mickey and tossed it over to him. "It'll put a little heat in your belly," I said. We divided some dried meat and sat down on the edge of the canoe. "Joe's taken plenty of trips at night," I said, washing down the meat with a shot of whiskey. "Says when the wind dies and there's a little moonlight the churning water from the paddles lights up the lake like stars. And we'll be home in a couple of hours," I convinced him.

We loaded our packs into the canoe and pushed off into the dark, choppy water. Arno sat in the bow and I took the back and steered.

"Just head into the wind," I shouted, feeling a spray of icy water bite into my face. We paddled strong and actually made good headway at first, but by the time we got halfway across the lake the wind really began to whip and howl around our ears. White froth blew off the tips of the black waves, and more and more water began to slosh into the canoe. Our clothes were soaked by then, but we were working so hard we didn't even notice.

"Maybe we should turn back," yelled Arno, his voice trailing away in the wind. "We'll freeze to death at the rate we're going."

Our boat reeled and lunged around in the water like an eggshell, which made the steering extra tricky, and we couldn't afford to be hit sidewards by even one wave or we would've been swamped immediately. The water was freezing cold, and if we capsized or were thrown overboard our lives would have been washed out in a minute. On top of that, I had to bail water out of the boat.

I glanced behind me and could no longer see the shore line. Straight ahead a dark, jagged outline of trees dipped and sagged in the pale moonlight.

"Let's just keep going," I shouted. I shook my head to clear my eyes. My heart was pumping like crazy and my breath was ice. "We're halfway there."

The paddle was slippery with ice and my mittens kept freezing to the handle. I pulled my hand out of the frozen mitten and wiped my raw, frozen mouth, feeling the icicles in my beard. Leaning forward, I rummaged clumsily around in the pack, pulling out the mickey.

"We're making good headway all right," I shouted. I took a drink and felt the burning heat travel down my gritty throat. "Here, this'll warm you up," and I handed Arno the bottle. "Don't worry. The wind's shifted a bit and it'll get calmer as we get closer to the other shore."

The wind had shifted all right. It blew from all directions and all we could do was keep paddling like hell and focus on the opposite shore. There was no turning back, and we had no choice but to keep fighting the heaving, rolling waves, which must have been a good six feet high by then. I had no time to think fear, no time to dwell on our situation.

Icy sweat froze on my face, and sweaty salt burned my freezing, cracked lips. I riveted my eyes on the water and the giant, coiling, black tongues spit froth and foam at us like rabid dogs. Suddenly Arno's arms and shoulders stopped working. He pulled the paddle into the boat and turned to me. All I could see were the whites of his eyes and a glint of his white teeth.

"You sure we're making headway?" he gasped.

"Yeah, I see the treeline, all right, but for cripes sakes you gotta keep paddling."

My wet clothes were frozen so iron hard by then I felt like I was in a straight jacket, yet I could feel my underwear next to my skin, cold and clammy from the sweat I had worked up. My feet were icicles of pain, but at least that meant they weren't frozen. Even though my concentration was solely on our survival, every now and then I'd squint my eyes tightly together and let a vision of Grete beam into my mind.

"C'mon, Arno, you gotta paddle for our girls," I shouted in a hoarse voice. "You can see the shore there." But in all truth, I felt like we were in no man's land.

He looked over his shoulder back to me. Just then a patch of moonlight hit our boat and lit up the water like shining black marble. Arno's beard and brows were frosty white, but his eyes were black slits.

"My arms," he groaned. "I gotta rest."

I would've traded places with him, but we couldn't risk tipping the boat. "You gotta keep at it," I hollered. "Here, have another drink," and I fumbled around with the cap, securing the paddle under my arm. I handed him the bottle and he guzzled the rest of it down like water. Then he hunched his back and started to rock.

I jabbed him with my paddle. "*Kreiz Donnerwetter,*" I hollered. "Get your paddle in the water. You want us to drown?"

"What's the difference? I'm already freezing to death," he croaked. "My hands . . . they're frozen."

"Quit your bellyaching and get that paddle in the water, or we will be done for," and in that second a wave sloshed over us. I hunched deep into the boat, feeling the black, freezing water whip at my face like slivered icicles. I bent my head sideways and concentrated on keeping the boat from capsizing.

Without another word, Arno dipped his paddle into the icy, black water and leaned his powerful body deep into the wind and began to stroke. Slowly we edged our way to the other shore where the wind became a little calmer. We had crossed the lake at a diagonal, so I figured we only had another five miles to go.

"We're almost there now," I yelled.

"Almost where," Arno groaned, pulling in his paddle.

"Don't give up now, you stupid bugger," I shouted, taking a good look at my paddle to make sure I actually had a good grip of it. "We're making plenty of headway. It's easy street from here on in."

"I'm all cramped up. We can pull to shore."

"That really would be the end of us. We'd freeze to death before we got a fire going. I don't think I could strike a match."

My arm muscles were cramping, and the numbed pain in my hands and feet made me begin to wonder if we really could make it. Along the shore we passed black looming rock bluffs and small rocky bays. Wisps of black clouds streaked the sky and the moon tilted over the mountain on our right. In the east a yellow tint began to break across the skyline, and at the end of the lake ice had formed all along the shore. Somehow we managed to keep paddling and I guess all those hours on the green chain really paid off. The last three hundred feet we chopped at the ice with our paddles to make our way to the edge of the lake. When we finally made it to shore and I stepped off the boat, wrenching jolts of pain shot through my feet and up my legs, leaving me momentarily dazed. My fingers were frozen into position.

"Let's leave the packs," Arno said from a stooped position. "You know the wolves'll never touch 'em."

We were both shivering so hard we must have looked like a couple of starving, frozen mongrels. "No, we better not take the chance."

He straightened up and glared at me through frozen eyelashes. His thick eyebrows and beard were clumped with frost and his clothes were frozen white.

"You look like you're from Siberia," I said, pulling his pack out of the boat. "C'mon, I'll help you load up."

With the last bit of strength we could muster, we made our way up the ridge and back to the cabin. The smell of smoke broke my lungs, and when I finally saw the outline of the roof I was dizzy with relief. I bumped Arno on the shoulder and pointed. He just looked at me from his stooped position with hard, white eyes.

The door of the cabin opened, and before we knew it, Little Max was stripping off our clothes. He put our feet into a pan of cold water to loosen the socks that had frozen to our skin.

"You guys look like a couple of frozen corpses," Max said, rubbing the ivory-white patches on our noses and cheeks with snow. "Didn't expect you crazy sons of guns back before afternoon."

"Get the coal oil, Max," I groaned. "Remember what George said about coal oil."

Max turned and poked around among the rubble of tools and pots and guns. He poured some oil onto a rag and rubbed it on my hands and feet and dabbed some on my face. Fiery pain rolled through my body and my face felt on fire. I clutched my gut and let out a moan.

"Okay, your turn," Max said to Arno.

"Not me," he choked, putting his hands up to his splotched face. "Keep your God'amn hands away from me with that stuff."

"You want to lose your fingers and toes?" I said. "You've got no say in this. Give it to him, Max. Coal oil's the best thing to get out frostbite."

Max must have worked us over for more than an hour. It was a long, agonizing hour until the throbbing pain began to ease out of my limbs and I could work my fingers again. I don't think I stopped shivering for a whole day, but I can tell you I was darn grateful to be alive. I pulled my feather bed over my ears and looked at Arno.

"You pulled us out of that one, Shorty," I said. "You see, we made it. We'd be loading up that canoe right now if we'd spent the night on shore."

"Shut up *du bloeder Hund*. Just shut up and sleep."

11. Trapping

IT TOOK A COUPLE OF DAYS before we could get around again without feeling like we were walking on broken glass. Except for losing a few patches of skin here and there, I was none the worse for wear and the frost-bitten pain in my hands and feet had subsided, but both Max and Arno had come down with the flu. You don't usually get sick when you're living so isolated, but I guess we had brought the bug back from Burns Lake.

It looked like I would be the one to make the next run on the trapline, and as I said before, I didn't mind going out on my own, but there were times when the weather turned and things got rough and you wished you had a partner along.

I loaded up my provisions and left the cabin at daybreak. Except for the crunch of snow under my feet, there was an unusual stillness in the air. Black-headed chickadees sat fluffed and frozen on gray, icy branches. Even the whiskey jacks were scarce. The pale sky was streaked with pink-gray stripes of rippled clouds. I moved cautiously among the mounds and clumps of frozen snow along the banks of the creek. Damp, frosty fog hung thick around the marshy areas, where bare willow and poplar branches shimmered with ice.

When I came to the first muskrat pushup, my fingers quickly turned cold and clumsy trying to unhinge a frozen muskrat. I stroked the thick, shiny brown fur. Another dollar in our pockets. After a couple of hours I had collected several muskrats and a couple of mink. My spirits were up. The bit of experience I had was beginning to pay off. If you took your time and used a little patience to learn the ways of the animals, you could be sure of a payback.

By early afternoon a cold, gusty wind out of the northwest had blown in heavy, dark clouds. The gusts soon became icy blasts, and snow began to swirl down and around the trees biting like pepper into my face. The heavier the snowfall became, the more difficult it was to locate the trail and slashes on the trees. It was time to make camp.

I found a protected gully among the spruce and worked quickly to set up a campsite, collecting wood and getting a blazing fire started. Then I searched around for some broken limbs and dragged them close to the fire, leaning them in the crook of a couple of windfalls. After covering the limbs with freshly cut spruce, I layered more branches on the floor of the lean-to. You have to work quickly in the fading light of a late northern afternoon to make yourself as comfortable as possible for the long night ahead. I hung a frozen muskrat carcass on a spit over the fire and pressed snow into a pot for tea water. Finally I wrung out my wet socks and moccasins and hung them on sticks next to the fire.

I reminded myself that I was doing exactly what I had set out to do when Arno and I left for the Babine. A little bit of raw weather here and there was all part of trapping and wilderness living. I leaned back on my elbows in the open shelter and stretched my legs out toward the warmth of the orange-red flames. The tingle of icy, melting snowflakes beat at my bare feet and I shivered like a hairless Chihuahua, wondering if it was worth putting up with the freezing cold and exhausting work trudging along a forty-mile trapline with barely enough return for provisions.

As I rubbed the frost out of my feet, I thought of home and how easy my life would have been had I gone along with the scheme of things. Had I humoured my mother a little more, been more patient and tried to understand her way of thinking, maybe she would have come around and seen my side of the story and eventually come to accept Grete. Maybe I should've established myself properly in the business, become a real partner with my old man, instead of making an impulsive decision to leave my homeland.

The dripping grease from the carcass flared up the flames and the smell of roasting meat made my mouth water. I pulled a pair of thick, woollen socks over my burning toes and tugged on the steaming moccasins, hoping they'd dry overnight from my body heat. Black tea bubbled in the pot, and by the time I'd washed down some beans and strings of juicy muskrat with a quart of hot tea, an easy warmth had spread through my arms and legs. I threw several more broken limbs onto the fire sending sparks high into the early night. The wind was howling through the tops of the trees and in the distance coyotes were yipping. My .22 lay handy, but you never had to worry about coyotes. It was the wolves that concerned me, especially since Arno and I had been trailed by a pack of them just the week before.

I burrowed into my warmed feather bed and tucked the tarp around me, wishing Max or Arno were along so we could take turns tending the fire during the night, but I wasn't worried about waking up because my body would tell me when it was time to stoke the fire.

My mind wandered to my sweetheart, but within minutes I fell into an exhausted sleep. I don't know how long I slept, but the next thing I knew, I was lying in a heap of branches, snow and flying sparks. The wind was still howling, and the fire was a jumble of sizzling, blackened wood. I quickly threw bits of shavings and dry twigs into the fire, protecting it from the wind with my body. When flames began to lick at the pieces of wood, I rebuilt the shelter and settled in with another pot of hot tea. If I wanted to stay alive, I knew I'd better stay awake and tend my lifeline. Heat from the flames glanced off my face, and as I sat there watching the snowflakes melt into the fire, my thoughts once again slid back to home and Grete.

I had been gone for sixteen months by then, but my feelings for Grete hadn't waned in the least. Out there alone in the bush they became even more intense. I thought of the letter I had just received from her—*no surprise . . . you wouldn't be home this fall— just as well you're not here . . .* Maybe she was beginning to think I might never come back, in spite of my promises. My eyes began to droop. I shook my head and stared hard into the flames. Drinking down the last of the tea, cold by then, I shifted myself into a more comfortable position. I forced my eyes to stay open.

Suddenly I saw myself standing like a block of ice on an open stretch of frozen, glittering snow under a brilliant blue sky. The howling of wolves echoed across the landscape. Then the sound came closer and in the distance a sleigh came veering toward me pulled by a team of huskies. My heart began to thump. There was Grete standing tall and proud in the sleigh, holding the reins taut. The howling dogs with their blazing, yellow eyes and stinking breath swerved past me. Dark, frightened eyes loomed large in Grete's ivory face, and as she swung by me she called out, but her words vanished in the wind. My pants were frozen to my legs and a sharp, biting wind stung my face. I reached out, voiceless, but she and the dogs had already become black dots against the expanse of white snow. All I could feel and hear was the icy grip of the wind.

I awoke to the sound of howling and at the same time felt troubled that I could freeze to death just sitting there without even knowing it. I checked my .22 and pitched more wood onto the coals, pulling my feather bed tightly around me. Then another long, bone-chilling wail cut right through me. Gooseflesh crawled up my arms. Longer, deeper quivering howls rose higher and higher and died away into the night. My heart was in my throat and I kept telling myself that it was too early in the season for the wolves to be hungry, that no animal would be out in a blizzard. I peered into the darkness beyond the moving flames of the fire. More howling. You think you'd get used to it, but when you're alone it sounds different, I can tell you. You don't know how big the pack might be and what the wolves will do, especially if they get a whiff of fresh hides. A log shifted on the fire and sent up a sizzling crackle of sparks. I threw on plenty more wood and boiled another pot of strong, black tea. I wouldn't sleep again that night. I sat quietly with the gun across my lap and listened to the knocking of my heart.

I had plenty of time to think and one thing that came clear to me sitting there in my miserable hovel, waiting for daybreak, was that it would take some special kind of woman to live in the wilderness. How could I expect Grete to settle for a life in a cabin and the challenge of living off the fat of the land, even if it would be for only a year or two? And maybe I was out of line to think she would even consider coming to Canada. She would have the freedom of long days rolling one into the other without a clock, and there would be no more twelve-hour days behind a sewing machine, but life wouldn't be easy either, even if we lived in a town. We would be broke to begin with, she would have to learn the language and the ways of a new country, and then she would probably miss her mother.

Few women would choose a wilderness way of life and give up the comforts of home, that much credit I had to give to Arno. You either had to grow up in the bush where courage and the ability to adapt to the unforeseen became second nature, or you had to have some tenacious, inborn fighting spirit that equalled that of a fearless mother bear with cubs.

But no matter what the outcome, whether I decided to go home or if Grete would come, I needed money. I know you're probably wondering why I didn't just push pride aside and wire my old man so I could go back home if that's what I really wanted, but you have to understand it wasn't that cut and dried. My pride was an important consideration, of course, and I particularly didn't want to be obligated to my mother, but I was still looking at the opportunity of holding homestead land as well as exploring a big chunk of the country out there that I hadn't seen or experienced.

By daybreak the snow had become so fine that it floated in the air like a haze. It had turned cold, damned cold, freezing up the sap in the trees and causing them to crackle and explode like gunfire. Snow hung heavy on the branches, and every now and then a gust of wind sent a sheet of snow plunging to the ground with a thump. Each breath of air sent a chill to the bottom of my lungs. At least the clouds had scattered and here and there patches of blue poked through. I had to get moving, generate some heat. I strapped on my snowshoes, figuring I could reach Teakettle Camp well before dusk, but by early afternoon I knew I'd never make it. Heavy drifts of snow made for slow progress, and locating the animal snares and muskrat pushups had become too much of a challenge. Reluctantly I made camp in the refuge of some protected spruce. Although I was dog tired, I stayed on my feet all night, drank thick, black tea, and kept a roaring fire going. I had no intention of falling into a black sleep and becoming animal bait.

At the first crack of light I headed for home. By late afternoon, with the sweat pouring off my face and near exhaustion, I came upon two Indians who had set up camp. My empty belly cramped and my mouth watered when I smelled the rabbit stew bubbling over the hot fire.

"*Hadi, hadi,*" they said, grinning and shaking my hand.

I returned their welcome and slipped off my pack. "Hmmm, something smells good. Been on my feet the whole day. Could you spare a bite to eat?" I asked.

The Indian in the ragged heavy mackinaw with black hair hanging out from under his toque scooped some steaming stew into a tin bowl. "Eat up good. Plenty rabbit this year."

I sipped the hot, tasty liquid.

We talked some about trapping and then one of the Indians said they had seen some unusually big tracks in the snow.

"We show you," the Indian said, lifting his chin.

"We never see big track like that," the other Indian said, spreading his rough, bare hands out wide.

"Where'd you see 'em?" I asked, fishing out a piece of meat. "I heard a big pack of wolves last night."

"Wolf hungry this year," he said nodding, "but no wolf track. Track back that way on trail," he said pointing. "You finish eating. We show you. Them no wolf track."

Several dried berries popped up to the surface of the liquid. *Wachholder Beeren.* Saliva glided over my tongue as I remembered my mother's sauerkraut flavored with juniper berries. I was surprised that junipers grew in the area as I hadn't seen any, and impressed that the Indians used them for spice. But my bowl stopped in mid-air as I was about to take another sip. You see, the Indians cooked every part of a small animal. They skinned it and cooked it whole. *Shit inside,* I thought to myself, and without blinking an eye, poured the black beads onto the snow.

"So let's find the tracks," I said, raising the bowl to my lips and carefully sucking up the last of the sauce.

We backtracked about a quarter mile, and when I saw the huge prints, I recognized them immediately.

"Cougar tracks," I said. They were the same unmistakable huge prints that Tobee had shown me back in Winfield when I had first arrived in Canada.

The Indians nodded their heads and cinched their eyebrows together, looking at me in surprise. "*Ahah . . . Booscho.*"

Cougars rarely ranged that far north, so it wasn't surprising that they didn't know the tracks. It was nearly dark by then, so I camped that night with the two Indians and arrived back at the cabin by noon the next day. When I told Max and Arno about the tracks, Max became quite excited.

"Hey, we can make a few fast bucks," he said. "I know from the Okanagan there's a forty-dollar bounty on cougars. It didn't snow overnight so the tracks must still be there. C'mon, Arno, it's time we get our bones moving again. We been holed up too damn long in here. I think I'm going bush crazy."

They packed up right away and headed back the way I'd come, taking an Indian dog with them. I hated to be the one to stay behind, but I was sore and exhausted and needed the rest.

Max and Arno didn't come back the next day, but I wasn't worried because they were familiar with the area and knew how to set up a snow camp. By the third day I decided to head out to Stuart Lake to an Indian camp where we had heard through bush telephone that some Indians had an eight-year old stallion for sale. There was a pretty good trail between Babine and Stuart Lake, and with snowshoes I could make good time.

Gray-blue smoke trailed out of the rectangular wooden houses. They were made of slabs of wood and poles and roofed with spruce bark. A dozen skinny dogs came running up to me barking and sniffing my legs. A tall, dark-skinned Indian poked his head out of one of the huts and swung his arms, yelling in Indian to the dogs. They scattered in a flash.

"*Hadi,*" he said, nodding his head in recognition and motioning for me to come inside. "*Suento?* You fine? You travel in no goot weather?"

He had a long, dark face with a scraggly beard, and two of his front teeth were missing. I recognized him from the fishing season.

"*Hadi*, Johnny," I said, stepping down onto the floor of the hut which was about three feet below ground level. "I'm doing okay."

A fire burned in the middle of the hut, and even though most of the smoke went out through a hole in the roof, it was smoky as heck inside and smelled of grease and smoke and hides. His missus was stitching a rabbit skin on her lap and next to her lay a sleeping baby in a basket. Three older children had moved away from the fire and huddled together giggling at me.

I handed some tobacco to Johnny.

"*Musi*," he said, reaching for his pipe. "You bring whiskey?"

I shook my head. "I've come to buy stallion."

"*Tsekeyaz nduda* . . . girl sick in camp. With whiskey mebbe you fix girl?"

I knew right away that the girl was probably so sick that it was too late to help, or he wouldn't have asked me.

"*Ah-ah*," I said with a nod. "I'll see what I can do."

Because I was a white man, the Indians expected I'd be able to perform wonders. Tuberculosis also was a problem among the tribes, and they had asked me on more than one occasion if I could help them out. It was pretty pitiful to find someone in the last stages of emaciation and not be able to do anything about it. But at least with pneumonia or pleurisy I could give them advice with what little knowledge I had.

"*Annee* . . . come with me," Johnny said, standing up. I followed him to another hut where a six year-old girl lay on some skins. Her mother and a couple of other women were singing to her in soft, chanting tones. The girl's face was a deep red-brown and she looked up at me with glazed, black eyes. I pushed her black hair aside and put my hand on her hot forehead.

"We'll fix you up," I said, patting her on the shoulder. "Don't worry. Can you open your mouth for me?" When she didn't respond I opened my own mouth and pointed to hers.

I turned her head toward the light and immediately saw that her tonsils were red and swollen and speckled with pus.

There wasn't a thing I could do except to bring down her fever. I asked Johnny to get some snow for me. I gently packed some snow on her forehead and rubbed it up and down her arms and legs. I stayed with her for nearly an hour until her temperature had dropped some and she seemed to have stabilized.

"You know what tonsillitis is?" I asked Johnny when we left the hut.

"*Ah-ah*, mebbe so," he answered, creasing his brows.

"She's very sick, you understand . . . and if she isn't better in a couple of days you should try to get her out to a doctor. Take her to Fort St. James."

I explained that if her fever went up again they should cool her down with snow and told Johnny that whiskey wouldn't help her. I never was too sure how much they understood, especially me with my broken English.

"Come, I show you stallion now," Johnny said.

We walked over to a makeshift shelter where several hobbled horses were bunched together against the wind. All of them were on the scrawny side.

"That one. Him with white feet."

The stallion's ears perked forward when he saw us coming, then snorted and trotted away from us. He was a tall, scrawny roan and his hair was long and shaggy, but he had a good solid chest and was plenty spunky. I didn't know much about horses and he looked good enough to me.

"How much you sell him for?" I asked.

"You take him. Him yours."

"I can give you some good skins," I said, remembering what George had told me about cheating the Indians.

He shook his head with a laugh. "You keep skins. Him peppy and halter broken. Him used to rope hobbles. You take him. Father of girl on hunting trip. Him happy when he come home."

It took me a minute to realize that he wanted me to take the stallion because I had helped the little girl, and I knew I'd insult him and her family if I didn't accept.

"Him fatten up in couple months when spring come. Him scratch for food. Him fatten up," he added.

"*Musi, musi* . . . thank you very much. Strong animal."

"Next time bring whiskey."

"You bet your boots," I said nodding and grinning.

Before I left the next morning, I looked in on the little girl. Her tonsils were still red and swollen, but she wasn't as feverish as the day before and her eyes had lost that glittery, dazed look.

"Keep her warm now and give her lots of good, thin soup," I told her mother.

I left with the stallion, talking softly to him and stopping every now and then to calm him down. Progress was slow through the heavy drifts and he yanked his head back at every opportunity, trying to break away and return to the Indian camp, but I kept a good tight grip on him.

A couple of miles from the cabin I saw a campfire through the trees about fifty yards off the trail. I gave a holler and these two guys stood up and looked in my direction. Sure enough if it wasn't Little Max and Arno. What were they doing camping right there in the bush so close to the cabin? They shouted and came crashing through the trees and heavy drifts of snow, dragging their packs.

"Never thought I'd be so glad to see you," yelled Arno.

The next thing I knew, the stallion reared and I was face down in the snow dragging after him. He had decided to make a clean break for it. But my fingers were wound tightly around the rope, and I hung on for dear life until I could upright myself and dig my heels into the snow to bring him to a halt. I finally got him under control and eased him back to where the guys were waiting for me.

"Cripes almighty," I said, trying to catch my breath. "What the heck were you guys doing sitting there in the trees like a couple of bush chickens?"

Little Max eyed the snorting stallion and stamped back and forth on his feet trying to keep warm. "Got lost. Had no idea we were next to the road. So you got the horse after all, eh?"

"What about the cougar?" I asked, looking from Max to Arno and back to Max again. "You get 'im?"

Arno shook his head and pulled off his toque, running his fingers through his coarse, matted hair. "We tracked the bugger for two days and no more sign of him."

"So, how you plan to feed the nag the rest of winter?" asked Max. "And what if the tie contract comes through?"

I shrugged my shoulders. "Even if it does, we'll be back. It's time we had a pack horse . . . and he can forage. So you didn't get the cougar, eh?"

Max shook his head. "Hadn't tracked him for more than an hour when we found a freshly killed mule deer. Darned dog got so scared of the scent that he hung behind our heels, shaking like a leaf. Was getting dark by then, but we dressed it and had ourselves some good, fresh liver for supper. Followed him the next two days, but didn't see hide or hair of him. Then it started to snow again."

" . . . and we didn't know where the heck we were," Arno said.

"You guys are a sight for sore eyes," I said. "Let's get a move on before it gets dark."

Next morning I took the horse over to George's place, and his eyes lit up when he saw the stallion.

"Easy, old feller," he said, carefully running his hand down the foreleg. "Looks good and sound. What's his name?"

I thought for a second. "Puma. We'll call him Puma. It's German for cougar."

George nodded his head and patted Puma's neck. "It's English for cougar, too," he said laughing. "A little patience with him and he'll be broke in no time a'tall."

"I was thinking that maybe I could keep him in your corral a few days til he settles down."

"As long as we keep him clear o' my Nelly. She'll put his lights out for sure if he gets fresh."

Later in the morning, Max, Arno and I went up the mountain to haul in the deer meat. But the deer had been pulled down off the tree and dragged about two hundred feet off into the bush, under some branches. Fresh cougar tracks were all over the place and a good part of the animal had been eaten.

By the time Christmas arrived we didn't have any meat left, and there was no sign of deer anywhere when we went out hunting. We snared a few rabbits, but we were getting really hungry for some good red meat. We weren't going to celebrate Christmas without a good roast dinner, so we chopped off a chunk of frozen meat from the old nag we had shot six weeks before for wolf bait.

We spiffed up the place by hanging a few spruce boughs in the cabin and asked George to join us. We browned the roast and let it simmer for half a day.

"My cabin ain't smelt like this in years," said George when he arrived, breathing in deeply. "Hardly celebrate Christmas here in the bush." He pulled out a hand-rolled cigarette and lifted the lid of the stove to light it.

Little Max poured hot water into the tin cups and added some sugar and rum. "You ever get alone by yourself up here?" he asked George, handing him a cup.

"Ain't never been by myself." He took a long inhale of the cigarette and slowly blew out the smoke. "I've got my animals, I get along with the Indians okay and I've got my peace of mind. I can think what I want to think and don't mind a bit hacking out my own existence. Me and Mother Nature understand each other fine and dandy."

We cut into the roast and made real hogs of ourselves, even if the meat was stringy and wild tasting. We refilled our cups.

"That school teacher lady," I asked George with my cheek full of meat. "Had you promised to marry her?"

His sharp blue eyes popped open and he shook his head. "Hardly remember anymore." He took a sip of rum. "Ahh, good stuff. I guess I just presumed we'd get hitched. You know how it is."

"Did you write her?"

"Sure, sometimes, but who had money for postage, and letters took a coon's age, eh, to get anywhere. Got anymore of that meat?"

We finished our supper and refilled our cups. We sang all the German Christmas songs we knew, and when we ran out of songs and had long, homesick faces, George got up to leave.

"By the way, Paul," he said. "You gotta let your horse range a bit. You don't want 'im to get trench feet now, you know," and he stooped slightly to go out the door.

"Trench feet? What's trench feet?" I asked.

George laughed. "Ah, don't worry about it. You know, back in the war. The poor buggers in the trenches got it."

The next morning we were all so sick from eating that old cayuse that we were laid up for a week, not knowing which end was up, and couldn't even run the trapline.

By mid January we had collected enough skins to sell, so Max and George went out to Burns Lake to get supplies. When Max returned he had our contracts from the C.N.R. for delivery of five hundred railroad ties each, and had made arrangements for us to cut the timber on François Lake, which was about fifteen miles south of Burns Lake. But best of all, he brought back some mail.

I tore open the envelope. It was a Christmas card with St. Nicholas on the front. When I finished reading it, Max and Arno sat there waiting for the news. They had mail from their families, but that didn't interest them half as much as mine. We all craved news, especially from home, especially from our girls. I cleared my throat.

"Grete's been extra busy at work. Has lots of alterations. People don't have money for new clothes." I strained my eyes in the dim light of the cabin.

"Her stepfather complains that since Bruening is in power nothing's changed. Still no jobs, and taxes have gone up so much there's no money left to buy anything. She writes the Nazis are now the second strongest party, and no wonder, when Hitler keeps promising more jobs, higher wages, and cheaper food. And listen to this." I said with a laugh. "A foot of snow fell overnight and she says she could use a pair of snowshoes. Can you imagine her on snowshoes?" I put the card down and stared out the window.

"That's all she's written?" asked Max.

I picked up the card again and fanned it in the air. "Well, she mentions the big Winter Ball that everyone's planning to go to . . . and she says to say hello to Arno. She wouldn't know you're up here," I said to Max. "And, oh yeah, she's been dreaming every night that we're wrapped in each other's arms and sleeping on a bear skin."

"She wouldn't write that," said Max. "I've known her longer than you. We went to school together, for chrissake!"

"And she wouldn't even know what a bear skin looks like," said Arno. "Max is right, she wouldn't write crap like that."

"She'd tell me her dreams all right," I said, feeling a little hot under the collar.

"So why doesn't she write and tell you she's dreaming of coming to Canada?" asked Arno.

"Maybe she will come. What do you know? Right now she's still expecting me to go back home."

Arno stood up and poured himself some tea. "I hope she has lots of patience. She'll have a long wait."

"You didn't get a letter from Marga?" I asked.

Arno shook his head. "Not this time. Mail takes months, you know how it is."

Before we left for François Lake the end of January, Arno and I took one last run on the trapline to spring all the traps. We collected one fox, three mink and a dozen muskrat. It was one of our best rounds. But to be honest, I was glad to be done with trapping and everything that went with it, at least for the time being.

We left Puma with George with the promise we would be back by March. We packed up for our long trek into Burns Lake, and on our way out said good-bye to Joe and let Old Sam know we would pay off part of his bill at the general store in payment for letting us use his line.

12. Tie-cutting on François Lake

"Y OU CAN PAY UP WHEN YOU GET YOUR TIE MONEY from the C.N.R.," Mr. Brunell said, stacking the goods up on the counter and tallying everything up. "You'll find somebody down at François Lake to haul the ties out for you."

We collected our mail and I had my reply from Immigration. I read it over and laughed, shaking my head.

"They expect me to put up a $2,000 bond until Grete arrives and we get married!" I said, waving the letter in front of Arno and Max. "Where in the heck am I supposed to come up with that kind of dough?"

What I didn't realize at that time is that the government had halted all immigration because the country could barely take care of its existing population. All of the provinces were suffering from the Depression, with the Prairies getting especially hard hit. Not only had world wheat prices collapsed, which in turn cut the incomes of the railways, but a severe drought had ravaged whatever possibility the farmers had of making any income at all. So one way Canada could protect herself was by making it as difficult as possible for foreigners to enter the country. Yet Europeans still arrived with work permits and stayed on permanently.

"We probably could've helped you out and pooled the money we'll make from cutting ties," Max suggested, "but I never expect to see the day when I have that kind of money in my pocket. Besides, now the decision has been made for you. You'll have to go back home to marry her."

So there was my answer. It was quite a let down for me, but I no longer had to worry or wonder whether Grete would consider coming to Canada or if her mother would allow her to leave. And when I thought it over, I must have been dreaming to think she would have left home to live with me in the wilderness. I had left the Old Country with high hopes of earning good money, but with the collapse of the economy, and especially as an immigrant, you could hardly make a decent wage to support yourself, let alone a wife and family. So the next best thing for me was to stick to my old plan and find my own way back home.

I was almost certain my mother would never totally accept Grete, even though I still held out some hope that my time away from home would soften her up and that she would accept my decision to marry my sweetheart when I returned. And there was always the possibility that Grete and I could emigrate down the road, though that seemed an unlikely prospect once I returned and re-established myself in the business.

We left for François Lake, which was about fifteen miles south of Burns Lake, and moved into a log cabin that was equipped with bunks and a cast-iron stove. An elderly man living in the area pointed out the pine and hemlock used for the ties and demonstrated to us what we had to do.

We went to work with our broadaxes, which weighed about ten pounds each, falling trees not more than a foot across the stump. The first couple of days we really let the handles fly with a fury. We got a good system going, with one of us felling trees, the other hacking off the branches and squaring off the logs on two sides, and the third cutting the trees into eight-foot lengths. Steam rose from our bodies like smoke, although the temperature must have been hovering around zero. By the third day, though, we had to throw down our axes. Our arms and backs were so sore and stiff we had to lay off work for a couple of days. After that we slowed our pace and every day cut no more than thirty to forty ties each. Remember, our contract was for five hundred ties a piece, which would have given us about a month of steady work.

Well, close to the end of February, around my twenty-first birthday, another one of those humid Chinooks blew in and the weather turned unusually warm. You wouldn't believe how quickly the snow can melt in a situation like that. Our cabin had a sod roof that began to leak like a sieve, soaking everything inside. Our feather beds got soggy, the stove steamed and sputtered, and we were wet day and night. But worse than that, we needed enough snow and cold weather to skid and haul the ties to Burns Lake by sleigh. Wet and miserable like we were, and stranded with our ties, we finally made a deal with a farmer who said he would finish our contracts for the C.N.R. He paid us $75 for the cut ties and promised to pay off our bill at the general store in Burns Lake when he cut all the remaining ties.

"You fellows back already?" Mr. Brunell asked, pinching his eyebrows together when we arrived back in Burns Lake.

"Yep. Darned Chinook did us in. You know Mr. Keller at Francois Lake?" I asked, setting my pack on the floor. "He'll be paying off our credit."

"Sure, I know the Keller boys. So where you young fellows headed now?"

I shrugged my shoulders. "Well, I guess it's back to the homestead again."

I almost had Arno and Max talked into sticking it out at least until early summer as there wasn't much possibility of finding a paying job in the southern Interior until then.

We picked up our mail and this time Arno was the lucky guy. He put the letter in his pocket and we headed for the beer parlour. It always felt like home when I sat down with a glass of foaming beer in front of me. The smell of cigarette smoke and thick, yeasty air made me think of Saturday nights in the *Sonne* that were filled with laughter and singing. And there we were with barely a cent to our names, our hope for a few dollars from tie hacking shot to pieces. Maybe it would be best, I thought, to leave the homestead behind, head south for Vancouver and catch the next boat home. All I had to do was wire for money.

Steaming hot stew and biscuits were set down in front of us and Arno read his letter while we ate.

"So what's Marga have to say?" I asked, wiping my sleeve across my mouth.

The muscles in his face tightened and he picked up his glass of beer, guzzling the last of it down.

"Everything hunky-dory?" I asked.

He nodded, wiping the foam from his chin.

"Only person I get mail from is my sister," said Little Max, scratching the bristles on his cheek. "It would be nice if I could write to a girl."

Arno reached for a biscuit and turned to Max. "You're not missing anything."

"So how is she?" I asked again.

"You know," Arno said, "I think it's time to light out of here and see what life has to offer in the city. There's no bloody way to scratch out a living up here, no matter what you say."

"What the heck you talking about?" I asked. "You want to leave us in the lurch? I've thought of walking out myself—but to just leave when we're getting into the swing of things?"

He nodded and began to pull the biscuit apart. "I bet they could use a good cabinetmaker down in Vancouver. I've been thinking . . . I'm going to pick up a freight and try my luck there."

His Adam's apple bobbed up and down and his face grew red. "Listen, if you guys want to join me, fine, but don't let me hold you back."

"Wait a minute," I said, grabbing Arno by the sleeve. "What's going on?"

Low laughter drifted across the room from a table where several men were playing cards. Arno's heavy, dark eyebrows tipped down over his eyes and in a gruff voice he muttered, "Marga got married."

Max and I didn't know what to say. Arno had been away from home for less than a year. Even though I felt quite confident there wasn't anyone back home that Grete could be interested in, and she had told me herself she was too young to marry when I had proposed, there was always that nagging feeling she might meet someone and forget all about me.

"Well, marry in haste, repent in leisure," Arno said, shrugging his shoulders. "If that's what she wants." He pushed the bowl away from him and ordered another beer. "I'm a free man now."

Both Arno and Little Max caught a freight out of town the next morning.

"I've had enough of the homestead to do me for the winter," Max said stomping his feet in the cold. "May as well head south myself and try to get my job back on the farm." He stuck out his chin and puffed out white clouds of steam. "A man can take so much of the bloody bush before it gets to you. Well, you know where you can find me if you decide to leave, Paul."

A part of me wanted to go along with them, but I had to tie things up back at the homestead. George was expecting us and I had the stallion to take care of, but it was more than that. Arno and I had built that cabin with our own hands and I had an attachment to it. I just couldn't walk away without giving things a fair shake. I wanted to see springtime on the Babine Lake, explore the surrounding country during the dry summer months. Maybe things would change and the price of beef would go up again. I could raise a few cattle. The soil was fertile, the lake was full of fish and wildlife was abundant. Like Joe had said, life was good there on the Babine.

So we parted ways. Arno left for Vancouver and Little Max went back to the Robertson farm in Westwold. I bought supplies with my last dollars and left Burns Lake before dawn the next day to take advantage of the hard, crusty snow, because by noon it would soften and get slushy which made it hard for travelling. The days had warmed up pretty good. I visited our old Hudson, which sat off the side of the road in deep shade, buried in snow. It would probably be there in fifty years, all rusted and bent. I wiped the crusty snow off the side window and looked inside. Stuffing stuck out of the seat and a side window had popped. Someday I'd buy myself a decent car, I thought, giving the door a kick. I moved on, wondering how Arno would make out in Vancouver and if Max would get his old job back.

By noon the next day I was back in home territory. I heard the yapping of dogs and saw several Indians fishing along the shoreline. I stopped at Joe's cabin, but he wasn't around. His missus told me he had gone to Cunningham Lake for a couple of weeks.

Dripping icicles hung from the roof of my cabin, leaving deep-blue holes in the snow. Sunshine filtered through the trees, casting long shadows across the snowy meadow. I pushed open the door and dropped my gear and supplies on the floor. The dark cabin was half frozen and smelled damp and musky. A pile of wood lay beside the rusting stove. I cut some shavings and started a fire. After a bite to eat and some good hot tea, I headed over to George's cabin, at times pushing through heavy drifts of snow and sometimes across gray, flattened meadow grass.

"Holy moley, I'm surprised you fellers are back so soon," he said, crinkling up his blue eyes. "Sit down, sit down. Where are the boys?"

"Oh, they decided to head south, couldn't take it no more, but I'm going to stick it out for awhile."

"Yep. Folks come and go. Try a bit of the wilderness and find out it's too tough or too damned lonesome." He picked up the pot of coffee and jiggled it around.

"How's Puma?" I asked.

"Been no trouble a'tall. There'll be plenty for you to do now that spring's almost here. You've got your horse, and maybe you can do a little muskrat trappin' yet before the season's over. Muskrat fur's really at it's best, you know late winter, early spring. Startin' May I could use some help planting. I got plenty of seed potatoes, and I can trade you a milk cow if you're a'tall interested." He poured me a cup of coffee and sat down.

I nodded. "Yeah, maybe I am." I swallowed some lukewarm coffee. "You know, before I left I mentioned there might be a chance my girl could emigrate."

"Yep, I remember."

"It didn't work out. I don't know. You think a woman would ever live up here?" I asked.

He shrugged his shoulders and set the can of tobacco in front of him. "Most would find it awful lonesome, I'd say. Never met a white woman myself that woulda liked it."

"Yeah, you're right, I guess. I don't know what I was thinking. So what would you trade for a milk cow?"

"Like I said, come end of May you help out with the plantin' and later on the haying and the cow's yours."

Sure, I thought to myself on my way back home. I'd be living off the land, scraping by, but wouldn't be earning one red cent. As the days passed, I kept myself busy enough, doing a little fishing and hunting. Then a storm moved in, leaving a couple of feet of new snow behind with temperatures back down to zero. I could have gone back out on the trapline, but muskrat skins just didn't bring in enough to make it worthwhile. I worked on the cabin a bit, re-chinking some of the moss that had fallen out from between the logs and went out everyday to gather firewood between the snow-drifts. I tried out new ways to cook rabbit and grouse, and reread the half dozen battered Westerns that were in the cabin. I worked with Puma everyday so that I could use him as a saddle horse, but every time I tried to mount him he would get real ornery and kick and buck and do his best to rid himself of me.

At night the cabin was so quiet that I found myself straining my ears to listen for some music from howling wolves and yipping coyotes. I would dream of Grete and wake up miserable. In the morning I threw bits of fat over the frozen snow for the whiskey jacks.

Then the grosbeaks returned and flocks of blackbirds and sparrows began to sing in the trees. The familiar quacking of mallards and the honking of Canada geese filled the air, but all the signs of spring only left me restless. Sometimes I wished I would have gone south after all with Arno and Max. I was torn between wanting to stay on the homestead, going back to the Old Country, and worrying about not having enough money to do either. Finally, after one long, fitful night, I packed up all the gear I could carry.

I took Puma over to George's place for him to keep or give back to the Indians.

"I'll never get back to the Old Country this way," I explained to him. "I'm heading down to Westwold where they might have some spring work at the ranch for me. I don't know if or when I'll ever get back."

George shook my hand. The wrinkles around his eyes and mouth deepened. "Well, you have my blessing, young man. You've been damned good company. I'm gonna miss you, miss all of you. And whatever you decide, the cabin'll be waiting for you."

We shook hands and as I turned to leave he put his hand on my shoulder.

"About that girl of yours," he said, "I wouldn't save on postage if I was you."

On the way out, I stopped by at Joe's cabin. Two of his children came running to meet me. The sweet smell of willow smoke and the pungent odor of dried fish filled my nostrils when I stepped inside. Skins lay heaped in the corner and chunks of wood lay in a pile by the door. Dried fish hung from the ceiling and several tins of tobacco and a large can of honey stood on a small wooden table that was pushed against the wall.

"I'm leaving, Joe. I've come to say good-bye."

"Too bad. You leave when best time of year come," he said. "Spring beautiful. You stay longer. I think you like it here more better."

I shook my head. "I have to go home, back to my own people."

"*Ahah*, I understand. Yes, but we don't say good-bye," he said grinning. "*Nan yse Tenlah*. We will meet again. Mebbe you come back one day."

Two days later I had joined up with several hobos who were waiting for a freight out of Burns Lake. The sky was streaked red and the sun felt cold and frosty on my face.

By then the Depression had set in hard and thousands of men were out of work. The government had made a feeble attempt to establish relief camps where guys got fed and paid about twenty cents a day for road work or any kind of work that was around. Farmers were subsidized five dollars a month to take on any help they could in return for room and board, but there were too many jobless, so when the men couldn't find work in one place, they moved to the next town via the cheapest possible transportation.

When Richard Bennett of Calgary had become Prime Minister the year before and had promised to get the country moving again, the prices just kept falling and there no longer was a market for goods. All his promises came to nothing and the bread lines kept growing longer. Attitudes had changed around the railroad, too. By then there was no more looking the other way by the railroad police if transients jumped off a freight at a station. It really was a ridiculous situation. Nobody wanted any jobless bums stopping in their towns, as they would have to feed them, and the railroad didn't want them riding for free either, so the railroad police were always ready with their clubs.

So there I was, just like the rest of the hobos, stamping around in the cold, out of sight off the side of the track waiting for the freight. I didn't have any experience grabbing a freight, except for that one time going to Shuswap Lake, and I guess this older guy in a heavy overcoat, who looked like a veteran of the rails, sensed my nervousness.

"You done this before, son?"

I nodded. He must have caught a funny look in my eyes because he just kept on talking. "The freight'll be picking up some speed by the time she rolls outta here, and we'll all be jumping on at the same time." He cleared his throat and sent a long, black stream of tobacco juice past my ears. "Don't get pushy. There's enough cars. Just watch your timing and grab the ladder nice 'n' easy."

The long, shrill whistle and the chug-chugging of the train as it pulled out of the station made my heart race. Billows of steam covered the old locomotive as it gained momentum. We crouched beside the track and even though the train had picked up some good speed by the time it reached us, we had no trouble swinging ourselves up and sliding open the door of the boxcar.

Crates of canned fish, which were being shipped to Vancouver out of Prince Rupert, rattled against each other. We did a little rearranging and made ourselves as comfortable as we could. Some of the fellows began rolling themselves a smoke and others took out their snoose can or a mickey. They offered me some, but I shook my head to both snoose and whiskey. I pulled the letter out of my pocket that I had picked up in Burns Lake.

January 15, 1931
Lieber Paul,
When are you coming home? We were expecting you back by Christmas and thought you might surprise us, until we received your letter. Ever since you left there's a big empty space in my heart. I know we disagreed sometimes, but when you came back from Berlin you at least added a little spice to our lives.

Anna and George Hertel on 25th wedding anniversary trip to Italy, 1931.

Vater misses you. He doesn't say, but I can see it in his eyes when I sing the old songs. Remember "Wo die Nordseewellen?" I always think of you when I sing it. I guess that's because I know you are far across the ocean somewhere. Mutter and Vater are celebrating their Silver Wedding Anniversary next month. We're having a big party and then they are going to Italy for eight days. Some day I want to go to Italy . . . Canada, too. Sometimes I even feel like running away from Rehau, just like I ran away from that private school. Remember how I ran away so many times they finally stopped sending me? I was so dumb when I climbed out the window and forgot about the snow and they followed my tracks all the way to my friend's house. But where could I run. It's not so bad working in the Sonne, really.

I can hardly wait for spring when we can go hiking and camping again. We have such a good time singing around the campfire. I always take my accordion along. I think I'd like it in Canada in that kind of wilderness you write about.

I've been going to the Sunday afternoon tea dances at Cafe Horn. Sometimes I see Grete there. She dresses very chic, you know, and I envy the shoes she wears. She must buy them in Hof or Nuremberg, where she sometimes goes with Mathilde. I think Mathilde has a brother who works in the Kaserne there ...

I folded my sister's letter carefully together and leaned back on the rusted wall of the boxcar, letting the vibrations of the moving train ripple through my body. Gusti's smiling eyes hovered in front of me as I nodded my head and tapped my foot in tune to the song "Where the North Sea Waves Break on the Sand." I should have had a letter from Grete too. I had written her often enough. She had sent only a card at Christmas. Now that I was going back to Westwold it would take weeks before any mail would get transferred from Burns Lake.

When we approached Prince George, we knew the bulls would be watching for hobos and that we had to jump before we reached the town.

"Jumping off is the toughest part," the old guy said, running his tongue behind his bottom lip. "You gotta be careful shakin' a freight. You can get thrown under the wheels with one slip. I seen it myself. It ain't a pretty sight. Just make sure you jump well clear. Throw your pack first and land on your feet, otherwise you can be thrown right under the train."

With my heart in my throat, I clung for a few seconds to the open door then threw off my pack and let myself fly, curling my knees under me. The wind hit my face and then I was bumping and rolling down the bank through the soft snow. I was safe.

"Now we gotta skirt the town and try to pick up the old girl again before she leaves," he said, brushing the snow off his clothes and picking up his pack.

I was hungry by then, real hungry. Some of the guys went bumming for food, but I decided to go with an empty belly. I hightailed it around behind the town and waited for the next freight.

We were on the train all night. We huddled together on the cold floor and I thought hard of better days and warm food. When we jumped off at Red Pass the next morning, which had nothing more than a section house and a small general store, I was surprised to find that we were practically back in the Rockies. In order for us to go south, we had to travel all the way east to Red Pass where we could catch the southbound freight from Edmonton. There were about twenty of us, and we would have to wait three days in Red Pass for the next freight coming through.

The following morning as we sat in the empty boxcar, all of us hungry as hell because nobody had a nickel to buy any food, we heard the roar of a plane. Airplanes weren't all that common in those days so we were pretty surprised when we looked out and saw this two-seater with float pontoons land right on the lake beside the tracks. Red Pass was at the northern tip of Moose Lake, and the river that flowed out of it was the beginning of the Fraser.

Although the lake was frozen where the water was calm, at our end the water was free of ice and moved at a good clip toward the river. The plane settled down nice and easy, but directly in the current. The pilot opened the door and threw us a rope, but it fell short and into the water. The plane began to turn and drift toward the railroad bridge which was two-hundred feet downstream and with less than a six-foot clearance above the water.

"The poor bastards," one of the hobos said. "Looks like they seen better days."

The pilot and co-pilot hollered and waved their arms as they floated toward the railroad bridge. We knew they were in trouble, and when nobody moved, I kicked off my boots and jumped into the freezing water with all my clothes on. I felt like I'd been hit with a jolt of electricity, but I didn't have time to think of the cold and headed straight for the rope. I wrapped it around my wrist and swam toward the bank for all I was worth, snubbing the rope around a tree. Fortunately there was a back eddy right there and by then several of the guys had rallied to help haul in the plane.

The fellows climbed out of their two seater and were really grateful to me that I had saved their plane and probably their lives. Well, one of the men threw me a box of matches so I could light a fire and dry my clothes. My teeth rattled and I shook so hard I could hardly strip off my clothes.

"You were a damn fool for riskin' your life," one of the men said, getting a good fire stoked up.

"I'll say. Look at you lookin' like a drowned rat and whatdidya get for it," said another.

I had pulled on my dry boots and wrapped myself up in my feather bed. Yeah, I thought to myself, they at least could have offered us a bite to eat.

But before long, one of the men came over and gave me ten bucks. The hobos' eyes lit up like firecrackers and we headed straight for the general store. I was able to buy enough food for all of us. The storekeeper even let me dry my clothes by the heater.

Several days later I arrived back in Westwold. The first thing I did was go to the Circle J Ranch to see if they had a job for me.

"You can work for your room and board for the time being," the foreman said. "That's the best we can do for you. Things're still tight with the cattle business."

What was I to do? At least I'd get fed and maybe, come summer, they would be able to pay me wages. They had about five hundred pigs on the ranch at that time, so he put me to work to help with the butchering. I was pretty lean from roughing it all winter, so for the next couple of weeks I filled myself up on all the porridge, potatoes, bacon, beans and all raw eggs I could find.

The first day I had free, I hitchhiked to the Robertson farm to see if Little Max was there. He had been rehired, but also worked for his room and board until the ground was ready for plowing and cultivating. He was pretty happy to see me. Big Max was still working in the area at another farm.

"Come on into the shed a minute," Max said, giving his jaw a jerk. "I want you to meet somebody."

I squinted my eyes in the low light.

"Hey, Adam," Little Max said. "We got a visitor." Adam dropped the wood he was stacking and I could hardly believe that another friend from Rehau, Adam John, had arrived from Germany just a few weeks before, on a work permit. I guess he must have heard enough about our adventures, and with the political climate and bad employment situation in Germany, thought he would look the country over for himself.

Adam was a tanner by trade and had worked in a leather factory in Rehau, and since I knew the Circle J needed a good tanner, I took him back to the ranch with me. The foreman was tickled pink when he realized that I had found a man for him who really knew his business. Adam taught me the tanning formula, too, so we both tanned cowhides and got busy fixing about a hundred set of harnesses. I had more than enough work then.

One day, Mr. Bulman, the owner of the ranch dropped by, and when he saw the kind of work we did with the harnesses, he offered us $25 a month each on the spot right from the day we arrived. Finally I was earning some decent money.

June was roundup time for the hundreds of horses that were scattered out on the range. The ranch had top cutters, even rodeo riders, and they would bring in horses and rambunctious stallions to the corrals in a cloud of dust, just like in the Old West days. I helped out with the branding and even tried my hand at roping, but they didn't have too much time to deal with a greenhorn.

There were a couple of Indians on the ranch that were breaking in about a hundred fifty broncs that were five and six years old. The horses had to be harness broken and worked in the fields for a couple of weeks before they could be sold. One day after work I asked if I could help them out sometime. The one Indian looked me up and down.

"You strong man?"

"You betcha," I said, lifting my arm and flexing my muscle.

"Come back tomorrow," he said grinning. "We hitch up four-horse team for you."

I went back the next day and they took three pretty wild looking broncs out of the corral. "We hitch old Charlie up with broncs," the Indian said. "Him breaking horse and don't run away."

The Indians had done the main breaking of the horses in the corral, so they harnessed up the horses and I climbed up on the wagon, easing the horses onto the road.

"Keep eye on lead bronc," the Indian shouted after me. "Hold reins short but soft . . . "

I kept the reins nice and light in my hands, but not giving the horses any slack, just like the Indian had told me. They pranced and tugged and I talked to them. "Easy now, easy now. Just follow old Charlie."

We were moving along the road pretty good, when all of a sudden the front bronc bucked and kicked the rear horse, and they took off like a bat out of hell in a tangle of straps and harness. I stood up in the wagon and put all my weight into pulling back on the reins. Tears streamed out of my eyes from the wind and I was bucked around in that wagon as much as if I had been riding one of those devils. They galloped down the road full blast, and I didn't think I was going to get out of that jam alive. I pulled with all my strength on Charlie's rein and was finally able to steer them off the road onto the soft ground of the field, but the wagon went over on its side and I took a nose dive into the mud.

It took me awhile to get the horses calmed down and the wagon upright again, but I worked those horses until they were ready to drop, and they didn't try to run away again. When the Indians had the next set of broncs for me, they nodded and grinned, putting me wise to start them off in the field instead of on the road.

I was having the time of my life on that ranch. The foreman even had me helping with the calving and giving vaccinations against black leg. I thanked my old man many times for the lessons he taught me caring for sick animals.

Then a letter from Grete finally arrived. I opened it with some trepidation because months had passed since I had heard from her. Her beautiful handwriting swam before my eyes. I had been away from my girl for nearly two years by then, but for every half a dozen letters I wrote, I only got one back.

February 10, 1931
My dear Paul,
I just received your Christmas letter and have your other letters, too. The mail takes forever and I never know where to write you anymore. I was surprised to hear Max is living with you, too. I don't

Grete (Wendler) Hertel,
ca. 1931.

expect you will be home for a long time, and the months pass quickly after all.

This letter will be very late for your birthday, but Viel Gluck zum Geburtstag anyway, and I'll be thinking of you. How do they celebrate birthdays in Canada? Or do you even celebrate, living in the bush like you do? Sometimes I think you must all be crazy to want to live in that wild country. I can imagine the crusty, sparkling snow, and the northern lights must be something fantastic, but chills go down my spine when you describe the howling of the wolves and the bitter, icy cold.

Mathilde and I went to see Charlie Chaplin's "Gold Rush"—remember? We laughed so much, but we thought about all of you out there somewhere in the freezing North.

Sometimes I complain about my long days at Frau Schoedel's and am very tired when I get home, but mother always has a bowl of hot soup waiting and a warm house, though sometimes the house isn't so warm and coal is very expensive. The apple trees look so bare and lifeless, but with spring around the corner they will soon be in blossom. Our gymnasts club is doing well and we are preparing

143

for our annual meet—in Bamberg this year. I love that city with all its beautiful canals and old timbered houses.

People don't laugh so much about Hitler anymore and you can be happy you're not living in Berlin where there is so much student unrest and street fighting. And the new movie "All Quiet on the Western Front" has caused a big uproar there because the Germans are so insulted by it. It hasn't come to Rehau yet. Do you hear much about Hitler in Canada?

A couple of weeks ago I saw the movie "Wild Orchids" with Grete Garbo. At least we can still go to the movies for 50 pfennige.

Fasching time is here again . . . with all the masquerade balls. 'A Night in Heidelberg' is the theme for the next Saturday night dance—two bands, prizes for the best costumes, a huge beer fass. We will miss you. I guess you don't celebrate Carnival in Canada?

Did Arno hear from his girlfriend in Hof? That she married? It was very sudden. I met Marga once at the Turnhalle when she was with Arno. She loved to dance. Does he have plans to come back home soon? And you? Will you even be home by fall?

My love to you,
Grete.

I felt pretty lightheaded for a few days and carried her letter around with me, reading it over and over every chance I had. I wrote back right away, of course, and told her about my stroke of luck at finding a well-paying job on the ranch, and that I would be home before her next birthday in November.

By early summer we were in full swing with haying. The land was very fertile and with the long, hot days, the first crop of hay was ready to be cut by early July. Haying was tough work in those days, but Mr. Bulman had purchased a tractor to supplement work with the horses, even though he never did believe in automation. He even said to me once that horses would come back one day. But that didn't stop him from driving around his ranch in his open car heaped with dogs and farm utensils.

Once the hay was cut, we had to turn it by hand so it would dry, then stack it and load it onto the wagon. From there we unloaded it into the barn. We worked without shirts and got as brown as leather. But I never minded the work. The air smelled sweet with fresh hay and the sky was as blue as cornflowers.

So the summer wore on and we had stacked, loaded and unloaded hundreds of tons of hay. I had saved about seventy dollars by then and was beginning to think about making plans for my return trip home when the foreman came up to me one afternoon. "R.C.M.P. here to see you, Paul."

I looked at him and couldn't figure why the police wanted to see me.

"They have a summons."

I lifted my hands and questioned him. "A what?"

"A summons. Don't you know what a summons is?"

I shook my head not knowing what was coming up, but it sounded like trouble to me.

"You'll find out, I guess," the foreman said. "Just follow me."

"You Paul Hertel?" the police constable asked, looking pretty important in his red uniform and broad-brimmed hat.

"Yeah," I said nervously, thinking I was in big trouble for riding the rails.

"I have a summons here from Burns Lake. You're to appear in court in ten days."

My stomach grew tight and I shoved my hands into my pockets. "In court?" I asked, taking a deep breath. "What did I do?"

He handed me a slip of paper and shrugged his shoulders. "You'll have to talk to the judge about that, and you've got ten days to get there before you get arrested."

My heart sank right into my toes. For the first time since I arrived in Canada, I was earning some decent money, had found a real niche for myself, and now a monkey wrench had been thrown into my life. I knew I would lose nearly a month of work by the time I got up to Burns Lake and back, and the trip would cost me a few dollars too, but I had no choice but to quit my job and head north.

13. Murder on Trembleur Lake

THE NEXT FEW DAYS GAVE ME PLENTY OF TIME to think about where I'd gone wrong. Maybe I should have stayed on the homestead. When you claim land you've got to live on it. Or maybe we shouldn't have been running Sam's trapline.

I hitched a ride with an elderly couple from Kamloops to Lillooet and caught a freight from there to Quesnel, but what I didn't realize is that the train terminated there. I still had eighty miles of hard road to cover up to Prince George before I could hook up with another freight to Burns Lake. There wasn't a single car or truck going in my direction the two days it took me to walk that stretch. By the time I hopped a freight going west from Prince George, my shoes were worn through and I was plenty footsore.

In Burns Lake I went straight to see the magistrate and he called in the game warden.

"Pleased to meet you, Mr. Hertel," the warden said, shaking my hand with an easy smile on his face. "I'm Dave Roumieu." He rattled some papers in his hand and looked at me with a question in his eye. "Looks like we have a small problem here, Mr. Hertel. I understand you sold fur for the Indians last spring, and it's my duty to inform you that it's against the law to sell their furs."

So that was it, I thought. "I only did them a favour," I explained. "I didn't make any money off 'em, not a single dime."

"Well, in that case, I guess it woulda been better to sell the skins under your own name," the warden said in a sympathetic tone, crossing his arms and nodding his head. "Then there wouldn't a been no problem a'tall."

"Somebody could've told me that when I sold the furs," I said, tossing my hands in the air. "All that money went to the general store to pay off their credit!"

The magistrate ran his tongue across his lips and shook his head. "Well, seein' as you're a greenhorn around here, I guess we can drop the charges. What do you say, Dave?"

"Yep, sounds fine with me."

I looked at them in disbelief, yet grateful that I wasn't getting fined or thrown in jail. "I quit my job and came five hundred miles for this?"

"Five hundred miles?" the warden asked, popping his eyes then looking over to the magistrate. They both shook their heads and began to laugh.

"It's no laughing matter to me," I said.

"Well, we can slap you with a fine, or throw you in the lock-up for a week," the magistrate said with a chuckle. "We can do that if it's gonna make your trip worthwhile."

I raised my hands in defeat and shrugged my shoulders, then shook their hands and told them in as polite a tone as possible that it was nice meeting them.

Before I got myself a bite to eat, I stopped at the post office hoping by chance there might be a letter for me, but no such luck. All the mail would have been forwarded to Westwold by then.

Back at the hotel I ordered a bowl of thick barley soup and a beer. I was thinking about George back on the homestead and how I'd like to pay him a visit before I headed south again when an elderly Swiss set down a glass of beer and extended his hand.

"Excuse me. May I join you," he asked in a Swiss-German dialect. "My name is Fritz Holz." He wore the traditional gray Swiss jacket and knickers. "You sound like a German to me." He pulled out a chair and plied me with questions about where I lived, where I was from, where I was going. Then he explained he was on his way out to the Coast looking for some good homestead property.

I finished my soup and wiped my sleeve across my mouth.

"I know good homestead property not far from here," I said, lapsing comfortably into my German tongue. "I've staked a claim and built my own cabin over on the Babine Lake."

He nodded his head. "*Jawohl*, I hear there's plenty of property around there . . . some of the gentlemen were telling me, but way in the bush and bitter cold in winter, isn't that true?"

"You get used to it. Cold didn't bother me, except for a time or two." What did he know, I thought. He had lived a couple of years in the Vancouver area and when he couldn't find any good land to claim decided to try further north.

"Out in Prince Rupert there's still good property and the weather mild, like Vancouver," he said. "You been in Vancouver?"

I shook my head. "My friend from Germany lives there."

"*Ach ja.* So, you hear much from the Old Country?" he asked. "Life is a little tougher over there from what I hear. I don't think the government knows what it's doing half the time, too many parties fighting for power."

I shrugged my shoulders. "Yeah, my girl writes. Says the Nazi Party is getting stronger. Don't think she likes Hitler or the Party much, but he promises to get the country back to work and higher wages."

"Huh, isn't that what they all promise? They should send that tramp back to Austria—that house painter." Fritz pushed his hands against the table and leaned in close to me. "All his talk of the pure Aryan race . . . preservation of the Volk. He's a rabble-rouser that's all. Trouble. And politicians, huh. They're all the same—promises, promises. You want another beer?"

I nodded. "So you think there's good property out on the Coast then?"

"There's still plenty available from what I hear. Say, why don't you come along with me and take a look around. The country's supposed to be beautiful—like Switzerland."

"Ever ride the freight?" I asked, rubbing my hands together and feeling an itch inside my shoe. A little detour out to the Coast wouldn't take more than a week or so, I thought, and there was new country to be seen just around the bend.

"*Jawohl!*" he winked. "How do you think I made my way up here?"

Next morning we caught a mixed train that carried passengers and freight. Of course, we travelled as blind passengers. Half the train consisted of empty fish cars with ice compartments, but the stink inside the box cars was so terrible we rode on top. The weather was clear and balmy and we sat up there feeling like we were on top of the world without a care, swaying back and forth, listening to the clackety clack rhythm of the wheels and enjoying the cool wind whipping at our clothes and whistling through our tangled hair.

"We wouldn't be doing this in the Old Country," I yelled to Fritz.

"That's why I like it in B.C. It's just like home with all the mountains, and no one asks any questions, except you have to watch for the railroad police."

Every time the train arrived at a division point, the bulls checked for non-paying passengers. We huddled inside a stinking boxcar while they walked along the top of the cars, lifting the lids off each icebox to chase out anybody they could find. But all they really did was take a quick gander into the dark interior and move on to the next car.

Through the Bulkley Valley and towards Hazelton, the tracks followed the west side of the Bulkley River. We were surrounded by high, snow-capped mountains, with the Hazelton Mountains on our west and the Babine Range to the east. The river basin was green and fertile with good farmland and waist-high grasses and wild peavine. If we'd been smart, we would've jumped off right there and tried to claim a homestead because that Bulkley Valley is one of the most beautiful valleys in British Columbia. Even the weather is more temperate there than in other areas in the North and has dry Indian summers that last well into autumn. Thinking back on that trip, the scenery through the Bulkley Valley and on out to Prince Rupert was one of the most scenic and spectacular trips I'd ever taken.

There was a layover in Hazelton so we had a bite to eat in a local cafe. South across the river stood a towering mountain peak which the Indians called *Stegawdun*, which means Brother. "And make sure you watch out for his Seven Sisters," the waitress told us. "You'll see the peaks along about forty miles west of here. They're never without snow."

Hazelton, which sits right on the confluence of the Bulkley and Skeena Rivers, had been an important supply center for gold seekers heading up toward the Takla Lake area. About twenty-five miles west of Hazelton we passed Kitwanga, an old Indian village, where I saw my first totem poles. They were as tall as trees and elaborately carved out of cedar. Weathered birds with long, curved beaks and wide, wooden wings, stood on top of strange animal shapes with yawning eyes and broad fish-shaped mouths. I only learned later that each pole told a story of an Indian family or clan, and represented a kind of family tree, and that totem pole carving even originated in Kitwanga. I guess totem poles are to the Indians what the coat-of-arms is to a European.

The vegetation was entirely different from the rolling hills of the southern Interior and the sparsely wooded Bulkley Valley. The evergreen forests of spruce and cedar and hemlock stretched across the mountains as far as the eye could see. I'd never seen such giant trees, and some must have measured eight feet in diameter. Along the Skeena, where the water was quite shallow in parts because of the time of year, grew groves of massive cotton-woods, and up the mountainside you could see where spring snowslides had torn out everything in their path.

The Skeena is known to the Indians as the K'san River or "Water of the Clouds" because of the heavy rainfall and the low-lying clouds that persistently hang in the river valleys. The Coast Mountains, which average about six thousand feet in elevation and not anywhere near as towering as the Rockies, are nevertheless just as impressive with their snow-capped peaks and green alpine meadows. As we clung to the top of the swaying box car, the Seven Sisters came into view, seven snowy peaks glowing pink in the last rays of the late afternoon sun.

When we arrived in Terrace, which was given that name because there are a series of terraces up the sidehill on which the town was built, a valley opened all the way to Kitimat Inlet in the south and the Nass River in the north. I didn't have an eagle eye, so couldn't exactly see the whole length of the valley, but I was to find all that out later.

Past Remo, which was a small settlement about seven miles from Terrace, and what one day would become more than a dot on the map for me, the Skeena became as wide as an inlet. As we chugged toward the Coast, each time the train passed through one of the many tunnels, the old Swiss and I took refuge inside the boxcar.

Until the railroad was completed in 1912, the only source of transportation to get supplies inland to Terrace and as far as Hazelton was by paddle-wheeler during the summer months; and during the winter, mail and supplies were taken in by canoe or dogsled, depending on how solid the river was frozen.

When we arrived in Prince Rupert a heavy rain was falling and the cold seeped right into my bones. The town has one of the best harbours in the world and is located on Kaien Island just off the Tsimpeen Peninsula. Old Victorian houses, shrouded in fog, were built up the hillside above the town. After warming ourselves with hot coffee and soup at a local cafe, we asked the proprietor how we could get to the Salvers River Valley, where Fritz had heard about some good land.

The balding man with a well-rounded belly pulled up a chair and asked if we knew anyone around there.

"We're looking for some good ground for settlement," I said.

"So you never been in those parts? There's plenty of land left there all right," the man said with a grin and a nod. " . . . smack in the middle of a snowbelt. Twenty feet's nothing. And a fifty-foot snowfall ain't no surprise either. But if you're a'tall interested, just pick up a train east and get off at Salvers. All the good land's been taken around here. Have you been to Terrace or Hazelton? Plenty of homesteaders around there."

We thought the man must have been pulling our leg with his fifty-foot snowfall story, so from Salvers we followed a bear trail up the Salvers River Valley. There were bear droppings all along the trail, and though we never saw any, we heard them breaking through the brush. Thousand-foot cliffs rose out of the valley floor, and we saw plenty of mountain goats picking their way among the rocks. The whole area was thick with alder and underbrush, and a jungle growth of devil's club tore at our hands and clothing. My face stung with pain from a branch that ripped across my face. The brush was so thick that we lost the trail. Finally I climbed an old cedar to orient myself. About twenty feet up the tree I found three inches of hard, crusted sand on a thick limb.

"I guess the guy was right," I said to Fritz after I climbed down the tree. "You'd need a Noah's Ark if you wanted to settle in this country."

We finally found a bear trail and made our way back to the tracks. That ended our interest in looking for some good land around there, but Fritz was still intent on finding good homestead property.

We grabbed a freight heading east for Terrace, which was a little more tricky, as this time the box cars were loaded with canned fish. We found a car that had room enough to stretch our legs and make ourselves comfortable. I leaned against a crate, feeling the motion of the swaying car vibrate through my body. I pulled out my pocket watch squinting in the dim light to check the time.

"This is Monday, isn't it?" I asked Fritz.

He shrugged his shoulders and patted down his pack. Slivers of light glanced off the crates of canned salmon and shrimp that would be shipped around the world. I checked my watch again. Five a.m. Grete would be back at work after her noon meal. I closed my eyes thinking I could have been back on the ranch in Westwold by then pitching hay, saving money for my trip home, and instead I was bumming around on a freight, not knowing for sure where I was headed. The clacking of the train wheels began to lull me to sleep. My parents were probably having their afternoon nap. The smell of fish and rusted metal clung to my nostrils. How disgraced my mother would have been had she been able to see how I lived and survived. She would never have understood my way of life , how every day offered a new adventure, and that not knowing what lay in wait around the next corner was for me as close to taking opium as I could ever get.

Sure, I wanted to get back to the Old Country, but I also knew that once I got there, my life would drastically change and I'd probably be stuck there for the rest of my life. I was afraid that once I got back home I'd begin to feel trapped and hemmed in, so I wanted to make sure I got the wilderness fever out of my system. Then there was the question of the relationship between my mother and Grete. I remained certain that the longer I stayed away from home, the better my chances would be that my mother would change her attitude and she would come around to my way of thinking. I hadn't heard any news from home in months, and as always, when I started thinking too much about the Old Country, I would start to feel sorry for myself. I pulled out Grete's last letter, which I kept in my shirt pocket. I could barely make out the words in the dim light . . . *you must all be crazy to want to live in that wild country . . . will you even be home by fall?* Running my fingers across the page brought her fine, white skin, her soft, blue eyes alive. I had been gone from home for two years by then. I could've stayed on the train and gone directly to Vancouver—wired my old man for money—he wouldn't have refused. I could've caught a freighter and worked my way around the world—been home by Christmas.

We got off at Terrace, right there on the Skeena, a nice little town that hadn't been on the map for much more than twenty years. It was a friendly town, too, that left a favorable impression on me. We met up with a German by the name of Gus Gaensbauer who worked in the local sawmill. He worked six days a week, ten hours a day and made about $3.50 a day. When we told him we were looking for homestead property, he invited us to stay with him and his family while we hiked around the area. Mr. and Mrs. Gaensbauer were a young couple in their thirties with a little boy and had left Germany a few years before I did. They made us feel welcome, and we chopped wood and did repair work around the place to help with our room and board.

Naturally, all the good land around Terrace had been pre-empted years before. The town, surrounded by mountains, was basically a farming community situated along the terraced banks of the Skeena. But I had no interest in settling there, not then, and besides, I had my homestead on the Babine. But I always enjoyed new scenery, new country and meeting new people. Fritz, in the meantime, met up with another Swiss-German who had lived around Terrace for years and decided to stay on for awhile. So, with a promise to the Gaensbauers that I'd come back to visit, I was on the freight the next day on my way back to the Circle J in Westwold.

The leaves of the cottonwoods and birch along the gravel bars of the Skeena were showing early traces of yellow and the nights already had a good nip in the air. I jumped off the freight in Burns Lake, tired and grubby, hoping by chance a letter might be waiting for me, but the mail clerk shook his head and I left dejected and empty-handed. I hoisted my pack onto my back, wondering where I'd spend the night, when I spotted a familiar team of horses. My face broke into a grin. I kicked my heels together, hitched up my pants, and sure enough, there was George Nelson sitting in the beer parlour with a few old-timers.

"Cripes almighty," he shouted, standing up and stretching out his hand. "What in hell's blazes brings you back here?" He grinned from ear to ear, obviously pleased to see me again, and when he asked if I would go back to the Babine with him, I didn't need much arm twisting. I used up the last of my cash for provisions and loaded everything onto George's wagon.

Late the following afternoon I was back on the homestead. The old cabin was cool and damp inside. I fired up the rusting stove and propped open the door with a block of wood to let the sunlight stream in. It was good to be home. A cast iron frying pan hung from the wall and a shovel stood in the corner. I unpacked my goods and settled in. The days were still warm and the marsh grass in the flats, tall as a cow's belly, rippled and swayed in the wind. The heady scent of ripened grass and pine needles drifted in the soft, breezy air. Every day I picked sweet, ripe blueberries and ate my fill. Sparrows and chickadees and whiskey jacks hopped around looking for handouts. Sky blue forget-me-nots grew three feet high along the creek, and on my way to George's cabin I bent over and picked a handful. "*Vergissmeinnicht*," I said out loud, thinking of Grete's beautiful blue eyes, hoping she would one day understand why I had come back to the homestead.

"This land, eh. It get in your blood," Joe said, when I visited him again. His black eyes smiled and he looked skyward, stretching out long, brown arms. "We never leave land. This spot sacred, eh. Mebbe you stay long time?"

The next couple of weeks Joe and I helped George with the haying. The sky was clear, the air dry, and every day we turned the mixture of peavine, marsh grass, and red top until it was dry enough to haul into the barn.

George had given Puma back to the Indians as he had no need of an extra horse and didn't want to feed him over the winter. I knew I could get him back when I was ready.

We were just finishing up with the haying when a forest ranger came along on a horse looking for fire fighters.

"We've got a bush fire about sixty miles up the lake. A dozen men are getting camp ready and we need all the reinforcements we can get. The government'll pay you."

I looked at George and he squared his heavy shoulders.

"I'm too damned old," he said, "but they'll need your help all right. You ain't seen nothin 'til you seen one of those timber fires burn outta control. I fought plenty years ago on the Coast."

I loaded my pack and left with the forest ranger. Several young Indians came along with us. Far to the west across the lake the sky had turned a thick, hazy gray. When we got to Burns Lake, the ranger gave me the job of finding reinforcements. I drummed up every farmer within a thirty-mile radius, and couple days later about fifty wagons loaded down with food, axes, picks, shovels and camping equipment were headed along the wagon trail to Babine Lake.

Acrid smoke hung blue and thick among the towering spruce where about three hundred men were camped close to the lake. Next morning, with our picks and shovels on our backs we made our way along the lake toward the fire. The smell of smoke clung to our clothes, even though the wind had shifted, sending the smoke west along the lake. Nobody seemed to be in any particular hurry to reach the fire.

"We're not going to get any fires out this way," I said to one of the men.

"Just don't you worry about it, you bohunk," said a dark-looking fellow with a heavy beard and a wad of snoose in his bottom lip. "You done your work. You done one hellofa job rounding everyone up, so just relax." Then he jerked his thumb and mumbled to the guy next to him. "We finally get us a payin' job and he wants to douse it with water and pick axes."

It was one against two hundred and ninety-nine solid-looking guys, so there wasn't much I could do. We dug in our heels, and that fire kept happily burning well into mid September when the rains came and finally drowned it. I didn't do any real fire fighting that time around, but I eventually had more than enough experience with forest fires. Although the fire put about $100,000 into the economy around Burns Lake, well over a 100 million feet of valuable old growth timber had burned.

We pulled up stakes, and before I headed back to Beaver Creek on the Babine, I wrote to my family, to Max and Arno, and . . . *to my sweetheart . . .*

How can I begin to explain to you why I am back here in the North instead of on a ship crossing the Atlantic on my way home to you? You must believe me when I say my plans were settled. I was making a decent wage at the ranch—I wrote you all about it—which would have afforded me the trip home, until I was summoned by the police to come up here, and all under a false accusation. There's so much to tell you! Then I had the opportunity to see the Pacific Coast with a Swiss I met. Grete, the country opened up new vistas and more friendly people for me. You may think this is a land uninhabited by women, but I met the nicest family, the Gaensbauers, in the town of Terrace, far west of here. The Gaensbauers are also from Germany and they love it in the North. Many families settle up here and the women aren't tough as shoe leather, if that's what you might think. Some dress quite fashionably, too. They can order just about anything they want by mail from a catalogue.

Travelling along the Skeena River by train was an experience I'll never forget. I wish you could have been with me to see the towering peaks covered with shining snow, the never-ending river, deep and treacherous in places, wide and meandering around miniature islands in others, heaped with forests of driftwood. Try to imagine travelling for miles and miles without seeing another soul. The Skeena is longer and swifter, I'm sure, than the Rhine—maybe not as romantic without the castles—but pure and wild and with its own Lorelei legends. The Skeena also has a famous rock

rising out of the water where the river god lives and demands a
sacrifice for protection.

Tomorrow morning I'm returning to the Babine homestead—
just for the winter. I need to try my hand at another season of
trapping now that I'm experienced, and if the winter's good and
cold, the furs will pay well. If I go south, back to the Circle J, I'd have
no opportunity to make a decent wage over the winter. You have to
understand, Grete, how important it is for me—for us—to remain
independent of my family, and I especially don't want to arrive back
in Rehau in threadbare pants and worn-out shoes looking like all
that is missing is my bowler and cane. And you don't need to worry
that I might settle on the homestead for good. It is far too remote,
even I will admit to that, and I could never, would never settle
anywhere without you.

The months will pass quickly, and soon, very soon, I will be back
home and we'll be together again. When I get back home I'm going
to build a small summer cabin in the forest where my parents have
property. I think of you and miss you always—every minute of the
day. Don't give up on me and write soon and often.

Your Paul

The deep blue of the Babine was a welcoming sight. The annual
migration of ducks and geese and flocks of cranes filled the sky
with V-shaped, swift-moving clouds of whirring wings and noisy
honking. A cool breeze rustled the shimmering yellow and golden-
pink leaves of the poplar and cottonwood, and as always I felt
overwhelmed by the force of nature around me. Some of the flocks
of Canada geese and ducks—mallards, pintails, teal—settled along
the lake in small sandy bays and were as noisy and quarrelsome
as children, flapping their wings and skimming across the water.
Another year was around.

The next afternoon I crossed the flats to the Indian settlement
and greeted the tribe from Stuart Lake that had returned to net
and dry salmon. Joe was hauling in a net with a couple other
Indians.

"*Suento*, Joe," I called out to him. "*Whudinzoo* ... nice
weather."

His long, black hair swung into his eyes. "Aha, you spend winter after all, eh?" he asked, letting go of the net and coming over to shake my hand. "Goot you come back. Mebbe we go hunting later, eh. Plenty more moose this year. Cold winter. Here, you try salmon?"

I prepared for the winter, drying and smoking my own salmon, hauling in dead wood, chopping green wood and preparing the trapline. I re-chinked part of the cabin and sealed the window with boards until I could replace it with glass or new cellophane. I went over to Stuart Lake to get Puma. Red kerchiefs for the women, some tobacco, and a couple of pints of whiskey, and I was on my way home with my stallion. I was patient with Puma and for the first few days didn't even try to ride him. He would paw and snort and every time I put a sack on his back he shifted away from me and tried to take a chunk out of my backside. But slowly we made friends again, and before long he whinnied and came to me when he heard my whistle.

One day early in November Joe asked me to go moose hunting with him, so we packed some gear and headed toward Cunningham Lake. Ice had formed on the slough grass swamps sending the moose to higher country. A few inches of snow lay on the ground which made tracking easy. I hadn't done any moose hunting or even seen any moose close up, so I followed Joe in quiet anticipation through thickets of willow and leafless poplar. Joe stopped and carefully studied some large moose tracks. Several moose were feeding off the willows and not moving in any particular direction. Joe put his hands up to his mouth.

"Uuuuurrrnnn-ungh," he cried, imitating the call of a rutting male, hoping to attract their attention. We waited awhile and then he called again. "Uuurrrnnn-ungh." Suddenly we heard a moose crashing through the bush, but away from us.

"Moose him no see too goot, eh, but have goot smell," Joe whispered to me. We trailed after him and through a grove of poplars spotted a huge brown bull moose with a broad rack of shovel-like horns, head in the air and ears perked. He turned toward us and Joe lifted his rifle and fired. The moose took off through the brush, but Joe went after him and another shot brought him down. A third shot brought down a smaller moose. I was right on Joe's heels and he was grinning, obviously proud of himself. The big bull must have weighed about 1300 pounds on the hoof.

"That'll give your people plenty of meat for the winter," I said.

Joe just laughed and shook his head. "Mebbe for month or so. Tribe come and help us with animals."

Moose was important to the Indians as it provided them not only with meat, which they cut into strips and dried, or froze, but the hides provided them with a good part of their clothing and blankets. We skinned the animals and cut out the tongues, hearts, brains, and livers, which were real delicacies and packed home as much as we could carry.

When we told the Indians about the moose, half the clan dropped what they were doing and went back with us. They took every scrap of hide, meat and bone that was left. They even cleaned out the stomachs.

"*Utsung 'i tazul ba unzoo . . .* make good soup."

In mid November George took a trip to Burns Lake, and when he returned a few days later, handed me a stack of letters. I think I must have been the happiest fellow north of the 49th parallel. I wet my finger and leafed through my mail. There was one from Gusti, letters from Little Max and Arno . . . and one from Grete.

"Don't take too much time readin' those, now," said George. "You and Joe gotta get the rest of the supplies up the lake before dark." George had left the sleigh at the end of the wagon road with the heavier supplies, and Joe and I were to go up the lake with his twenty-foot flat-bottomed boat to pick up the rest of the goods. I went back to the cabin to add a layer of clothes for the trip and, of course, to read my mail.

Both Maxes and Adam were still in Westwold, and Arno was down in Vancouver working at any odd job he could get. He wrote we were fools to stay up North and that we should come to the Coast where the weather was mild year round. Gusti sent a post card from Neuschwanstein, a fairy-tale castle in Southern Germany which had been built by a mad prince ... *We've been hiking for a month now, going from youth hostel to youth hostel. Herrlich. Wunderbar. Come home soon, Pauli!*

Then I tore open Grete's letter.

July 10, 1931

My dear Paul,

You mean you have actually settled down on the ranch? Does this mean you will earn enough money to be home by the fall? Your life sounds right out of a Karl May book. I can hardly believe that nearly two years have passed since we said good-bye. You really will be home by fall? If you don't come back soon I will forget what you look like, and from the last picture you sent, you have changed so much. You are very thin and I hardly recognize you in a beard.

Life goes on here, much the same as always, except for all the Nazi propaganda and Nazi parades. Mother says that the fear of starvation from the Great War still sticks in the bones of the Germans, and all the promises of work that Hitler offers are a ray of hope for people desperate and out of work. He declares himself as the last hope for the millions of Germans looking for a job! More and more people are joining the Party, especially the young people. What else is there for them to do, that's what they think. Anyone out of work can find a job with the Party—they put on a uniform and march up and down the streets carrying flags and collecting money.

I saw a movie about a month ago that you would like—"The Blue Angel" with Marlene Dietrich who plays a night club performer. It's a talkie and she sings in it. She has a beautiful, sultry voice. Do you ever go to movies? I don't suppose you would have heard that Anna Pavlova died in January. She was already fifty. You're lucky you saw her perform in Berlin. I read that at her villa in London she had a lake filled with swans. Did she dance the Swan Lake when you saw her?

I sometimes wonder if you will like it here when you come back home. Rehau doesn't sound very exciting compared to all the wild things you do. I'm not sure that I'll write to you again since you might be catching a train or a boat for home by the time you receive this letter. I sometimes try to imagine what it will be like to see you again. It's been a long time, you know. The wild roses are especially beautiful this year. They remind me of you—when we walked across the fields. I hope you like the picture I'm sending. It was taken last December in Nuremberg at the Kristkindl Markt.

My love to you . . .

Grete

I lay the letter down and picked up the picture. Grete wore a dark coat and a felt hat that looked like an upside-down bowl. Her fancy high-heeled shoes had straps like Gusti had written about. I shook my head, thinking how out of place she'd be in the wilderness. But she must still think of me, I thought, or she wouldn't write a'tall. Her full, rounded cheeks and soft lips smiled out at me. I put the picture and letter back in the envelope and tucked it into my shirt pocket. Pulling on my hat and jacket, I ducked out the door and breathed in the fresh and crisp air. I let out a howl and went off on a run down to Joe's place. Grete would have heard by then that I wouldn't make it back home until the following year. I missed her like all blazes, but I knew that when the time came and I was really ready to pack up and go home, I could rely on my parents to bail me out, but that would be a last resort.

The sun was directly overhead when Joe and I left with his boat to pick up the supplies, leaving us not much more than about three good daylight hours. When we got to where the supplies were stashed, ten miles up the lake, the wind had picked up and the waves were rough and choppy. Tears ran out of my eyes from the cold and I didn't like the looks of it one bit.

"We'd better make camp here for the night under some trees," I told Joe. This time I wasn't up to taking any chances, even if Joe did have a good outboard motor.

"My motor powerful," he said grinning. "I ride even bigger waves with no trouble many times. And extra gas can, too."

So we loaded up the supplies and steered the boat away from the rough shore line, but we still smashed down hard on the waves. About five miles down the lake the motor conked out. I grabbed a paddle to keep us from getting beached while Joe fiddled around with the motor. One wave after another sloshed against the boat, sending an icy spray into our faces. Then a rolling wave broadsided us and the boat capsized. The waves rolled over top of us and the frigid, water had us soaked and freezing in seconds. We hustled to get everything out of the boat onto dry land, but the sacks of sugar dissolved before we even got to them. The sacks of flour and rolled oats were soaked, too, but salvageable, and the pails of syrup and cans of jam and the other tinned supplies were okay.

We were thoroughly frozen by then and wasted no time to find a sheltered spot and gather some wood. I pulled out my watertight matches, and in minutes we had a roaring fire with red-hot warming flames shooting several feet into the air. Suddenly my hand went to my chest. Grete's letter. With shivering fingers I pulled it out, and sure enough the water had run the ink together, but it didn't matter as her words were already in my memory. The picture was still okay, though a deep fold ran right through Grete's face. We wrung out our clothes, pulled them back on even though they were still wet, and turned ourselves round and round in front of the hot fire the whole night. Next morning Joe miraculously brought the motor to life and we made it safely back home with our mess of groceries.

About a week later—I'd just come back from a run on the trapline—Joe came up to the cabin accompanied by the R.C.M.P. and the fisheries officer. I invited them in, wondering what the heck they were going to knock me for this time.

The young Mountie leaned his .30-.30 against the wall. "Just a few questions, Mr. Hertel," he said in a deep, serious voice, turning his brown Stetson hat round and round in his hands.

I nodded and told them to sit down, thinking they were going to get me for trading Puma for whiskey, but then the Indians were pretty tight-lipped, and had they talked they would have put themselves into jeopardy. I knew the officer as he was the same guy who had been around the year before, but when I looked at him his eyes shifted away from mine.

"You familiar with Trembleur Lake?" the Mountie asked.

I shook my head. "All I know is that it's north of here, north of Stuart Lake, but I've never been there."

"And what about Fort St. James? Ever done any dealings around there?"

What did he mean by dealings, I thought. I shrugged my shoulders and hoisted up my pants. "I know it's at the end of Stuart Lake and that it's a Hudson's Bay post, but, no, I'm not familiar with the place."

"You don't know anyone from there?"

"No, nobody," I said. "Only people I know on Stuart Lake are the Indians."

"Well, we're asking you these questions," the Mountie continued, "because two Germans were murdered at Trembleur Lake last spring. You'll have to pardon me, but since you're German, we have to do some routine questioning."

"Well, what happened?"

"It was late last spring after the thaw. Three Germans had bought a canoe at Fort St. James and went up the Tachie River to Trembleur Lake, but several weeks later only one returned, sold a lot of goods and left for the Prairies. We got news of the murders a few weeks later, and after we investigated and made a search, we found the bodies. The man was finally apprehended in Prince Albert, Saskatchewan."

He paused and pulled up his pant legs. "He's going on trial for his life in Prince George, and we just thought if you knew anything a'tall, we could use your cooperation."

I couldn't help them, and as it turned out, the accused man was condemned to death in Prince George, but at a later trial in Kamloops he was acquitted and deported to Germany.

Sometime after the Mountie had talked to me, I heard the real story from an Indian who claimed to be an eyewitness to the murders. He was a little drunk when he told me the story, and I wasn't sure that he was telling me the truth, yet there wasn't any reason for him to make it up. Apparently, the Germans had taken two cases of whiskey up to Trembleur Lake and traded it with the Indians for their winter catch of fur. Once the Indians got a little whiskey into them, it was easy to bargain with them, and the Germans realized that it was a simple way to get rich quick. But the trick was to be gone before the Indians wised up. Well, these three guys were contentedly sitting in their tent one night when one of the Indians sobered up enough to realize they'd been cheated out of their winter's catch of fur. By then a few other Indians wanted their skins back, too. A gunfight ensued and two of the Germans ended up dead. Of course, the one that escaped knew how serious the offense was for peddling liquor to the Indians, so he was afraid to report the murders to the authorities.

My work on the trapline became pretty routine, and there was so much for me to do that I never even thought about getting lonely anymore. Besides, I'd acquired a dog from the Indians, so he was good company for me at the cabin, although I couldn't take him along on the trapline for fear he'd go after the bait and get caught in a trap or a snare.

One night shortly before Christmas, Joe came over to the cabin about ten o'clock to tell me there was a light across the lake. From the edge of the lake we could see the flickering of a fire like the eye of a cyclops glowing in the dark, but we had no idea who it could be. But out in the back country like that, if anything looks suspicious you always check it out, so about five in the morning Joe and I loaded some blankets and extra clothes into the boat and took off down the lake to investigate. It was still dark when we broke ice at the edge of the lake, but by the time we got to where we could see smoke from a smouldering fire, a milky yellow sky had begun to form behind us.

We pulled the boat up on shore and scrambled over some logs to the fire. "Well holy moley," I said to Joe, and immediately began to shake the two men by the shoulders who were lying like stiffs in about two inches of water with a caking of ice. There lay my best friends, Little Max and Adam John, with the black sleep of death hovering over them.

"Get the blankets and clothes, Joe," I yelled, shaking the guys to life. We re-stoked the glowing embers of the fire and got them quickly into dry clothes.

"You guys're a godsend," said Max shaking like a dog. His face was chalk white against his beard that was frosted with white ice crystals. "I'd never have known, I'd never have known," he kept repeating.

Adam's teeth were chattering and his whole body was trembling. "I don't think we'd ever have woken up if you hadn't come along," he said, his face contorted with pain. His cheeks and nose had little white patches of frostbite.

We wrapped the men in blankets and got into the boat. All the way back I gently rubbed their noses and cheeks to get out the frostbite. They weren't frozen up too badly and after a few cups of hot coffee they began to feel alive again.

"We walked all the way from Burns Lake yesterday, hoping to make it to the cabin in one stretch," croaked Max, sticking out his heavy jaw.

"You oughtta know by now how long that trip takes and that the days are short. George and I always take two days, even in summer." I thought back on the reckless night Arno and I had spent on the lake.

"Well, I made it once before. But no matter. We got caught in the dark and couldn't see where we built the fire. Had no idea we were on swampy muskeg."

During the night the warmth of the fire had melted the ice underneath them, and they must have become so numb with cold and sleep, they didn't even feel the water.

Of course, Max and Adam wanted to surprise me for Christmas, and it was a pretty good feeling to have my friends with me again. They had brought special food—canned peaches, O'Henrys, strawberry jam, a bottle of rum. For Christmas dinner we had moose chops fried in bear grease with heaps of mashed potatoes supplied by George. But there was no mail for me, a repeat from the year before. By the time Grete and my family had heard I was staying another winter it would have been too late for them to send Christmas mail. Max and Adam, of course, had no intention of spending the rest of the winter with me, but I tried my darndest to persuade them.

"I can always use help on the trapline. We can trap muskrats through March, that's when their fur is prime. And you'd probably enjoy a few runs with me, Adam. Think of all the furs you could tan. You guys aren't making wages over the winter anyway, so stick it out here for a few months."

Max had finally developed into a man. His chest and shoulders had filled out and he had grown to his full height of 170 centimeters. He shook his head and laughed.

"I'm surprised you're not bushwhacked yet. And how can the trapline support all of us? At least back on the farm I know where my next meal is coming from."

"Since when did you miss a meal around here? You just have to step out the door and you have your choice—fish, bush chicken, meat of your choice. You guys could even think of settling here and we could try our hand at ranching, raise a few head of beef cattle like George. There's plenty of open meadow and good rich grass. The beef market could turn around and we'd be ahead of the game."

"You know, you're so full of malarky sometimes it won't be long and your hat won't fit," Little Max said, pushing his straight, black hair out of his face and jutting out his large, bony jaw. "You know damned well there's no bloody money in cattle and won't be by all the signs. Cripes, I know of a rancher who sent two carloads of prime steer to the Vancouver market and all he got for them was a bill for $38 from the C.N.R. for freight. And what happened to your plans about going back home? Has Grete given up on you, or what?"

"No, she hasn't given up on me," I said raising my voice. "I'm heading home in the New Year for sure with the money I'll make off the furs. She still writes and she knows I would never renege on my promise to her."

The boys didn't stay for more than a couple of weeks and I missed them badly when they left. Maybe I was being pig-headed, but I still wanted to finish the winter out, hoping to get a good cache of furs, but I knew that after the season, I, too, would probably leave the Babine Lake for good and give up the idea of claiming the land. I took another run on the trap line and picked up a few more skins. When I got home, my dog wasn't around, which filled me with some foreboding. I always left him tied up at the cabin and had an Indian throw him some fish when I was gone. I figured he must have tried to follow me so I went back out on the trapline. Sure enough, one of the snares was sprung and when I came to the next snare, I found him choked to death. I felt like I'd lost a good friend.

By March I decided to wind up the season. There was no future for me there on the homestead and the loneliness finally got to me. I came to understand what Little Max had meant when he talked about going bush crazy. But I had no regrets about the time I spent there on the Babine and came away with a great respect for the people that lived there and the land that supported them.

I remembered my friendship with the Gaensbauer family in Terrace and how they had urged me to return, so I figured if Gus could help me get a job in the mill at $3.50 a day, I would earn more than at the Circle J and be able to set some money aside to get back home to my sweetheart. From Terrace I could go straight to Prince Rupert and take the ferry to Vancouver.

I bartered another horse from the Indians so I could pack all my gear out, but before packing everything up, I went over to George's cabin to have one last cup of his specially brewed coffee. I stood in front of the small glass-paned window imprinting on my mind the slope of the land, the swift rise of the mountains, the peaceful marshes.

"Sit down, Paul," George said, pouring some whiskey into my cup. "No need for the long face. If I was your age and could do it over again, why, I'd probably be long gone myself." He picked up some tobacco and carefully sprinkled it onto the cigarette paper. "Your friends have left, your girl is waiting for you, and except for the challenge and beauty of this country, there's nothing holding you here."

The warmth of the hot whiskey spread through my body.

I leaned back and stretched out my legs. "You're right," I said nodding. "It's been lonely without them, and as much as I'm attached to this place and enjoy your company—get along with the Indians—it's time to move on. You've been a real help to me, and to Arno and Max, too. I hate to see the land go back to the government, though."

George lifted the lid of the stove to light the tightly rolled cigarette. "Yeah, but you don't owe nobody any taxes," he said, inhaling deeply.

We sat in quiet for awhile in our own thoughts.

"Maybe that's one of my biggest regrets," George finally said, blowing out a stream of smoke. "Never marrying, giving up too soon, you know how it is, and suddenly the years pass you by. But I got used to the solitary life and the years have been good."

When I stood up to leave, George looked me straight in the eyes. "Just make sure you get back home to your girl in time. A girl as beautiful as that."

"You've been a helluva friend, George, and, yeah, some woman did miss out."

I loaded up my bale of fur, bedding, cooking utensils, all of Grete's letters, and the few supplies I had on the pack horse. Puma was well broke by then and no longer minded being ridden. We had become good pals and he never failed to come up and nuzzle me and whinny when I was close by. I stopped by Joe's place on the way out. The snow had melted around the cabin, exposing brown, matted grass, and pussy willows were breaking out of their shells.

"Someday, my friend, you come back, eh," he said in his quiet, clipped manner of speaking. His dark eyes lit up. "Your word for goot-bye . . . *Aufwieder . . . sehen*, same as our people's word, eh. We see you again?"

I grinned and laid my hand on his shoulder. "*Ah-ah*, yes, *Nan yse Tenlah*. I'll never forget you, Joe Hansen," I said. "You're a good man. And damn rights I'll get back here somehow, someday."

When I left, I was looking forward to easier times, a regular job, and my trip back to the Old Country, but how could I have known what lay ahead of me, and that I was to walk from one adventure right into another.

14. Disaster on the Copper River

JANUARY 19, 1932

Dear Paul,

Your last letter arrived two weeks ago and the one before that in November, three days after my birthday. And I thought you would have been back in Rehau by then! I guess there must be some truth about the pull of the North. Why would you otherwise stay in a part of the country where the winters are long and icy cold and the living so primitive you may as well be back in the Stone Age? Do you have magnets in your feet? Maybe plenty of women do live in the North and dress fashionably, but I couldn't imagine such a life.

On my birthday Mathilda and some of our other old friends met on the Sunday afternoon at Cafe Koeberling for a tea dance. Everyone always asks about you, but you may as well be in Siberia as far as they are concerned. We danced and sang songs and then somebody pushed the zither in front of me. I played all the old pieces and we had a good time. Mathilde and I went to a Zither and Mandolinen Konzert here in November. With forty players you can imagine how beautiful the sound.

Don't you ever get lonely? And you're really staying another winter? At least when you come home a job will be waiting for you. My stepfather says that 6,000,000 people are out of work now, and around Rehau some of the farmers are afraid of losing their property. He says young men only join Hitler's brownshirted SA because they are promised tobacco and chocolate and new boots with real leather. Who doesn't have a shirt on his back can wear a brownshirt is the motto, he says. Are things really so bad in Canada too? I read in the Rehauer Tagblatt last fall that hundreds of miners in Saskatchewan went on strike. Is that close to you? They were led by Communists who carried Soviet flags. They got into a fight with the police and two strikers were killed and many injured.

We recently saw the American film "Jack Diamond" which was about murder and alcohol smuggling. Next week "Nur Wieder Liebe" with Lilian Harvey, the sweetest girl in the world, is playing. You probably think that all I do is go to movies. The propaganda before the movie begins gets tiring, though. There's always a short film about Hitler—'One Nation, One Leader, One Volk.'

You probably never heard of Hitler's niece, Geli Raubl. Well I hadn't either until she shot herself in Munich last September. She had been living with "Adolf" and the Frankische Tagespost reported a "mysteriousness" around the whole affair. Mathilde and I heard about it in Nuremberg.

The winter has been unusually warm. Already snowdrops are pushing up through the ground, but there also has been heavy flooding from so much rain, especially in Dessau on the Mulde.

Fasching time is here again and next week is the Winterball at Cafe Horn. And you are still living in a world of white, bitter cold. This time I won't ask when you will come home, but keep well.

Love . . . Grete

My heart was in my throat, I can tell you, when I read Grete's letter, but at the same time there was a tightness in my chest because I felt a distancing in her words. She had waited until after Christmas to write, and that she had dropped the "My" from *Dear Paul* didn't go unnoticed either. Maybe she wouldn't be waiting for me when I got back home, regardless of my reassurances, but that was a chance I had to take.

When I thought of all the unemployed in Germany, though, it didn't mean much to me. My homeland was becoming more and more disconnected in my mind, and other than Grete, I thought of home less frequently, though that vague feeling of *Heimweh* or homesickness, or maybe it was lovesickness, never quite left me.

I sold my skins and picked up a few supplies from Brunell's grocery.

"So you're headed for Terrace," Mr. Brunell said, setting a bag of rolled oats, a slab of bacon and canned beans on the counter. "You may want to check out an old pack trail through the Hazelton

Mountains," he continued, crossing his arms over his broad chest. "Might save you some time and a lot of miles. Don't know that it's been used much in the last few years, but ask about it when you get to Telkwa."

The next few days I rode Puma, with the pack horse trailing behind, along the dirt road going west and spent the nights at different farms where people were always more than happy to put me up. When I arrived at Telkwa, I asked an old man with thin, watery eyes and a heavily lined face if he knew about the condition of the trail.

"Oh, that trail ain't been used hardly a'tall since the turn of the century, I don't think. Don't know if anyone's been over it in thirty years."

"But it's passable?" I asked.

He shrugged his shoulders. "I don't rightly know, but if you go into Tutty Mines," and he pointed his finger across the Bulkley River, "... you can follow a road along the Telkwa. You'll find a watchman still there. The mine's closed, though."

I pulled out my map. By shortcutting across the mountains, I could save a lot of miles. Although there was a road from Telkwa up to Hazelton and on to Terrace, it was an old wagon road made out of corduroy and from what I'd heard, it was as rough as walking on a railroad grade.

"You know how many miles through the mountains from here to Terrace?" I asked the old man.

"Oh, I'm not sure, but you should save yourself a good eighty, I suppose."

I thanked the fellow and hopped up on Puma, giving him a few pats on the neck. He was as gentle as a lamb by then. It took me the rest of the day to get to the Tutty Mines. The watchman was there, all right, an old stringy-looking guy with a handlebar mustache.

"There's a trail, yep; you might find some old markings along the way still, I'd say." One of his eyes turned westward. "If you want, you can spend the night here and get off to an early start. Over there's an old corral you can use," he said pointing a long skinny finger.

"I sure appreciate that. I'll take you up on your offer," I said. "When's the last time *you* been over the trail?"

He sat down on the steps of his cabin and puffed on his pipe. "Me?" He laughed and shook his head. "I don't hike nowhere no more, young man. And I don't even remember the last time I seen someone come through there. But I used to hunt some a ways in there." He stuck out his chin and pointed to the mountains. "There's a natural pass right through Hunter Basin. You might even find an old campsite or two."

"Any rivers to cross?"

"I'd say," he said nodding his head. "You probably have to ford the Copper. May be a little high with spring runoff, but if you're careful and find a shallow crossing and don't hit too much rain, it shouldn't be no problem."

I left the next morning, leading the horses along an old trail that followed the Telkwa River. The trail was overgrown with willow and alder, but still passable, and here and there I'd spot old slash marks on the trees. We hit some heavy rain but by the next day the dark clouds had blown away, and after steadily climbing the mountain pass through jack pines and spruce, we came to a beautiful open basin of alpine meadows which made the going easier. Along the way I shot rabbits and blue grouse for a good, hot evening stew. Blue grouse were always an easy catch as they wouldn't fly until you were almost standing on top of them. Patches of snow still lay on the meadows, and up on the cliffs I spotted white dots of mountain goats.

But it wasn't all easy going. The fourth day out I got quite a scare. We had come into a forested area, and I was still able to pick up the trail, but there must have been quite a wind storm at one time because there were a lot of downed trees.

I checked if I could get the horses around the slash, but there were cliffs going down on one side and up on the other, so I had no choice but to move on through the jungle of windfalls that were strewn in every direction. On top of it, they were overgrown with vines and brush. The horses could easily have broken a leg if they got stuck between the logs and couldn't move left or right. I had to take them over the logs one at a time and it took some patience with a lot of pulling and coaxing.

After a lunch break we were on our way again. A wind had kicked up and the pines were swaying overhead. Suddenly Puma stopped in his tracks and began to snort and back up. He snapped back his head and I really had to hustle to pull him up short and get both horses in control. Only then did I see a huge, tan-colored grizzly lumbering toward us with two cubs, not more than a hundred feet away. My body prickled with electricity. I knew through the grapevine that grizzlies could really travel when they got mad, but they were also shy, especially of humans, unless you ran into a mother with her cubs. The fur on her front haunches rippled in the streaked rays of sun as she grazed, moving slowly toward us. The wind was blowing in our direction so she and her cubs kept ambling along unaware of us. She hadn't smelled us, and to my surprise, hadn't heard us either. With trembling fingers I pulled my rifle out of the pack and slowly cocked it. Puma yanked back on the reins and whinnied. The bear's head shot up and her ears flattened. She let out a loud huff and stood up on her hind legs, swaying back and forth and sticking her nose in the air. Then she turned her dish-shaped face toward her young ones and to my relief pivoted on a dime and hightailed it out of there with her family.

The next day we arrived at the Copper River. The high milky-blue water boiled and churned along at a good clip. The river ran north and south and I was quite concerned about the prospect of crossing it. I rope hobbled the horses and hiked up and down the river looking for an easier crossing, but there was nothing. At least from that point there was a nice sandy landing a few hundred yards down the river, and after sizing up the situation I felt confident enough that my stallion and packhorse could handle the current. They were powerful animals and used to water.

I made a fire and boiled some water for tea. Dark clouds hung low on the mountains and I could smell rain in the air, but rain didn't worry me any. The thought of the icy water is what gave me the willies. After eating some smoked fish and finishing off the pot of hot tea, I lay back on the grass for a ten-minute nap. I awoke to big drops of water splatting on my face and jerked up my head, not knowing for a moment where I was. Puma and the gelding were grazing peacefully a few yards away, tearing and crunching at the new shoots of grass. I got up and walked over to them.

"Okay, boys, time to get your bathing suits on. We're going for a little swim." I rubbed Puma's nose. His nostrils felt as soft and warm as velvet and his big brown eyes no longer held the fear of a white man. His big, warm lips nibbled at my fingers and he let out a soft snort.

I took off my clothes and put on my rubber pants and a rubber coat, packing everything securely on the horses. I looked up the river hoping there might be a break in the flow. Down river a back eddy swirled around the sandbar close to the landing. It took some coaxing to get the horses into the swift-moving water, but I knew that once they started to swim they'd make a beeline for the other side. Puma pawed and snorted and refused to leave the bank until I put a willow stick down hard on his haunches. I firmly gripped his tail with one hand and the packhorse's rope with the other and plunged into the searing, icy water, feeling like the air was being sucked out of my lungs. The horses swam strong with their heads high, but the landing came up in seconds, and as we approached the other side the swift water propelled all of us downstream away from the sandy bank. The river was deep and fast and I was surprised how quickly the heavy undertow pulled us along. I tried not to panic, as there wasn't much I could do but hang tight to Puma's tail.

"Just take it easy, old fella. We'll find a spot. Easy now, easy now." I could hear his heavy breathing as we drifted toward a narrow canyon area where the water became more turbulent and headed downstream at an even faster clip. I let go of the pack-horse's rope and was already so cold that my legs began to cramp and I couldn't bend a single joint. The horses and I drifted down river for probably close to a mile with no way in sight out of the steep, rocky sides, but I knew my only chance to survive, was to get out of that water darn quick. I forced my fingers to bend and at the next opportunity grabbed some overhanging branches. The water pulled me down, but with a heave I swung myself onto the bank on the same side of the river that we had entered. For the first few minutes I was so freezing cold and disoriented that I ran around in circles. Pain hammered through my limbs and I was sick to my stomach, but more sick about losing the horses, especially Puma. I told myself they would somehow find a safe landing and eventually rip the packs off their backs by rolling or brushing against some trees.

It took me some minutes until I realized I had lost everything— my gear, my guns, my old faithful feather bed that I'd brought over from the Old Country, the last of the money I had made from the furs, and Grete's letters. I had no shoes, no food, and worst of all, no matches. My rubber overcoat and pants, which felt cold and clammy next to my skin, were the only protection from the wind and the cold, sleeting rain. The old saying about being up a creek without a paddle really hit home.

Things didn't look encouraging, but the only chance I had was to return to Telkwa along the trail through the mountains. I started off immediately and hiked until dusk. The only way to keep warm and dry, I figured, was to make a pile of moss and spruce needles and burrow underneath like an animal. The rain was still falling so I put the rubber coat on top of my makeshift bed to keep the water off. I kept warm enough overnight, but every time I moved, the moss and needles prickled and irritated my skin.

As soon as daylight broke, I was on my way again, itching and scratching. Water was plentiful, but that didn't help the sharp and gnawing hunger pangs. Along the way I ate grass and dandelions and tried to catch minnows in pools of water alongside the river, but that did little to relieve my stomach cramps. The rain kept pouring down and I kept moving along at a good pace to keep myself warm. That night I made myself the same moss and pine needle bed. After two days my bare feet were sore and bleeding and I would stop to rest and soak them in the icy river water. Grouse flew up from under my feet and several times I almost had one in my grasp. My mouth watered at the thought of raw meat. I'd stalk them, crawling over moss-covered logs and through the undergrowth, but all I got were feathers in my face.

I began to think of Charlie Chaplin in *The Gold Rush* and how he at least had some leather boots to cook up when he didn't have a bite to eat. After five days the rain stopped and steam began to rise from the ground with the first rays of the warming sun, but soon the no-see-ums and mosquitoes came out in full force. Welts covered my body and I itched like dynamite. I still made myself the same bed every night because it was the best way to keep warm and protect myself from the mosquitoes. I was bone tired but all I could think of was food. I'd dream of feasts my mother had prepared—apple cakes, potato dumplings with rich, brown gravy, bratwurst dipping in grease. "*Iss, doch,*" she'd tell me. "Eat!" But I couldn't eat and when I finally reached for the food my fingers were too stiff and clumsy to pick it up.

I kept track of the days by marking a walking stick that I used. I stumbled along on swollen feet and by the time a week had passed, my legs ached constantly and I had to stop frequently to rest. The sharp pangs of hunger had given way to a dull, gnawing ache. I scratched around for roots and sometimes I'd find sprouts of wild stringy onions. One morning I didn't have the energy to hoist myself out from under my spruce-needle bed. It would have been easier to fall into an endless sleep, and the temptation became great, but I thought of Old George swinging his scythe, and saw the golden, rippling marsh grass. I imagined Grete running across the meadow toward me, her soft, blue eyes laughing in the wind. Her pictures and the pocket watch were somewhere in the Copper River, but her letters were all in my head. I read them over and over in my mind and recited them out loud. The words gave me the strength to keep going.

Sometimes I lost the trail and had to double back. The endless bush was a torture and each step a painful effort, but I drove myself to keep moving and never gave up hope that there would be help around the next bend.

On the ninth day, in the late afternoon, I reached the Tutty Mine. The watchman's eyes were as big as saucers when he opened the door to my knocking.

"Well, I say, you are a poor son of a gun. My . . . your eyeballs'r swollen shut, lips all cracked."

My mouth moved, but I could only croak out a few words. The watchman sat me down on his couch and pulled off my rubber clothes. He wrapped me in a blanket and spoon-fed me some hot soup before I fell into a dead sleep for hours. When I awoke he had a tub of hot water waiting for me. I stunk like a polecat, but after a long soak and some more good hot soup, I began to feel better. That watchman saved my life, no doubt about it. He gave me shoes and clothes and all the food I could eat, and believe me, I had such a yawning appetite that I kept eating whatever he put in front of me, which was the worst thing I could have done because I ended up paying for it dearly. But I couldn't seem to get filled up.

A couple of days later I caught a freight out of Telkwa and got off at Smithers. When I explained to the police what had happened, they gave me a couple of bucks to help me out. I went into the Chinese cafe and ordered myself a delicious meal. From there I caught the train to Terrace. When I knocked on the Gaensbauer's door, they were shocked to see me, especially in the condition I was in. But they welcomed me and Mrs. Gaensbauer made sure I got more than enough to eat.

After a few days, just when I thought I had recovered from my ordeal, I got so sick I couldn't get out of bed. My hands and arms began to swell and my legs looked and felt like white concrete pillars. The family called in Dr. Mills, who diagnosed me as having Ludwig Angina, better known as trench feet.

"Trench feet?" I asked. Cripes almighty, I thought to myself. That's exactly what George Nelson said I wouldn't have to worry about.

"Too long in the wet and cold, and filling your belly didn't help, either," Dr. Mills said.

Well, he tended me like a baby, putting on hot and cold compresses to ease the pain and lessen the swelling, but everyday I just kept swelling up more and more. No matter where I was poked, a hole would remain. My body accumulated so much fluid, and the pressure got so intense, that I began to have difficulty breathing. My heart pounded so fast it sounded like a roar and I felt as if my life was being squeezed right out of me.

When Dr. Mills sat down on the bed with deep furrows in his forehead, I knew I was in trouble. "We gotta get you to Prince Rupert right away," he finally said nodding his head. "No use taking you to my two-room hospital."

By then I didn't care what kind of help I got or whether I got any. I remember being loaded onto a stretcher and hearing the clacking of the train wheels. When I arrived in Prince Rupert, a doctor operated on me immediately. I remember a nurse's soft, cool hand on my forehead and someone muttering it was midnight. They made an incision in my throat and drained out all the excess fluid to take off the terrible pressure—that's what I was told later.

When I woke up from the anaesthesia the first thing I did was sit up and say, "Gee whiz, I feel fine." But I was far from fine, and if I hadn't reached the hospital in the nick of time, I almost certainly would have died of a heart attack.

"You're tougher'n a boiled beaver," the nurse told me, patting me on the shoulder. "You just take it easy for awhile and you'll be like brand new."

"If I weren't tied to this bed, I'd take you to a dance," I said. The anaesthesia hadn't quite worn off because she must have been old enough to be my mother, but I was higher than a kite. "What's a beautiful girl like you," I asked, winking at her, "with a pair of legs like that doing out here in the bush?"

"They always babble after a dose of laughing gas," she said with a smile, taking my pulse with her warm hand.

I was feeling my oats all right, but I was damn glad I was alive, and grateful for the good care. After a week in the hospital, where they nearly starved me to death so my body could slowly adjust to food, I was discharged with a clean bill of health and even given a train ticket back to Terrace as a regular passenger. I sure felt good when I got out of the hospital, but by then it was the end of June and somewhere I had lost nearly six weeks.

15. The Balancing Act

LOUISE AND GUS GAENSBAUER WERE QUITE relieved when I returned to Terrace because they thought for sure they had seen the last of me when I was carried away on a stretcher.

Gus introduced me to his boss, George Little, who not only owned the local sawmill, but was one of the founders of Terrace and an all-around shrewd and successful business man. But business was pretty tight and Mr. Little couldn't help me, which was just as well because I was still unsteady on my feet and needed time to recuperate.

A few days later I met a Swede by the name of Jens Erlandson who told me about some beaver meadows north of Remo on the Zimacord River.

"Nice little valley dere," he said in his sing-song accent. He was tall and heavy shouldered with blond, thinning hair. "I got a cabin dere easy to find—about six miles up the river. Trap dere every winter. Why don't you look around. Stay as long as you vant. Rest up a liddle."

The Gaensbauers loaned me a gun, fishing gear, bedding, and loaded me up with a few provisions. I caught a speeder from Terrace to Remo, where I turned north on the Zimacord and followed a fairly good trail along the river bank. The days were warm by then and the thick growth of cottonwood, cedar and spruce kept the trail shaded and cool.

I found the cabin, on the fork of the Zimacord River and Erlandson Creek, which was set back from the river on a sloping meadow. Tall grass grew up to the doorstep and when I pushed open the door, cobwebs wrapped around my face. I felt quite fatigued from my trip and after I started a fire in the stove to make a pot of tea, I relaxed on the stoop in the warm afternoon sun. Beyond the river tall reeds and cattails swayed in the soft breeze and beyond the slough a dark forest of mixed timber sloped up the snow-capped mountain. Toward suppertime I threw my fishing line into a dark pool along the bank and within minutes caught a half dozen Dolly Vardens, enough for a good supper.

I dug in my heels and for the next six weeks did nothing but fish and shoot the occasional grouse and rabbit and enjoy the three-ring circus that life offered me. In my weakened condition, the location was an ideal paradise for my convalescence. You probably think it was a fool's paradise, a *Schlaraffenland*, as the Germans say, where laziness is revered and hard work frowned upon, but my body had a chance to recover, and I lived out there in nature feeling comfortable and right at home as I was quite experienced with the wilderness by then.

The weather was in my favour too. The summer sun was hot, the days long. Every afternoon I took a dip in the icy river water, feeling the burn move like fire through my muscles and tendons. Then I'd flop in the meadow and let the warm sun dry my tingling body. I breathed in the scent of the grasses and wildflowers while watching the clouds drift by. The colors of pink and red fireweed, yellow buttercups and dandelions, wild bluebells and lupins washed across my face like a painting. I'd yank at a stalk of grass and chew on the milky stem, vaguely aware of the humming of bees and insects.

Every now and then heavy thunderclouds rolled in and a cool shower freshened the air. Much of the time I sat up on the river bank and watched the black bears fishing for salmon. As long as I didn't get in their way they didn't pay any attention to me. Even the mothers with their cubs were harmless, but only as long as I kept a respectable distance. One day I saw some huge bear tracks in the sand that measured sixteen inches. I'm quite convinced that, years later, I encountered that same bear. I never tired of watching the bears. They'd flop and dive into the water and when they had a fish between their jaws they'd be out of the water in a flash. They would staple the struggling fish to the ground and tear and pull off a few bites, leaving the rest to the ravens.

Overhead the bald eagles circled, gliding and dipping their wings, watching and waiting for a salmon to surface. In those days they weren't at all popular with the farmers, and there was a government-sponsored bounty on them, which really cut back on the eagle population. But I revered those big white-headed birds with their seven-foot wing spans and hooked beaks, and was fascinated by their ability to suddenly swoop down and catch their unsuspecting prey.

During the long twilight of the evening, which lasted until nearly midnight that time of the year, I would fall asleep to the peep, peeping of the nighthawks. Warblers and crossbills, robins, redpolls and gray jays all joined in the chorus of nature. Early in the morning and late evening deer would arrive in the meadow, their spotted young fawns tagging close behind. At first they made themselves scarce when they saw me, bouncing away with their white tails poking skyward, but after a couple of weeks they didn't bother to run off anymore. They would quietly lift their heads and stare at me with their round black eyes. Occasionally I would catch a glimpse of a coyote or two disappearing silently into the forest.

Wild strawberries and raspberries were in season and orange salmonberries hung full along the creek. Berry-picking bears were my worst enemies.

At first I didn't feel lonely. Oh, sure, I missed Grete. An hour didn't go by that I didn't think of her, and especially in that small paradise of mine I wished she could have been there. But I had been away from home for nearly three years by then, living on the brink of adventure every step of the way, and it was a chance for me to think things through and let the days roll over me. I'd just come through a near-death experience, and living there in nature, which was teeming with life and doing so well without man, made me feel in one way like an intruder; but on the other hand I felt as if I'd been given a chance to coexist with a finely tuned orchestra that was being conducted by something unknown. Lying in the deep grass watching the white, shining clouds grow into thunderheads made me believe that Mother and Father Earth had laid gentle, healing hands on me and given me a chance to slow down, to take a fresh look at life.

After resting for a couple of weeks, I hiked up the west fork of the river to the beaver meadows. About seventy acres of dry meadows were located at the base of the mountain range which was very similar to the Beaufort Range in the Alberni Valley. Snow-packed peaks ringed the valley and beyond the meadows forests of cedar, fir, hemlock and spruce flowed dark and majestic up the mountainsides. Even though I was much closer to civilization than down at the end of Babine Lake, I was in a real wilderness area where you could live for months without the sound of another human voice. As I gazed across the dry marsh land, I visioned it as perfect grazing land for a few head of cattle. The beavers had been nearly trapped out, otherwise the streams would have been dammed and the meadows would have been ponds. A few jays squawked at me from the willows and hawks circled overhead. I had found my own world where no one else had lived, not even the Indians. Maybe I should have thought more about that, more about why the Indians had never settled in that valley, but there was plenty of country around in those years that was still unsettled by any man.

After several weeks, I had regained most of my strength and the wound on my neck no longer drained. I began to think more and more of home and wondered how my old man was getting along. He'd be fifty-five the coming November, my mother forty-six the end of October. I thought about the last letter from Gusti. She had written that Jette had a boyfriend but *Mutter* didn't think much of him because his family didn't own any property to speak of. My mother would never be happy with anybody we wanted to marry unless it was someone of her choosing.

Naturally, when I got to thinking about my family, the old feeling of homesickness always got the best of me, even after all that time. One morning I woke up and packed together my gear. I'd had enough of living alone in the bush with no job to count on and no place to call my own. I decided right then and there the time had come for me to return to the Old Country and marry my sweetheart, provided she would still have me. I would wire my father from Terrace for the fare back home to Germany and worry about consequences later. To heck with pride, I thought. Deep down I knew my family wouldn't let me down. My heart skipped a beat just thinking that I could actually be home by the end of September, ready to face the music.

"Harry Frank has been looking for you," Louise Gaensbauer told me after she had inquired about my health and general well-being. "He said he wanted to talk to you as soon as you got back from the Zimacord."

I walked over to the Frank's farm and Mr. Frank didn't beat around the bush. He shook my hand and without further ado asked me to run the new butcher shop in Terrace. During the six weeks I had been away, the Farmers' Institute had decided to build a shop so they could sell their own meat. Pat Burns also had a shop in Terrace, but he didn't buy the local pork and beef because he could purchase meat from the Prairies much cheaper, including the cost of shipping, which didn't sit too well with the local farmers.

Mr. Frank was president of the Institute at the time, and I felt quite honoured to be asked. In fact, I didn't have to think twice about it. Suddenly I had the chance to earn a good, honest dollar with the kind of work I knew best and it was something my old man would have been proud of. So the telegram home, my family, my marriage to Grete—all my plans settled like a horse into quicksand. I'd be my own boss, and that was an opportunity I just couldn't pass up. I had to give it a try.

I paid Louise and Gus $20 a month for room and board, but I didn't see much of them as I worked from daylight to dark to get the business started. I didn't mind the hard work, in fact relished the challenge of running my own business. At first I did everything. I did the butchering, the meat cutting, and even cured the meat and made fine German sausage, which was quite a specialty there in Terrace; but at the same time it was a tough struggle to turn a profit when I had to compete with Burns, who had a meat shop down in Vancouver and other businesses around the province.

I finally hired a young man by the name of Walter McConnell and trained him to cut meat, as it had become impossible for me to handle all the work myself. As busy as we were, though, we still didn't earn much of a wage. To supplement our income, I bought beef from around Burns Lake and shipped it to Bill Jones' shop in Prince Rupert. For the first time since I arrived in Canada, I began to feel settled. I'd had that feeling before, especially when I worked on the ranch in Westwold, but this time it was different. I really felt that once I got established there actually might be a future for me in the area. If the business proved profitable, I would seriously consider asking Grete to immigrate. By then I knew a lot of people around the town and it was as nice a place to live as anywhere. The winters weren't as severe as further inland and the summers with their long, northern days were warm and pleasant enough.

Of course I wrote Grete about my good fortune, but I felt it was still too soon to mention anything to her about immigrating, knowing full well she would probably turn me down. And looking over the situation, I felt it would be best to take a trip home, no matter what. I owed that much to my parents and to Grete. I wrote my family how hard I was working and how successful the business was, and assured my father that I could apply some of the new ideas to our business back home.

The fact of the matter was that I broke my back every day trying to eke out a living. Those Depression years were lean. By that time close to a million people were unemployed in Canada, a significant portion of the population. And no matter how hard Walter and I worked, we couldn't seem to make any headway in the business. There was just no money in beef. All I could get was two cents a pound dressed. But I had a certain sense of pride, and as long as we could keep the business going I wasn't going to quit.

Then one day around the middle of December Louise Gaensbauer handed me a letter from Grete. I sat down at the kitchen table and tore it open.

October 17, 1932
Dear Paul,
I guess you have made a real home in Terrace, now that you have your own shop and are doing well. Thank you for drawing a map so I know where the town is. You have written so often to say you are coming home, and then another letter arrives telling me you've found some other job, that I don't know anymore what to

believe. As I said before, you are probably best off there anyway. Business can't get worse here. Mother is hoping for a warm winter so we will have enough coal to see us through. In the last seven hundred years only twenty eight other winters were as mild as last winter . . . statistics from Rehauer Tagblatt. But imagine lilacs blooming in early April!

This year there has been one election after another, and everywhere you turn are Hindenburg posters or Hitler posters or Communist posters. Papen is our new Chancellor, but not much respected. And President Hindenburg, my stepfather says, is getting too senile to know what he is doing, but nobody else seems to know what to do either. He says there are too many parties in the stew and if people don't get back to work the whole country will boil over. There were street riots in Prussia last summer between the Nazis and Communists, and many people were killed.

Mathilde talks about moving to Nuremberg. Her brother is in the army and stationed there. We were there in September when the big Nazi rally was going on in the stadium. Brownshirts marched up and down the streets with their drums and banners shouting, "Sieg Heil, Sieg Heil."

We just saw "The Man from Nevada" with Tom Tyler, a real Wild West film. The country looks wild everywhere in America. Do you ever hear from Max and Arno? Are they planning to come back home? Well, until I actually see you in person, I won't believe you are ever coming back, no matter what you say. I think the apple tree will bear a ton of fruit before you come home. By the way, do you remember Frau Katherina Hertel? She passed away last summer at 73.

I wish you a Merry Christmas and lots of luck and adventure in the New Year. Best wishes . . .

    Love Grete

I think my fingers trembled more after I read the letter than when Louise handed it to me.

"Bad news, Paul?" she asked, a worried look clouding her eyes. She picked up her baby daughter off the floor and patted her on the back.

"No," I said, shaking my head and running my tongue over my lips. "No bad news, Louise. I just miss my girl, that's all. She doesn't think I'll ever go back home. What can I do," I asked, looking into her kind, sympathetic eyes. "I promised the farmers I'd give the shop a good try and I can't just quit because business is bad."

"Don't you worry now, Paul," Louise said, putting a hand on my shoulder. "If she's a smart girl, she'll wait for you."

I nodded, wanting to believe her. I reread the letter, searching between the lines for an answer, but in truth, it may as well have been from a friend, or from my sister. Was there another man in her life? Would she tell me if there was? Had she given up on me, like my parents? I felt as nervous as an old billy goat, but all I could do was sit down and write to her, and as hollow as my words seemed, I reassured her I would be home the summer of '33.

That Christmas there were no surprise visits from the guys. Arno was still down in Vancouver, and Little and Big Max had stayed in the Okanagan. Adam John had decided to strike it rich and had left the beginning of the summer for Dawson City in the Yukon.

Then on January 30, 1933, we heard over the radio that President Hindenburg had appointed Hitler as Chancellor of Germany. It didn't mean Hitler was the Fuehrer, but that appointment was all he needed and all he wanted so he could get his foot in the door. Only three of the eleven ministerial posts belonged to the Nazis, which gave Hindenburg and the Social Democrats a false security that they'd be able to control the Nazis, but Hitler didn't waste a minute to call for immediate elections so he could gain a majority. With heavy Nazi propaganda via radio and press and Hitler flying all over Germany to make speeches, the last democratic election under the Hitler regime was held in March '33. The Nazis still didn't get the majority of the vote, but Hitler declared a victory and by decree became Dictator of the Third Reich, leaving Hindenburg on the sidelines as a worn-out puppet president and at the same time luring a tidal wave of Germans under his umbrella.

But I knew nothing of that in those days. There wasn't much news in the *Terrace Times* about Germany. It was mostly local stuff, and who knew in Canada and the U.S. what was really going on anyway. One thing I have to say, though, is that nobody ever bothered me in those days because I was German, even though Germany had lost a war just fifteen years before.

Spring rolled into summer, and Walter and I still barely turned a profit, though we worked from dawn to dusk, six days a week. But it wasn't all work either. In the evenings or on Sundays I taught gymnastics to some of the young kids there in Terrace, remembering quite well everything I had learned back home as a youth. Or sometimes a group of us would go to a Saturday-night dance. One time a bunch of us young guys took off to Remo late one Saturday afternoon. We walked the seven miles along the railroad track, but for us that was no distance a'tall. We arrived early and were hanging around the ferry dock where a cable spanned the Skeena River; the river that was used to ferry boats back and forth.

"Hey, Paul, a free bottle of beer if you walk the cable," someone yelled, pointing out across the river.

My friends knew I was quite agile, good at balancing, and always ready for a dare. I looked up at the fifty-foot cable tower, then at the cable that stretched across the Skeena about a quarter of a mile or so. It was tight as a drum and I took one look at the fellow and grinned.

"You find me a nice alder pole that I can use for a balancing stick and you've got a bet."

Within minutes a long, supple pole was in my hands and a small crowd had gathered. Never in my life had I walked on a cable or tried any kind of a stunt like that. But I thought to myself if Chaplin could do it, why couldn't I, and as a teenager in Berlin, I'd seen tight-rope walkers in their colorful tights and black satin shoes, walk a taut rope which was stretched across the street from one gable end of a high building to another gable end. One would take a wheelbarrow across, another a chair—even sit down on it. I'd hold my breath and crane my neck until the drum roll stopped and they'd be safe. And in Rehau as a kid I was always in the front row when roving acrobats and jugglers arrived on holidays and entertained us for a few *pfennige*.

I was as cool as a cucumber. Nonchalantly I took off my shoes to get a good feel for the cold, winding cable on the soles of my feet. The whole thing didn't look dangerous to me because if I fell it would have been into the water, even though it was swift, swirling dark water, and the rope walkers I had seen never used nets.

I felt the weight of the pole in my hands and climbed up the cable tower, not feeling the least bit of fear. Dewey Atkinson, who later lived in the Alberni Valley and was a good friend of ours, was the ferryman there at the time.

"You sure you know what you're doing, young fellow?" he asked. His shoulders were slightly stooped, and he looked at the crowd and back to me. "I don't want no trouble now."

I gave him a wink, put my right foot flat on the cable and kept my left toe balanced on the platform. It took me about a minute to get the pole perfectly balanced. Then I eased along, one foot over the other. The only thing that existed for me in that moment was the feel of the pole in my hands and the cold, wiry steel of the cable under my feet. My heart beat a slow, steady thump in my throat. The poplar pole felt cool and smooth in my hands. I kept my eyes straight ahead and eased along until I got to the middle of the channel. By this time the cable began to sway a little and the pole started to dip back and forth. My muscles tightened and quivered. That's when I knew I had come to the end of my rope. I stopped and began to teeter, unable to take another step forward, but turning around was even worse. My ears buzzed, and I must have wobbled there for a couple of minutes, doing a balancing act with that pole. Finally I took a deep breath, leaned carefully into my knees, and did a Pavlovian pirouette. I teetered back and forth, and when I finally got my balance, I inched my way back toward the dock, keeping my eyes steadily on the cable. Only once did I catch a glimpse of blurred, white faces on the bank. My panic passed. Nobody said a word until my two feet were on the ground. Then they let out a cheer. That's when my knees began to knock and the reality of what I had done set in. I don't even remember whether or not we went to the dance afterwards. As thrilling as that dance-on-the-wire act was, I had no intention of ever repeating it.

The summer of '33 passed and my promise to Grete had indeed become hollow. But I wrote to her again, explaining the circumstances and obligations, reassuring her that if the business didn't improve over the winter, I would definitely leave for the Old Country in the spring, no matter what. And this time I really meant it. I asked her not to give up on me and assured her my heart was still in the right place—right next to hers.

I had let her down, but my feelings for her had never diminished in all those years, and as long as she remained single, I remained hopeful. So while we didn't make much profit in business, at least we were establishing a name for ourselves, and I kept hopeful the economy would soon recover.

In the fall of that year I took several hunting trips into the mountains. One time I went out with Jack McCullough, a young man I'd met in Terrace. Later on, his family also settled in the Alberni Valley, but Jack married and stayed in Terrace. He liked to hunt, so we went up the Zimacord River and hiked up a mountain creek bed to get high into goat country. I climbed ahead up a fairly steep ravine. When I stopped and leaned into a rock wall to rest, I saw Jack put his hands on a huge boulder to boost himself up a steep incline. Suddenly I heard a grinding crunch, and the boulder began to shift and tilt.

My hands flew up. "Jump, Jack! Jump, the boulder!"

He looked at me with a surprised stare and without a word disappeared like a cardboard dummy underneath the rolling, sliding boulder. I felt the blood drain out of my face as the boulder crashed and bounced down the mountain through the bush. I never expected to see Jack alive again. The boulder must have come down with a snowslide during the winter and had precariously settled there. I threw down my gun and rushed down to Jack's side, fearing the worst. He was lying on his back in a trough that had been formed by erosion. His head faced down the mountain. He fit in between the shoulders of earth and rocks as if he were lying in a coffin. I expected to find his body crushed and mangled, but before I even touched him he opened his eyes and lifted his head. My temples pounded and I kept asking him if he was okay.

"I'm okay!" he shouted and gave his head a shake. "Help me get the hell out of here for chrissakes!"

All that boulder did was squeeze his chest a little as it rolled over him. We, nevertheless, were both badly shaken up by the incident, and I must have been as white as he looked, but after a rest and a good laugh, we continued up the mountain and bagged a good-sized billy that gave us a couple hundred pounds of meat.

Before I knew it, another year was around. I hadn't received a single letter from Grete, and even though I still thought of her and wrote every few months, I no longer checked every day for the mail. My parents no longer wrote, but one day there was a letter from Gusti, overflowing with all her good news.

September 30, 1933
Dear Paul,
So much has happened this year and my days are so full of work that I barely have time to write to you. Now that Hitler is in power people are getting back to work and things are changing. You know, I'm training to be leader of the Bund Deutscher Maedel, The League of German Girls. Tomorrow morning I'm leaving for Stuttgart for another week-long training session. There's so much to do. Over the summer I spent weekends at different Youth Hostels where I helped train the younger girls how to throw the shot-put and the discus. The young people are the hope for the future—that's what Hitler says.

I just got back from Nuremberg where there was a special Sports Day event. It was herrlich, Pauli, wunderbar there among the cheering crowds with waving flags and banners. The festival days are back and we march and sing all the old folks songs. You would be proud to come home to your Fatherland. We finally have a future.

Ja, we thought you would have come home long ago, but I'm glad you're earning good money from the butcher shop. Vater doesn't understand why you have to run a business there when you should be here where you're needed. He looks so tired and sometimes I think he has lost hope you will ever return. Mutter doesn't say much either, but I think they're worried you won't ever come back. Pauli, when are you coming home? That girl in Wurlitz is married. Mutter, in one of her dark moods, said you had your chance.

Even though life is better now, most of all I'm looking forward to the day you do come back. Jette is fine. She still goes out with Karl and Mutter doesn't seem to mind anymore. Let us know when you are coming back home so we can meet you at the train in Hof? I miss you every day.

Your Gusti

My little sister had become a real Nazi *Maedchen*. But I couldn't have known then what it all meant. I couldn't have known that Hitler had found a perfect target in the German youth. Prior to 1933, the German Youth Association was probably the strongest youth group in the world with about ten million members, and Hitler, realizing their potential took it over, Nazified it, glorified it, and stuffed the young people with Nazi indoctrination. My sister Gusti was a perfect pawn, loving the outdoors as she did and being the talented musician she was.

Along about November, when winter began to close in on us, I met a fellow by the name of Berth West in Prince Rupert who was interested in taking over the shop. That was the spark I needed to finally make the decision to get out of a losing proposition and make definite plans to return home. At least I had the satisfaction to see the shop kept open and that I had done everything in my power to turn it into a successful business. Any idea I had about settling in Terrace had become exactly that, an idea.

I had run the shop for a year and a half, by then barely turning a profit, but written home that my business was a success. So more than anything I wanted to return home without asking for help.

Having heard of the possibility to catch a freighter out of Vancouver and work my way back to Europe that way, I took just enough money out of the business for a boat fare from Prince Rupert down to Vancouver.

In January, 1934, I said my farewells and headed south. British Columbia had turned out to be everything and more than I had ever dreamed about, but my heart was truly back in the Old Country. Once my plans were settled to return to my homeland— and this time I was determined that nothing and nobody would change them—I couldn't get there fast enough.

16. Riding the Rails

A COLD, ICY FOG HUNG OVER THE WATER as we left Prince Rupert, but by next afternoon it lifted and you could see fingers of long fjords cut inland between the heavily forested mountains. I had hoped to spot some gray whales, but I guess they had been hunted almost to extinction by then, though there were plenty of sea lions, clustered thick on islands of rock. The noise of our passing boat sent them spilling into the ocean. I stayed on deck most of the time fighting seasickness and watching the squawking gulls hover and dip in the wake of the boat.

The boat docked in downtown Vancouver at dusk, and the big city lights, the screeching wheels from the trolley cars, the smell of slick streets and exhaust set me back ten years when I had first arrived in Berlin as a young boy. Yet the city of Vancouver in those days was peanuts compared to Berlin with its miles and miles of majestic old buildings and broad, tree-lined *allees*.

Arno lived down in the West End near Stanley Park, so I asked directions and walked from the pier to his rooming house. He was quite astounded to see me. His face had thinned out, and his thick, dark hair was combed straight back off his face in waves.

"It's been one hellova long time," he said, gripping my hand hard and patting me on the shoulder. "Thought you might have left for the Old Country some time ago."

He had found steady work in the shipyards and lived quite comfortably in an old Victorian rooming house that was circled by a large, overhanging porch. He had all the comforts of hot and cold running water and even had a radio in his room. We sat up late over a few beers and got caught up on all the news.

"So what are the guys up to?" I asked. "I heard sometime back they left the Interior."

"Oh, yeah. Little Max has rented a farm around Duncan, just across the water on Vancouver Island, and Big Max has settled in Victoria—they came through last fall. They like the nice mild climate down here. And Adam's on the Island, too, back down from the Yukon."

"You ever hear from Marga again?" I asked.

"She did me a favor," he said, lifting his heavy brows and giving me a half grin. "I've met a girl from Austria. She's beautiful . . . and graceful like a porcelain figurine."

"Can she dance?" I asked jokingly.

He nodded. "Oh, yeah, I'll say she can dance, but we don't go much, you know. She's a widow . . . has a little boy, Ronnie."

"Oh yeah? What happened to her husband?"

"Killed. Fell off a scaffold about a year and a half ago. Was a house painter."

"Must have been a young guy."

"Yeah," he said nodding. "It's still tough for her at times. Her little boy was only a few months old when it happened. What about Grete? She still single?"

"I hope so. Haven't heard from her in awhile, but Gusti would have told me if there was someone else."

"Well, if she's still single that must mean something. But you really think she'll still be waiting for you after all these years?" He opened another beer and set it in front of me. "Maybe she would have come to Canada. Did you ever ask her?"

I shrugged my shoulders. "No. After that bond issue fell through I gave up on it. I would have, though, if my meat business in Terrace had been profitable. But I've promised her all along that I would go back home and marry her. More, I couldn't do."

"Well, it's taken you long enough to make up your mind, but I wouldn't count my chickens," he said, leaning back in his chair. "What I don't understand is how she's still under your skin."

"I can tell you one thing," I said. "She brought me through some pretty tough times. You know that yourself. I've never let go of her, never stopped thinking of her. Maybe I don't have enough common sense, and yes, I probably should've gone back to the Old Country long ago, and I'll find that out soon enough, but I still have a chance, and you'll see, if I play my cards right, I bet my mother will even come around after all these years."

"Huh. She'll come around all right—in a big circle. As I see it, if Grete gets caught in the middle, you'll be right back where you started."

I drummed my fingers on the table. "Too much time has passed. Things'll be different when I get home."

I picked up the bottle of beer and took a long drink. Five years was a long time, but I knew I could handle my mother and soothe away any differences. Grete was my greater concern.

The next day I met Ida and her little boy, Ronnie. She kept house for an elderly couple somewhere across the Granville Street Bridge. She had her own room with a small kitchen.

"*Gruess Gott*," she said in a tinkling Austrian dialect. She took my rubber coat and hung it on a hook. "Please. Sit down, Paul. Arno has told me so much about you."

She had short, light brown hair and sparkling eyes that changed color with the shadows and light. She looked like one of those wind up Vienna dolls and fit Arno's description perfectly. Even with high heels and her curly hairdo, she didn't reach my shoulder. Her little boy clung to her legs and wouldn't come near me. I had shaved off my beard, had a bath, and made myself look quite respectable, but he didn't want anything to do with a gaunt, dark-haired stranger.

"I have some good lentil soup," she said smiling. "I'll have it ready in a minute."

"You two really like it here in Vancouver?" I asked.

"I've made a new life here," Arno said. "You can't beat the climate, though it's a little wet sometimes. I don't know how you stood it up North the last couple of years. And when I hear what is going on in Germany, I don't think I'll ever go back."

"So what brought you to Canada?" I asked Ida. "And how did you manage to immigrate?"

She shrugged her shoulders and laughed. "Mostly *Wanderlust*. My friend Martha and I had heard so much about Canada from my brother, Joe—he immigrated in '28—that we wanted to leave too. We first went to Edmonton where I worked for a Jewish family who had sponsored me, but I didn't like the freezing weather so came to Vancouver."

"And where do you come from in Austria?"

"Near Graz, in Steiermark," she said, cutting thick slices of rye bread. "I never wanted to stay there."

"Well, I wish you both luck," I said, feeling a little sad that I'd soon be leaving my good friend for who knew how long. "I almost decided to stay in Canada myself, but it's time to go home and take care of business there."

Ida set steaming bowls of soup in front of us. "I wish I had more to offer you."

Arno put his arm around her waist and looked up at her. "It smells delicious. I don't think Paul's too fussy." Ida sat down at the table and began to butter some bread.

"Things won't be the same when you get back, Paul, do you know that? Huh, and to think we used to laugh about Hitler. Remember?"

"Yeah, but who knows, if it hadn't been him it could have been the Communists. And you better hope the same doesn't happen in this country, especially if the economy doesn't turn around."

I left Vancouver a few days before my twenty-fourth birthday with fifty cents in my pocket. There were no freighters needing extra hands out of the Vancouver harbour, so the next step for me was to cross Canada by rail and try to get one out of New York. Arno had no money to spare, but he gave me some heavy underwear and a thick sweater so I wouldn't freeze to death on the freight ride across Canada. Ida gave me a ring of bologna and some cheese.

"All the best to everyone in Rehau, eh," Arno said. "And be sure to write when you get home." He flashed his big white teeth. "Someday we'll get back for a visit," and he squeezed Ida around her waist and looked down at her. "Hey, Ida?"

When I arrived at the freight yards, I recognized immediately that the railroad police were out in full force. About eighty men were stomping around in the cold, unrelenting drizzle of rain, waiting for the next freight to leave.

"You bastards scram and keep behind the fence," a railroad policeman shouted, swinging his club. "You keep off railroad property you hear? And don't try no funny stuff until the train gets moving." At least they were cooperating with us to some extent.

The authorities were just too darn glad to see us leave the city, and as long as we didn't try boarding the train while it was sitting in the switching yards, they looked the other way once the freight got moving out of the yard. They dumped the job onto the train crew to bump the hobos, but there was never enough crew to handle the job, and once on board they couldn't very well throw anybody off a moving train.

We had to wait a couple of hours until the train leaving for Winnipeg began to pull out of the freight yard. We all hunched into our coats trying to keep dry in the cold, steady rain. My fingers trembled and I was chilled to the bone. I wore the same rubber coat I had on when I swam the Copper River and lost the horses. At least it kept me dry.

The bells began to clang and white clouds of steam hissed into the air. Saggy eyes popped open and heads turned. The train whistle shrieked and I heard the old familiar puff, puff, puff coming up the tracks. We crouched low in the ditch. My heart pounded and the adrenalin began to rush through my body. I felt like a cougar ready to pounce on its prey.

The engine passed us at about fifteen miles per hour, followed by a tender car filled with coal and then some refrigerator cars and flat beds piled high with lumber. When the boxcars came rumbling along we leaped up and ran alongside the train, stumbling over the ties, trying to grab for a door handle. I clenched my pack in my teeth and made a jump for it, grabbing the handle as tight as I could. I leaped onto the stairs, yanked the door open and waved to those behind me that the car was clear. The boxcar was half full of crates so there was room for at least fifteen guys inside. Being in the middle of winter, the more guys in a boxcar, the warmer it would be. When everyone was in, we made sure to put a stop in the door so it wouldn't close completely as there was no way for us to open the door from the inside.

We looked like a sorry lot. But you could tell the veterans from their clothing and the tired, sorry look in their eyes. Their mouths sagged and their beards were uncombed and scraggly. Some wore coats several sizes too big or too small and some had the elbows out of their sleeves and knees out of their pants. Their torn rubber boots were held together with tape. Some of the better-class guys had proper fitting jackets and decent shoes. We were all starving by then and broke open whatever food we had along. Some of the guys hadn't eaten in a couple of days and were grateful for anything we could share.

"I wouldn't be here if I had steady work," one young kid said, biting into a piece of dry bread he had pulled out of his pocket. Blond hair hung out from under his cap, and he couldn't have been more than fifteen.

"Oh, yeah?" one of the older fellows with sunken cheekbones said to him. "If I was you I'd git right back along home where you belong before you git sucked in. You ain't even dry behind the gills. I been at this for more'n a few years. You hear that train whistle blowin' and it gits in your blood after awhile."

The boy shook his head and looked down at his feet. "No room for me at home." He pulled off his cap and smoothed back his hair. "My old man's on relief. They've enough mouths to feed without worryin' 'bout me. My old man says there might be work back East."

The man with the hollow cheekbones gave a dry laugh, relaxing his hands on his knees. "Did you try the loggin' camps? You look like you'd make a good whistle punk," he said to the kid, but didn't wait for an answer. "I just wish someone would make the goddamn politicians ride the rails sometimes. Let 'em find out what it's like when you can't squeeze a nickel with a shoehorn out of some fat-bellied bloater. You just be careful, son," he continued. "It's a dangerous business on your own, and you don't want to wind up greasin' the rails."

"The politicians are all crooks, riding 'round in their big Buicks," somebody from the corner chimed in, "and all we get is week-old bread."

They talked a different language down there along the border. The guys were savvy, and being out of work for months, especially over the winter, they were bitter. Most of them rode the rails out of necessity, but at least they were accepted among their own kind and no one looked down at them for being jobless. I wanted to tell them to get out of the cities and live off the land, but in the middle of winter that advice wasn't very sound either. At least they had free food and a place to spend a night in the cities as long as they didn't loiter, and most of them were good at panhandling, too.

"Things'll get better. Next spring, next spring. It's a goddamn chant with the politicians," said one guy with a clean-shaven face and a decent-looking gray hat.

One young fellow who was sitting next to me, who was about the age I was when I left the Old Country, was on his way home to Calgary. "Where you headed?" he asked me in a quiet voice.

"Back to Germany," I said with pride.

"You're gonna need more than that raincoat to keep you warm when you hit the Prairies."

"I'll find some newspapers around for extra insulation. I'm used to the cold."

"You want my mackinaw?" he asked, his eyes lighting up. "I'd as soon be wearing your rain coat."

I looked at his thick, warm jacket. His bony wrists stuck out of the sleeves. "Why do you want my raincoat?" I asked, already unbuttoning it. "It won't keep you warm."

"Mackinaw's a relief coat. I don't want my family to know I been on relief."

I nodded my head and grinned, thinking he must be nuts to give it up.

"They think I been workin' see. No one in our family ever needed handouts, if you know what I mean. Don't want to worry them none."

Just before we got into Lethbridge in Alberta about three days later, we had to drop off the train again. The temperature was well below zero and we all headed for the relief station, hoping for hot soup and a place to warm up.

To my surprise, the people running the place handed us a piece of soap and a small towel, and sent us to the showers. Then they gave us a bowl of watery soup and a couple of slices of dry bread.

I was still hungry as a horse, as were the rest of the men, but there were no seconds. Then they showed us a room where we could sleep on the floor.

The next morning we were given a bowl of steaming porridge and moved out early. We caught another freight and headed for Winnipeg. I was among professionals and really got an eye opener on that next leg of the trip about the different sort of people that rode the freight. It sure wasn't the sort of life I would have wanted to lead, even with the adventure that went along with it. Although most of the men rode out of necessity and were an honest bunch, there always were a few you wanted to keep clear of.

I started talking to this one guy who tried to tell me how easy it was to get around and make a living. "Ya just hafta know the ropes. It's easy to pull the wool over people's eyes. Look at me. See this?" And he hunched up one shoulder and contorted his leg. "Lotsa times I make out to be a cripple. People feel sorry for ya, see. You tell 'em a good sob story and they'll fall for it every time. There was a time I could easy panhandle a couple a bucks a day, but not anymore."

I again was reminded of Charlie Chaplin and the many movies where he played a tramp, a vagabond, an immigrant, but by then the romance and comedy of riding the rails and adventure had been drained out of me. It was pretty sad to see teenagers riding the rails. I saw quite a few of them and most of them stuck together like glue for protection. All the guys I'd seen ride the freight in B.C. were labourers who had been uprooted by the tough times and were decent men looking for work, but on the mainline there were all kinds. Some of the hobos were die-hard bums who had been hooked into the life of vagrancy. They were the sort who either weren't interested in finding steady work, or just couldn't hold down a job when they did find one. They went from whistle stop to whistle stop getting odd jobs here and there, nickel and diming whoever they could, spending their night at relief stations or hobo camps.

That trip through the Prairies the thermometer dropped to forty below zero. We had to keep dancing on our feet all night long just to keep from freezing to death. One of the hobos had brought along a bucket half filled with sand and soaked in kerosene. It would burn for hours and at least we could warm our hands up a little. Sometimes someone would crack a joke or we'd get to talking about our favorite food.

"I can't wait for some of that sky pie when we get to Winnipeg," one of the fellows said.

"Yeah, they always have plenty leftover, too."

My mouth watered at the thought of a good pie. "What's sky pie?" I asked.

There was some snickering and a couple of guys laughed.

"The relief stations is famous for sky pie . . . You ain't had none yet?"

When we got off at Winnipeg, we didn't have far to go to find a relief station as it was close to the railroad, but as usual, there was a long soup line. While we waited, the rumour went around like wildfire that two luckless fellows had been found frozen stiff as boards in one of the boxcars. They had been locked in all the way from Vancouver.

We were handed a tin plate and given a couple of scoops of beans and stew and two slices of bread. There wasn't much meat in the stew, just some pieces of tripe floating around in it. I sopped up the last of the gravy with my bread then remembered the pie. "Where's our sky pie?" I asked a familiar face.

He laughed. "Hey, he wants some sky pie. Did you hear that?" he yelled to the guys. "Don't you know, you crazy bohunk," he said looking at me with a half grin on this face, "that it's pie they served last week, or yesterday, or maybe they'll tell you not until next week."

We didn't have much time to get warmed up before we were on the road again. We had no trouble catching a freight out of Winnipeg as the railroad police were happy to see us leave the city, but when we got to a division point this side of Thunder Bay in Ontario we ran into some trouble. About seventy men were aboard and we all jumped off about a half mile before the train stopped. We hustled down the tracks to pick it up again when it left the division point, but when we got there several railroad police were on the lookout to make sure nobody got on. The wind was blowing to beat the band and icy particles of fine snow bit into my face. I don't think the police would've given a damn had we frozen to death in the ditch.

I surveyed the situation and knew there was no way we'd get on if we stayed in close. It was late morning and I figured with the limited visibility I'd be safe a good quarter mile or so up the track.

I crouched low in the snow-covered heather. The bells clanged and I could hear the engine strain forward. Through the fine swirling snow I saw a bunch of stick figures make a dash for the cars, but then I heard a release of steam. The police must have signalled the engineer to stop the train. Even from where I was, I could hear the police hollering and going at it with their billy clubs to chase the guys clear of the tracks. Well, the engineer stopped four times so the police could send the hobos packing.

On the fifth try, the freight didn't stop and by the time it got to where I was, it was coming fast. The stack spit out dark smoke and sparks, and I felt the vibration of the thundering wheels under my feet. I clamped my pack firmly between my teeth and adjusted the bedroll tied around my back. My legs felt like springs and a flash of white heat rushed through my body. I'd never caught a freight moving at that pace. Down the line I could see the shadows of several other men crouching in the ditch among the heather. My heart knocked fast and heavy in my throat.

I sprang up and started to run. There wouldn't be a second chance once I made a dive for the handle. I shot through the air and grabbed a handhold on the boxcar. My body slammed against the side of the car and my arms almost jerked out of their sockets, but my fingers locked their grip. I began to wheeze and gasp for air. I held my grip, but my body sagged down and my legs banged and knocked along the ties like a kid running a stick along a wooden picket fence. With all the strength I could muster, I hauled myself up and rolled into the boxcar. I fell flat on the cold, metal floor gasping for air. My pants and longjohns were ripped to shreds and my knees were raw and bloody. I was the only man in that boxcar, and I guess for the few other guys who made it on, the engineer didn't figure it was worth stopping another time. I cleaned my knees as best I could and huddled miserably into my flimsy blanket.

I was a sorry sight when I arrived in Sault Ste. Marie. I was sick of the road, tired of being cold and hungry, tired of watching out for the railroad police, and tired of sleeping on hard metal. All I wanted was to get on a ship and home the quickest way possible.

I jumped off the train before we got to the yard. The bitter cold cut through my tattered clothing, but at least the daytime temperature was above zero Fahrenheit. I limped up to another guy who had jumped out of a car. We were just skirting the yard, when we noticed two girls running across the tracks. They wore overalls and heavy, black mackinaws. With their toques pulled down over their ears and their hair tucked up, they looked like young boys, but I could tell they were girls by the way they moved. I was surprised girls would risk riding the rails. A clump of hair fell out of one of the girls' caps. They walked on ahead at a quick pace and the fellow beside me said. "Whores. You don't see 'em much in winter."

All of a sudden two police came out of nowhere and grabbed them. "They gonna arrest us too?" I asked. "At least if we went to jail we'd get a hot meal and have a place to sleep."

"No such luck. They always take the whores to jail. Maybe they think they're gonna reform 'em. They send us packing, but they throw the girls in the clink."

I was so hungry and freezing cold that I thought a couple of days rest in jail would be just as good if not better than holing up another night on the floor of some sleazy mission, if I was lucky. And, besides, I was curious about what went on behind bars. So I went up to the officers and asked if they'd take me in too. They looked at me and laughed.

"If that's what you want."

The next thing I knew I was shoved into a Black Maria and driven to jail.

The next day we went before the magistrate. One of the girls was crying and her face was streaked with tears. She didn't look like a whore to me. She wore no lipstick and had combed her matted blond hair and didn't look a day over eighteen. I remember thinking it was a good thing her parents didn't know where she was. Or were they going crazy wondering where she was? Or maybe they didn't care, but I sure felt sorry for the girls and wished I had money to bail them out and send them home.

The judge banged down his gavel. "Ten days in jail," and then he looked straight at me, his eyes glaring. "And if it hadn't been for the girls, I would've given you thirty days."

"Your Honor," I said very politely, "if it hadn't been for the girls, I wouldn't be here."

His eyebrows pulled together and he leaned slightly forward. "One more word and you'll *get* thirty days."

I clammed up fast when his hard, cold eyes bored into mine. We were escorted on the train by police to Sudbury, Ontario and put into the big penitentiary. I felt pretty smart about that, too, as I was at least gaining miles. But I found out in a hurry that once those prison gates slam shut behind you it doesn't matter whether you're in there for riding the freight or for murder. We all had to follow the same discipline. But I thought it was a big joke and sang and whistled in my cell, which I shared with several other guys. Every time a guard walked by I had something smart to say to him.

"What's the weather like outside, boss? Hey, I've got a good joke to tell you."

Well, the head warden didn't think I was funny. On the fifth day I was escorted into his office.

"Do you know where you're at?" he asked.

"Yes sir," I said, lifting my chin.

"Do you know there are rules to be followed in this prison and we don't consider this place a holiday joint?"

"Yes sir," I nodded, feeling the smartness drain out of me.

"I think you need to be taught a lesson, young man. Maybe the rest of your time in solitary confinement might teach you some respect."

My face crunched together, and before I had a chance to protest, I was handcuffed and taken to a cubbyhole that was about five feet wide and eight feet long with no windows. I just about went berserk in there. Even a rat in a cage got better treatment than that. I lost all track of time and had no idea about day or night.

When I wasn't sleeping I was pacing back and forth. I found out what whistling in the dark was really all about.

I recited every poem I had ever learned. Every German kid had to learn "Erlkoenig" in school, but it was still one of my favourites. "Who rides by night in the wind so wild?/It is the father, with his child." I think if my father could have seen me then he wouldn't have been too happy about me coming home.

I thought of Grete and became filled with such longing for her that I broke down and bawled. In my mind, I read her letters over and over, and looking at the dark wall of the cell I could almost see her graceful handwriting like a work of art.

I sang songs in German and in English. "Oh my darling, oh my darling, oh my darling Clementine . . . "

They brought me bread and water three times a day. When I finally got out of there, five days later, I couldn't even open my eyes in the harsh, winter sun. That was one of the lowest points in my young life. Even when Arno and I rowed for our lives on the Babine Lake, even when I was barefoot and starving to death after I'd lost my horses, I never felt as humiliated and degraded as I had been made to feel in that cell. I was sent packing out of that hole in my rags smelling like a skunk.

One more freight ride and I finally got to Montreal. I found my way to a mission where I was given clean clothes, food, and a bath. I finally felt human again.

From there I tried to locate a freighter going to England, but so many guys wanted to work their way back to Europe that it would have taken several weeks for me to get on. I finally broke down and set pride aside.

I went to the North German Lloyd and wired my parents for money. Within the day enough money arrived for my fare to go by train from Montreal to New York, then by ship to Bremerhaven. When that money was in my hand I kissed it and with a double kick in the air was out the door.

17. Rehau, Germany, 1934

ON MAY 7, 1934, I WAS FIRST IN LINE to march down the gangplank in Bremerhaven. I drew in a long, deep breath—relishing even the thick smell of fish and salt air. Adventure and homesickness were behind and I was back in my homeland among my own people. All the resentment I had toward my mother was long gone, and I was confident that her attitude had also changed during the five years I had been away.

Once again the old, familiar cobblestones echoed under my feet, and a language comfortable to my ears rang out like music. Blood-red swastika flags hung bold and impressive from the storefronts, flapping in the wind. The smell of grilled bratwurst with fat bursting through the skins drew me to a cart on the corner of the street. I gave the peddler a fifty pfennige piece and he flipped a sizzling sausage between a bun and passed it to me. I crunched my teeth down on the bratwurst and the spicy juices squirted in my mouth.

I continued along the street, savouring the smells of freshly baked bread and cooking fat, the cling-clang of the trolley cars, the rich colours of the flags and the displays in the store windows. Suddenly people moved aside and some stretched out their right arms in a salute. I looked down the street and backed uneasily against a shop window. At least forty steel-helmeted police in black uniforms and tall jack boots marched past, goose stepping in precision.

Further along I asked an old peasant woman in a colourful kerchief and black coat directions to the train station, but she took one look at me and firmly shook her head. Then I asked a man selling turnips from a wagon if he could help me.

"Number three *Strassenbahn* straight ahead," he mumbled, pointing his finger.

I lifted my cap and continued walking. My eye caught the smeared words "Jews Not Welcome" on a shop window. Everyone bustled about their business with grim faces and eyes straight ahead. People flung up their right arms and snapped out a "Heil Hitler" when a uniformed officer marched down the sidewalk. Suddenly the air didn't smell so good to me.

Posters on an advertising pillar had slogans in bold print. "*Ein Volk, ein Reich, ein Fuehrer*—One People, One Nation, One Leader!" Another had a colourful picture of a black Hakenkreuz with an iron-jawed, straight-nosed storm trooper standing in front of it. "The Organized Will of the Nation" was printed across the bottom. Hitler had been in power just over one year but the Nazi presence was indisputably visible. Bells began to clang and the number three streetcar came rattling down the middle of the street. I climbed aboard.

When I arrived at the train station, I made my way through the crowds, listening to the nuances of different dialects. Hawkers sold newspapers, pretzels, cigarettes. Others sold all kinds of Nazi souvenirs from different stalls. Small swastika flags hung tied in bunches from racks. Painted plaques with "Heil Hitler" and "Sieg Heil" were displayed on counters and beside them stood porcelain cups with Hitler's sober, mustached face.

I bought my train ticket and wired my parents, letting them know my arrival time in Hof. Between naps on the train I took note of the clean and orderly countryside. The rolling hills and meadows were all under cultivation and even the forests were so neat you could almost see through them. The villages with their church steeples and town halls were immaculate, without a scrap of clutter. I had to chuckle when I compared them to the little towns in B.C. that had been thrown together with slabs of lumber, tarpaper, and logs. I thought about my old log cabin on the Babine, and about all the friends I had made in the North and left behind. Nevertheless, I was back in the country where I belonged, and most important, I'd be with my girl again.

When the train pulled into the station in Hof, my mother and Gusti were waving excitedly from the platform. I stepped off the train, and Gusti, nineteen by then and no longer a girl, threw herself into my arms, laughing and crying all at the same time.

"*Ach, du, Pauli.* You're home. You're home," she sobbed. "*Mein Gott*, how we've missed you."

My mother, tall and somber in her dark dress and heavy black shoes, grinned and held her arms open to me.

"*Siehst. Du bist doch endlich wieder nach haus gekomme',*" she said. Sparks of light shone in her almond-shaped black eyes. "You're finally home. I had given up on you ever returning." She leaned back and looked at me, shaking her head and holding me at arm's length. Tears welled up in her eyes. "Look how you've grown. You're a man now, but we need to fatten you up some."

She hadn't changed much except for a streak of gray running through her dark hair and a softening around her chin and neck.

"Where are *Vater* and Jette?" I asked.

"*Ach, Paul, du sollst wissen.* You know today is Saturday and the *Sonne* is a busy place. Come, hurry so we can catch the train to Rehau. I have a new suit for you," she said, pushing a package into my hands and telling me to throw out my old clothes and wash up. I couldn't blame her for wanting her son to look respectable after having been away from home for so many years.

When we arrived at the vine-covered train station in Rehau my heart began to thump like crazy. I glanced with longing and some foreboding up the hill to the Regnitzlosauerstrasse where Grete lived, and as much as I wanted to drop everything and run to her doorstep, I took a cue from my mother that there would be no detours, even though she didn't say a word or turn her head.

As we walked down Bahnhofstrasse, people kept greeting me and shaking my hand. With friendly faces in front of me and the old, familiar landscape around me, the years dropped away. "*Bist du aber lang weg gewese! Ach*, it's good to see you again, Paul. And how was it in *Kanada?*"

I felt like a celebrity walking down main street, and I was grateful to be wearing decent clothes and not looking like Charlie the tramp in baggy pants and a shabby jacket.

The late afternoon sun lit up the bright red flags that hung on the shop fronts, and as we got closer to our inn, The Golden Sun,

I stepped up my pace. The *Sonne* still had the same golden mustard walls, but now a deep red swastika flag hung by the doorway, flapping in the breeze.

The door swung open and beer mugs were pushed into my face. Old friends, singing and shouting, gathered around me. Some wore brown uniforms with a red armband and the black swastika emblem.

Jette's dark eyes were shining when she hugged me. "Paul, we've missed you so much."

"*Ja, Paul, endlich bist du da*," my father said, with tears in his eyes. "Finally you're home." He looked shorter and his face was pale, but he was smiling.

"*Gott sei dank.* Thanks to God you've come back," my mother said, resting her hand on my shoulder. Then she turned to everyone. "*Ja, Kanada* has made a man out of him, isn't that true," she said laughing. "Free *Schnapps* for everyone. Sit down, *Junge*, sit down," she said, patting me on the back. "You must be hungry. We have fresh pork hocks and sauerkraut for everyone today."

Before long, the *Sonne* was in full swing. Gusti played all the old songs on the accordion, and when her deep, mellow voice filled the room with "*Jagerland, Heimatland, wie bist du so schoen*," I shook my head and let the tears roll. Yes, I thought . . . homeland, homeland, how beautiful you are. I hadn't realized how much I really had missed my home all those years. Everyone wanted to know all about Canada. I had so much to tell them that it wasn't long and my throat went hoarse.

You probably think the first thing I would have done was to visit Grete, and as great as my desire was to do just that, I knew better than to rush things. I didn't want to start off my welcome on the wrong foot. It was good to be home and to be on good terms with the family. I knew I had to be patient for awhile and get my bearings straight, but there was another reason I had to remain calm, which I found out about the next morning.

When I came down the stairs Gusti cornered me before I even had a chance to sit down to some fresh coffee and my favourite crispy rolls.

"I've got to tell you something, Pauli, before you get any ideas."

I caught a strange look in her wide, dark eyes. "What do you mean?" I asked.

She lifted her hands and opened up her long fingers. "*Ach, Pauli,* I wanted to write to you, but I just couldn't." She creased her forehead and pushed her black, wavy hair out of her face. "Grete's been going around with someone."

My face went hot and I shoved my fists into my pockets. "So what's that all about?" I asked, tossing back my head.

"He's from Schoenwald," Gusti said with a frown. "Everyone knows about it."

"Well, I don't think it means anything. We wrote regular all those years, after all. And so what if everyone knows about it. She's not engaged is she?" I asked, feeling like all the stuffing had been knocked out of me.

"No, she's not engaged . . . at least I don't think so," she said, pursing her lips together.

"Is he good looking?"

"*Ja*, he is. I mean, I don't really know him."

I turned to go back up the stairs intending to see Grete immediately, but Gusti grabbed my arm.

"For heavens sake, Pauli, there's no rush. You want to keep peace in the family, don't you? Take your time now," she cried, almost in a whisper. "Come, sit down and have breakfast with us. Jette has put out all your favourite sausage."

She pulled me by the sleeve and sat me down at the table. Fresh, cool air blew in through the open windows, clearing out the smell of stuffy cigarette smoke and beer. The place was empty. Dishes banged in the kitchen.

"Smell the fresh rolls," Gusti said, smoothing her hand across the red and white linen cloth. "I picked them up especially for you. Eat now." Then Gusti put her hand on my shoulder and leaned in close to me. "*Mutter* hasn't changed, you know. And you can bet she's gloating over the fact that Grete's been seeing someone else. She probably has some girl lined up for you. You wait and see. That's why you have to be careful, take it easy a few days, get her on your side.

"She had a match for me, too, you know . . . a *Metzger* from Marktredwitz." Gusti sat down across from me and began to laugh. Her white teeth gleamed. "But I'll never marry him. She's not too happy with Jette's boyfriend either, but at least she hasn't kicked him out. He's quite a fine cabinetmaker, you know."

She poured me a cup of coffee. "Come, eat, you look as skinny as a broom handle. Now that I'm the leader of the BDM, you know, The League of German Girls, I don't have time to think of getting married."

I looked up at her, hardly hearing what she had said. "Ja, you mentioned something in your letter about the BDM."

"*Ach, Pauli*, it's so exciting. I haven't told you anything. Did I write you that I was in Berlin last summer for a sports training course in Gruenewald just outside of Berlin? *Es war herrlich.* Wonderful! I'm leader of thirty girls. Come, now . . . eat."

I poured hot milk into my coffee and took a sip. There was nothing like good, strong German coffee. So Grete had a boyfriend, I thought to myself. Why should I have been so surprised. And Gusti, a *Bund Deutscher Maedel* leader, taking her accordion everywhere she went. She knew all the old German songs, had always excelled in sports, especially the discus, shot-put and spear throwing, and was just the right age. The young girls would have followed her like rats after the Pied Piper of Hamlen.

"Pauli," Gusti said shaking my shoulder. "Don't take it so hard. It's been a long time. What did you expect?"

"She's still my girl as far as I'm concerned, but what about you? You believe everything Hitler raves about?"

"The country is changing," Gusti exclaimed, throwing up her arms. "We're on our feet again. People have work, food in their bellies. We can be proud of our country again."

Quite frankly I didn't know a heck of a lot about the political situation when I returned in '34, but I had already seen enough in the short time I had been home, with the strong military presence and the propaganda, that I was more than a little leery of the new leadership.

"What does *Vater* say about all of this?"

She shrugged her shoulders. "What can he say? There's nothing to say—everyone's joining up." She flashed her white teeth. "You don't understand. It's so exciting on festival days . . . the flags, the parades, the bands. Even here in Rehau we have more celebrations now, more music."

The door opened and my father came in. "*Gruess Gott, Junge,*" he said, patting me on the shoulder. "So, how's it feel to be back in your homeland? You sleep well?"

I nodded my head and tried to speak with some enthusiasm. "It's good to be home again, *Vater.*" I looked around at the cloth-covered tables, the tall arched windows with the deep window sills, the potted plants. "What's nice is that nothing has changed. I almost feel as if I had left yesterday, though the room looks like it has shrunk."

"*Ja, Kanada* is a big land," my father said, pouring himself coffee and pulling out a chair. "You just take it easy for a few days. Rest up good. You look tired and need some fat on your bones." Then he turned and hollered. "*Jette, komm, doch. Mutter.*"

"I learned a lot about business in Canada, you know."

He nodded. "*Ach,* you always knew the business. And don't worry. We have plenty of work for you. At least people always have to eat."

"So you're doing all right?"

"*Ja, Ja.* We have the land rented out," he said nodding. "Times seem to be getting better, that I have to admit."

"People are smiling again, *Pauli,*" Gusti broke in. "We can buy things and travel. Oh, you can be proud of your Fatherland again."

Jette and my mother came in and sat down and we had a family breakfast just like old times. Soon old customers began to arrive for their noon meal, and I began to tell my stories all over again.

That afternoon I had a decent haircut, bought some new clothes and began to feel like a new man. And I had calmed down a little about the fact that Grete was seeing someone else. As long as she wasn't married, I still had a good chance to win her back. She would have heard that I was back in town and was probably wondering when I would come by to see her. But I took my time and waited a good eight days, sticking close to home and getting into the swing of things. Besides, my mother had her eyes on me like a hawk, and every move I made she asked where I was going and when I'd be back. So I just put myself into idle for awhile.

The next time I was in the sausage kitchen alone with my father, I asked him what he thought about Gusti and her girls in uniform.

"*Ja*, times have changed," he said, lowering his voice and automatically looking left and right. "It's best to go along with the Party if you don't want any trouble, see. Lots of young people are joining the Hitler Youth, it's not just Gusti. That's what some do, even if the parents don't like it. I don't want any trouble, see, so I hang out a flag." He wiped his hands on his white apron and picked up a bundle of cured sausage. "What does it matter to hang out a flag? It doesn't hurt anyone. And Gusti? She's a born leader, you know that. And they do harmless things—sports, they sing. At least it's good for them, and as long as she does her work here, what can I say."

"You're a member of the Party then?" I asked, taking the sausage out of his hands and hanging it on a hook.

He leaned in close to me, shaking his finger. "There are some things out of my control, even under this roof, but you're my only son. You don't have to join, but you don't want to talk out of line, talk against them, do you understand?"

He picked up a few pounds of fresh sausage and set it on the scale. He stepped back and took a deep breath, squinting his eyes. "Hitler is very shrewd, very crafty, if you want to know," he said, facing me. He waved his arm and straightened his sticky fingers. "And he runs things with a touch of his fingertips. Young people . . . they just don't know, don't know what it's like lying in the trenches in a foot of mud, soaked to the bone and freezing to death. The Great War is still in my throat! All I hope is that we're not moving toward another one."

"So, what do we do?" I asked.

He shrugged his shoulders and sighed. "*Ja*, what can we do? I'm an old man. We do what we have to do. The Nazis make sure of that."

In a small, rural town like Rehau, business pretty much went on as usual under the new regime, and because Rehau had a very small Jewish segment, discrimination wasn't apparent either. There were no street riots, and the brownshirts were quietly tolerated and didn't make trouble for anyone as long as you didn't make trouble for them. People were no longer starving, unemployment had dropped and the economy was on an upswing.

But nobody talked about what was really going on, nobody dared. The newspapers were under Nazi censorship, all the political parties and state governments had been destroyed, there was no freedom of speech, no labour unions, even the social life of the Germans had become regimented.

But as I said before, I didn't know a whole lot about the political situation at the time. I lifted my arm and said "Heil Hitler" instead of "Gruess Gott" and in no time flat it had become habit. Uppermost in my mind was Grete, and finally the day arrived when I couldn't stay away from her one more minute.

She still worked for Frau Schoedel, according to Gusti, and lived with her mother and stepfather in the same house. So on a Sunday afternoon, eight days after I had returned home, I carefully dressed in my new dark suit and black shoes. I sized myself up in the little mirror above the dresser and ran my fingers through my receding hairline, pushing my waves forward to make my hair look thicker.

When the coast was clear I slipped out of the house, not wanting to run into my mother. The rays of the sun warmed my back as I clattered over the cobblestones in my new shoes. Lavender and white lilac bushes spilled over wrought-iron fences, and the musky scent of blooms hung thick in the warm, moist air.

I studied the long, spindly vines of the old rose bush that twined along the wall at the side of Grete's house, giving my heart a chance to settle back into my chest. Finally I knocked on the door. It opened a crack and I began to grin. Then the door swung wide.

"It's you? Paul? *Mein Gott!*" Frau Doetsch, Grete's mother, stood there, her eyes wide. She wore a black dress with a white lace collar and her dark hair was swept back off her face in a loose bun. We

Frau Doetsch (name by
second marriage; first
husband killed in WWI),
Grete's mother.

shook hands and she asked how I was and said she heard I had
returned from Canada.

"If you have come to see Gretel," she continued, "she's not
home this afternoon." She folded her hands together and lifted her
chin. "She's gone to Schoenwald."

My stomach muscles knotted and I stepped back. "Well, I'll see
her another time, then. It's nice to see you again and when Grete
gets home tell her I stopped by."

"You know, Paul," Frau Doetsch said, crossing her arms and
running her hands up and down her sleeves. "The best would be
that you don't see her again. We don't want any more trouble."

"But I've been gone five years," I said, stepping forward again
and gesturing with my hands. "... and I'm just back. I'd at least
like to have the chance to say hello to her!"

"*Ja, Ja*, I know, but Mr. Doetsch and I don't want trouble, you
see, and neither does Gretel." She shook her head and continued.
"I'm sorry, but it's better for everybody; you must believe me."

"Frau Doetsch, we've written to each other all these years."

"I understand, Paul. I'm sorry, but that's how it is."

I stared at her for another moment, not able to grasp what she was talking about. Now I was getting it from both sides.

"Good day then," I said, shaking her hand again. "It has been nice to see you, and I really hope I'll see you again very soon."

I left her standing at the doorstep with a skeptical look in her eyes. I could understand how she would want to protect her daughter, but I felt I had a right to hear it from Grete herself. And why would there still be trouble after five years? Who would have remembered the slurs my mother had made, and surely the old-fashioned ideas about marriage would have changed since then.

The next evening I waited for Grete up the street from the dressmaker's shop. I leaned against the wall and pressed my nose into the bunch of shivering purple violets I had purchased from the flower shop. I was so nervous about seeing her that I felt like eighteen again. I had to think back on the pictures she had sent to me to remember what she looked like. After all those years away I could hardly believe the moment was finally there. But moments can be long and I waited and waited, shifting back and forth from one foot to the other, thinking of what I would say to her.

 Suddenly she was walking towards me. My palms broke into a sweat and for a second I thought I was back in Canada in some crazy dream. Was that really the girl of my dreams coming up the street? But she wasn't a girl anymore. She was a beautiful young woman. Her flowery, short-sleeved dress swished back and forth as she approached me. She patted her hair and pulled a shawl around her shoulders. I didn't move, I couldn't have moved. I finally pushed myself away from the wall, hoping that the pound-ing pulse in my neck wouldn't show. Then she saw me. She stopped and her white hand flew up to her face.

My face cracked into a grin. The moment I had dreamed about for years was right there. People walked around us, but I was oblivious to everything. All I could think about was how we would embrace, how I would pick her up and swing her around, how my fingertips would touch her soft, round cheeks, and how her blue eyes would talk to me . . . how she'd laugh. Her skin shone like the pinkish glow of a wilderness sunset. She was more beautiful than she had ever been. Her hair was longer, her waves heavier, her body fuller.

"Paul?" she said, stopping a couple of meters away from me. A red flush rose on her neck and cheeks.

I wanted to run to her, hold her, but where was the joy in her eyes? The movement in her arms? The air between us turned quiet and still.

"I'm just back," I said, wanting to tell her I had always loved her and had never stopped thinking of her, but I couldn't get the words past my lips.

She gave me a quick handshake and began to walk slowly toward her house. "I know when you returned," she said, looking up at me. "You've been back for over a week."

"I wanted to come sooner," I said, leaning toward her and gesturing with my free hand, "I wanted to see you first thing, you have to believe that." I stroked her shining hair for an instant then turned and began to walk backwards.

"Grete, listen to me. I needed time to iron things out with my family. You know how it is with them."

"It doesn't matter anyway," she said, shaking her head. "And after five years, what's one week."

"Grete, you must understand why it took so long for me to come back from Canada. I explained everything to you in my letters—how I didn't want to owe my parents, especially since I only wanted to come back home to you. That's why I had to earn my own way. And everything matters to me."

"You've been gone a long time," she said in a matter-of-fact attitude. "I truly didn't think you would even come back after all these years. What do you expect? And Arno and Max? Why haven't they returned?"

"But all those years we wrote. You sent pictures."

"You wrote to me so I wrote back," she said with a shrug of her shoulders. "And I haven't written to you in over a year." We came to a corner and she stopped. "Listen. I don't want any more trouble, and it's better if we're not even seen together. I'm sorry, but I really have to go. We'll talk . . . .we can talk some other time."

"Grete, wait, I've missed you so much." I touched her shoulder, but she only shrugged and pressed her lips together.

"Here . . . the violets," I said, crushing them into her hands.

Her cool blue eyes gazed at me for a moment as if she were noticing my thinning hair, my skinny body. She looked down at the flowers and gently touched the leaves.

"It's good you're back," she said glancing at me, then up the street. "Your family must be happy you're home again, your father especially. And . . . I am glad you're safely home, but it's . . . it's just better if we don't see each other. I really have to go now. My mother will have *Abendbrot* prepared."

No words came. My spine bristled and a dull pain pulled together inside my chest, but when my eyes followed her up the street, the graceful movement of her blue, flowery dress made me forget my anger. She hadn't given me a direct no, after all, and she hadn't told me there was somebody else, so I made plans when I could see her again. I wasn't going to give up without a fight, not after all the years away.

I was back again the next day. "I told you," she insisted. "We can't see each other anymore."

"But why?" I persisted, pressing her with all kinds of sweet talk and reaching out to her. "We promised each other. How can you let go of all that after all this time. I've only thought of you. I promised you . . . "

"What are promises? Besides, don't you know yet?" She paused and her dark eyebrows pinched together. "Don't you know there is somebody else?"

When she actually told me, even though I knew, my face prickled with heat and I felt my body flinch. "He's the guy who lives in Schoenwald then?"

She lifted her chin. "It doesn't matter where he lives," she said, dropping her eyes. "I have to go. Please."

My dander was up, but I just swallowed hard. "You know, you're the most beautiful girl in the world." She pulled her jacket together with a shrug and began to walk away.

"I've never stopped thinking of you," I called after her. "Not for a minute. I'll see you tomorrow and every single day until you change your mind."

And I did. Every day I offered her flowers, oranges, chocolate, even *Knackwurst*. But the more determined I was, the more deliberate and cut and dried she became. Nothing worked so I decided to change my tactics. Even though so much had happened in the intervening years since I'd met Grete and we had both changed, I couldn't believe she had stopped caring for me. I just wasn't ready to accept that.

I dug up my old man's bowler, a tail coat, a cane and a mustache and waited in a quiet lane close to her house. I thought about how long ago it was since I had first met her at Carnival time and danced the Charleston with her.

People stared at me. Some shrugged their shoulders and laughed. It was a good thing not everybody in town knew me. I just tipped my hat and grinned. When Grete came up the street everything was in my favour. No one was around. I stepped out in front of her and bowed before she had a chance to say one word.

"May I have the next dance, please, Mademoiselle?"

Her eyes shot open in surprise, but instead of turning away, she shook her head and began to laugh. I didn't waste a second. I took hold of her soft white hands and kissed them and squeezed them.

"You haven't forgotten after all," I said and she made no attempt to pull her hands away. My heart beat around my ears. "Come," I said, wanting to jump in the air and give my heels a click. "Let's go for a walk." I tossed the mustache, hat and cane and tucked her hand under my arm.

"No," she said, "I can't, I really can't. I have to prepare for a trip tomorrow. Don't you remember that it's *Himmelfahrtstag*?"

"Come, let's go," I said. "Forget Ascension Day. We'll go somewhere."

"No," she said, shaking her shining, chestnut hair and smiling. "I really must go." She eased her hands out of mine. "You were gone so long, you know, that you almost didn't exist for me anymore."

"But I wrote to you as often as I could, and you were with me every minute all those years."

She began to walk slowly along the sidewalk. "Nothing has changed, you know. I have never spoken a single word to your mother since the day you left. But people still talk."

"What happened between you and my mother was so long ago you don't even have to worry about it. She's just too damned happy I'm back."

Grete began to nod her head and smile. "You don't know your mother. For her it's not long enough . . . and wait until she finds out you are seeing me again. You know very well that if we went for a walk, the news would be all over town."

When she said the magic words "seeing me again" I knew I'd won her over. "Let's forget my mother," I said, grasping Grete's hands. "What can she do? And the Wurlitzer girl is safely married."

By the beginning of June, the Schoenwald guy was out of the picture. I bought a gold ring so I could propose to my sweetheart in style. I was the happiest man alive. Somehow the news hadn't filtered back to my mother, but Grete and I had been careful and kept our meetings as secret as possible.

One Sunday morning Grete and I went for a long walk. Clover, white daisies, and forget-me-nots bloomed along the edge of the fields. Dandelion seeds drifted lazily through the warm, humid air. We followed a well-worn path into the cool forest of lean fir and spruce which grew in rows like marching soldiers. The only disorder came from the wild singing of the larks and blackbirds and the thrushes and finches that flitted through the trees. No giant cottonwoods, no cedar or balsam grew up in disarray through thick, scrambled underbrush. No windfalls, salmonberry bushes, tall ferns or heavy moss covered the damp forest floor like in the rugged forests of British Columbia.

We sat down in the tall grass alongside a stream, enjoying the peaceful trickling sound of the water. I plucked a daisy and stuck it in Grete's loose, thick hair.

I was convinced she would say yes, but I knew that underneath she feared my mother and the backlash that would follow. The ring burned into my pocket and I felt like a herd of wild horses was pounding across my chest. I picked up her hand and kissed her fingers, gazing with longing into her eyes. Clumsily I slipped the band onto her finger.

She began to blush and for a long moment we froze in motion like a couple of pantomime artists. Finally she looked down at the ring and twisted it around with her right hand not saying a word.

"I'm never going to leave your side as long as I live," I said to her, holding her warm face in my hands and kissing away the tears that had welled up in her eyes.

"Your mother will always try to get her way," Grete said, slowly shaking her head. "I just don't see how we could ever be happy."

I put my arms around her. "You won't have to live with my mother. You won't even have to see her."

"That's easy to say," she said, looking at me with large, somber eyes, "but I know I would never feel comfortable."

"Then we'll move away. My Aunt Gretel still lives in Berlin. She would be glad to help us out."

She drew up her knees and put her arms around them. "No. I couldn't live there. Not with everything that has happened—the riots, the mobs of people, the book burnings. So much changed after you left. You were gone so long. Sometimes I really get scared with everything that's going on. People get beaten, even shot, just for saying the wrong thing, for saying something against the Party. I've even had to sew Nazi flags." She picked up a stalk of grass and tossed it into the stream. "Some paradise Hitler promised!"

"Right now I don't care about Hitler," I said, turning her face to mine. "All I care about is you and that I want to marry you." She pulled out a hanky and dabbed at her eyes. "Grete, I know you're worried," I said, kissing her damp cheeks and stroking her shining hair. "I don't like what I see either, but what can we do?"

"You know, Paul," she said, leaning forward again and smoothing her skirt over her legs. "Maybe there is another way."

I rested my arm on her shoulder, trying to figure what other way there could be. But any idea she had I was willing to listen to. I would have done anything, gone anywhere for her.

She plucked a dandelion and gently blew the seeds, scattering them across the stream. She twirled the stem around in her fingers and the corner of her lips turned up in a smile. Then she glanced up at me with a gleam in her eye. "We could go to Canada."

"Canada?" *Mein Gott*, I thought to myself and almost stopped breathing. I jumped up and pulled her to her feet. I couldn't believe what I was hearing, especially since she had once written that she could never imagine herself in that country. I clutched her arms. "You would actually go to Canada?"

"I would," she murmured.

"If I'd known that! Do you know that I tried to get Immigration papers for you? And that I would have had to put up a two thousand dollar bond to bring you to Canada?"

"I had the money," she said laughing.

"I would never have dared to ask you."

"And I probably would have thought you were crazy if you had."

I threw my hands into the air. "But what about your mother, and your stepfather. They would never let you go. And your mother would never forgive me for taking her daughter away."

"I'll go if I want," she said, lifting her chin.

"But would you really leave, just like that?" I asked, beginning to grin. "Do you really mean it?"

"The further away I get from here, the better off we'll be," she said gloatingly.

I took a deep breath. The idea of returning to Canada never occurred to me. I had been home barely a month, had just started working in the business. What would it do to my old man, I thought?

"I don't have any money," I said, shrugging my shoulders, "and the old folks sure won't pay a second time for me to leave, especially when my mother finds out we want to get married."

Grete's eyebrows lifted and a smile slipped across her face. "Well, if you truly want to marry me and you would take me to Canada, I have plenty of money for our fare."

"You know I'd go anywhere for you, Grete, but would you really be willing to take a chance and leave your homeland for me?"

She nodded her head and I pulled her into my arms and kissed her, caressing her cheeks, stroking her hair. Here I not only had my girl, but we would return to the country I loved. I put my arm around her waist and began to waltz her around right there beside the stream.

"If you insist on marrying a poor guy, then we'll leave next spring," I said, stopping and holding her at arms length. "That way everybody would have time to get used to the idea, including my mother."

"Oh, no," she said firmly. "If we go, we leave this summer. I've lived in this town all my life and I want to get out. And the sooner the better. Once your mother hears that we're getting married, we will be in big trouble."

Suddenly I began to have misgivings, feeling I had misled Grete about the wonders of British Columbia.

"It's a hard life in Canada," I explained to her. "Times are tough there, too, really tough, and jobs are scarce. It won't be easy for us," I said, shaking my head. "And you might not like it . . . you don't know the language."

"I don't care. I can learn the language. Just think, Paul, our life will be our own, and we'll be free."

I picked her up and swung her around. "If you're absolutely sure, then I'll make all the arrangements. We'll leave as soon as possible."

18. Farewell my Homeland

THE NEXT MORNING MY MIND was still spinning. Grete was going to be my wife and that's all that mattered. But by the time I sat down for breakfast, I again had doubts about leaving my family so soon, not to mention how my mother would take the news of our marriage.

My mother set a jug of coffee on the table and touched my shoulder. "So, *Guten Appetit*, Paul. I've made some soft-boiled eggs just the way you like them, and fresh from the farmer."

My father sat across the table from me. "*Ja, Guten Morgen.*" He picked up a roll and cut it in half. "Nothing better than fresh *Broetchen*. I bet you missed the good bread in Canada," he said, spreading it with thick goose fat.

My mother left the room and I heard her shuffle down the stone steps in her slippers. My parents were happy I was home again, no doubt about that, and maybe, just maybe, my mother wouldn't object to my marrying Grete. I figured that if I talked it over with my old man he might be able to convince her that we could work things out. I had been gone for so long that I couldn't believe she would still have any objections. I grabbed a couple of buns from the basket and began to juggle them.

"What's the matter with you," my father asked, washing down the bun with some hot coffee. "Come now, eat something."

I tossed the buns back into the basket and stood up, shoving my hands into my pockets.

"What is it then?" he asked, his mouth full of bread. "What's the matter with you?"

I took a deep breath and faced my father. "Grete and I want to get married this summer."

His mouth stopped moving and his face turned a deep red. "*Spinnst du wohl?*" he spit out in a whisper. "Are you crazy? Your mother won't hear of that, you should know that by now."

"I thought if you would talk to her—somehow convince her . . . "

"After all these years and you're still stuck on that girl? I thought she was engaged!"

"Listen, *Vater*," I pleaded, motioning with both hands.

"You've got to make *Mutter* understand. I'm going to marry Grete and that's all there is to it. You want me to stay in the business, don't you?"

He shook his head and pushed back the chair. "Your mother has her own ideas and I'm not going to put myself in the middle. Sometimes she's as stubborn as an ox and nothing and nobody can change her mind. You tell her yourself," he said poking out his chin. "You'll find out, but just leave me out of it."

I pulled out my chair and sat down again. "I want you to know, *Vater*, I just want to warn you . . . if things don't work out, well . . . if things don't work out, Grete and I are planning to leave for Canada."

His face went white as plaster and his shoulders slumped. He ran his hand back and forth along the edge of the table. Finally he looked up. "If that's what you had in mind," he said, "we could've saved your return fare."

"It's not what I had in mind, believe me. Please, *Vater*, just talk to her."

"I know she won't change her mind," he said tightening his lips and shaking his head. "I don't even have to ask." He ran his hands over his balding head. "Why don't you at least wait a year, give her some time."

"*Donnerwetter!* I've waited five years already. I know darned well if *Mutter* doesn't want us to get married now, she's not going to change her mind in a year."

"You're the son. You're to inherit this place," he said, wagging his finger at me. "It's a law that all land is to be passed on to the eldest son. This place is yours. The land is yours. Hertels have been in this town for centuries and you're the last of the Hertels in our branch of the family, don't you know that? If you leave and I die there won't be anyone left to carry on our name."

"I'll have sons. And we'll come back some day."

"*Jawohl*, after I'm dead and gone."

"*Vater*, the business means everything to me, but I can't run it without Grete in my life. That's why I want you to talk to *Mutter*. If I try to talk to her I know she'll be insulted."

He took a deep breath and sighed. "All right. All right. I'll talk to her. I'll talk to her this evening."

The next morning my mother was not to be seen. I went into the sausage kitchen where my father was measuring out spices.

"*Morgen*," I said, tying my apron around me.

He nodded and continued to carefully measure out one spice after another—garlic, sage, thyme—not looking at me. I picked up a pile of sausages to be hung on the rack. I sized up the situation and it didn't look good at all, but I knew it was best to leave my father in peace until he was ready to talk. We worked along in silence for awhile. When he dumped the last of the spices into the ground meat and began to mix it in with his hands he looked over to me.

"When you were a boy, Paul, and used to play the violin. Do you remember?"

"Sure," I said with a nod. "I remember all right."

"You had an ear for the instrument. I used to sit in the next room and listen to you play. You had a feeling for that violin."

"I never liked to practice."

He stopped mixing for a minute and tasted the sausage.

"This formula, you know, it's been handed down from your great grandfather. We pass it on from one generation to the next and make the best *Knackwurst* in town. Where was I?" he said, pausing. "Oh, yes, that violin. I liked nothing more than to hear you learn a new piece, hear you play some Beethoven with Jette. I always felt sorry your mother had no patience with you, didn't give you a fair chance. You might have become quite a good violinist."

"I was happy when I didn't have to practice anymore."

He shook his head. "No child wants to practice, but once they get over the hurdle . . . Your mother saved that violin, you know.

It's still under the bed cracked in half with its broken strings flying around."

He let out a deep sigh and the two of us continued to work side by side, deep in thought. I wanted to ask him directly about the matter at hand, but the moment was gone and to pursue it would have been a mockery.

That afternoon I found my mother upstairs in an easy chair, shuffling through some old photos. Her jaw was set and she barely gave me a second look.

I cleared my throat, dancing from one foot to the other. "I guess *Vater* has told you that Grete and I are getting married and leaving for Canada this summer."

Without a word she just kept looking at the pictures. Behind her on the wall hung two large hand-painted plates decorated with deep pink roses and blue and mustard-yellow daisies. My mother shifted in the chair and glanced up at me.

"Those plates are very old, you know. They were here when your father and I married. Here, look, this picture of the three of you as children."

"*Mutter*, did you hear what I said?"

"*Freilich*," she said, irritated. "I have nothing more to say." Her jaw set and her dark steady eyes focused on mine. "Except that this family will not be at your wedding."

I threw up my arms. "I don't understand. Grete is a fine, intelligent woman." My voice cracked and I dropped my hands. "And I love her. We love each other."

She gave me another hard look. "You heard me!"

Her words cut hard, but this time the feeling didn't last long because I wasn't alone and I knew where I was headed. I have to admit, though, that I would never have had the guts to pull up stakes a second time without Grete behind me, never would have considered it. But by that point, I don't think hell or high water could have stopped the two of us from leaving.

That very afternoon I applied for a marriage licence, but first I had to get proof from Canada that I had never been married over there. I sent a telegram to Arno and asked him to forward the information to the proper authorities in Victoria and have them wire it directly to me. Grete and I also had to apply for passports and visas, which would take several weeks. We had endless forms and questionnaires to fill out. We had to be examined medically, criminally and ethnically. We were questioned, fingerprinted and photographed. I booked passage on the S.S. *Bremen*, which was to leave Hamburg August 19th, and we set our wedding date for August 14th. Gusti and Jette couldn't believe I was leaving for Canada again.

"At least if there's a war, you won't be killed in it," Gusti said to me one day when we were picking up empty beer mugs from the tables.

"There have always been wars, so no use worrying about it. Even Canada could go to war, no one knows."

"Maybe I'll visit you someday," she said with a sad look in her dark eyes. "Do you think I'd really like it in Canada?"

"It would be just the country for you, I always told you that. You could hike for days without seeing another person and when you're really out in the wilderness away from the world, there's no feeling like it."

Once Grete and I had booked our passage, I couldn't think of anything but our future together in a country without boundaries. Although I felt guilty about leaving the family, and this time I knew it would be for good, the remaining weeks before our departure filled me with a restlessness I knew would only be cured by leaving with Grete. Even though I had been happy when I first returned home, I came to realize that if I stayed in Germany, I would forever be bound to the business and the town.

But any doubts I may have had, and Grete had none whatsoever, were quickly squelched the beginning of July when we heard over the radio that a group of S.A. leaders, heading the Storm Troopers, had been shot by Hitler's S.S., the elite, black-coated *Schutzstaffel*. Roehm and other S.A. leaders were dead, General von Schleicher, the former Chancellor just prior to Hitler's takeover in '33, was dead. Even Schleicher's wife had been gunned down. There were all kinds of rumors and nobody knew what to believe. According to Hitler, they still would have been alive had they not resisted arrest and if others hadn't committed suicide. In truth, Roehm and his followers no longer served Hitler's purposes, so he eliminated them. No one knew how many S.A. members had been gunned down, but the numbers probably ran into the hundreds.

Some say that Hitler became absolute master of Germany after that night of June 30, 1934, known as the Night of the Long Knives. Others say it wasn't until Hindenburg's death just over a month later that he gained complete mastery, but by then he let it be known that "everyone must know for all future time if he raises his hand to strike the State, then certain death is his lot."

But as I had mentioned before, life in Rehau wasn't affected as much by the Nazi regime, and things were quieter than in the big cities. Life went on, the swastika flags flew and the ever-present brownshirts were people we knew. Then two weeks before we were to get married—the church bans for our wedding were up—I came home to find my father in a real uproar.

"Did you hear President Hindenburg is dead?" he asked.

I shook my head. "What's it mean?" Hindenburg was an old man well into his eighties by then.

"*Ja*, what do you think it means? Nothing can stop Hitler now." He wagged his finger and shook his head. "You wait and see."

For Grete and me, our personal freedom was about to begin, but little did any of us know what the next decade held in store for Europe.

My mother and I were barely polite to each other the last few weeks I was home, but the Saturday morning of our wedding she knocked on the door when I was getting dressed.

"It's open," I said.

Her dark figure filled the door frame. "*Also, wir sehen uns nicht mehr*," she said.

"Naturally we'll see each other again. I'll come back to visit in a couple of years or so."

"You could've married anybody . . . anybody, you know."

I straightened up and looked at her hard. Then I let my shoulders sag and nodded my head. "I know, *Mutter*, I know." I touched her arm. "Where's *Vater*?"

She shook her head dejectedly and shrugged her shoulders.

I took one last look in the mirror and saw a reflection of troubled dark eyes. I pulled at my collar and adjusted my bow tie. "Do I look okay, *Mutter*?"

She nodded and turned to leave. "*Ya*, so is that life. Maybe one day you'll understand."

My throat felt tight and I kept swallowing. I stepped toward the door and reached out to her. "Don't worry, *Mutter*. It's not so bad. Grete and I will have a good life together and we'll come back—anytime you'll have us."

"*Ja*, so is that life," she said again. Suddenly she put her arms around me and held me tight. "Keep well, keep well," she said and disappeared into the dim hallway.

I walked over to the window and looked down into the street. A horse-drawn wagon filled with barrels of beer was parked in front of our *Gasthof.* The horses were shaking their heads up and down and jerking the harness. The Rehauer Kronenbrau beer was the best in the world, I thought to myself. I pulled on my jacket and took a deep breath, looking around the room one last time. Everything was ready. My trunk and suitcase had been sent on ahead to the station, and Grete was waiting for me at the church.

Last night's cigarette smoke still hung in the air in the downstairs parlour where my father sat drinking a cup of coffee. He didn't look up when I came in. His big hands lay awkwardly on the table.

"I'm leaving now," I said, trying to keep it light.

He pushed back his chair and slowly stood up. His eyes were lined with wrinkles. "*Macht's gut, gelt?*"

I knew years would pass before I would see him again and I wanted to smooth things over, but what could I could say.

"*Danke, Vater*," I said, taking a deep breath. "We'll do good. And things will blow over in time. Don't worry."

"*Ja*, I know. You'd better go now before you get late." He ran his hand across his balding head. "We'll get along."

"*Also, auf Wiedersehen*, then," I said.

He put his heavy hands on my shoulders, looking at me for several seconds, his eyes dark and filled with worry. I gave him a last hug and patted him on the back.

I felt as if I were going to a funeral when I walked out the door and turned to wave one last time. Shadows from the morning light fell across the dull, mustard walls of the *Sonne*. My father waved without a nod of his head, without a smile. Then I heard Gusti and Jette at the open window upstairs. They put their hands around their mouths.

"We'll see you later, Pauli."

I could hear the bells pealing all the way up the main street. When I arrived at the church, my Aunt Gretel, who had come from Berlin, was outside waiting for me.

"You were practically like a son to me, all those years you were in Berlin," she said. "I wouldn't have missed your wedding for anybody. Why, Grete's a lovely girl, such a lovely girl. Your mother is making a big mistake."

I put my arm around her shoulders. "It means a lot to me that you came. We could've worked things out here I guess, but Grete wants to leave."

"She's not Jewish, is she?"

"No, that has nothing to do with it. It's a small town, and she would never get along with *Mutter*."

"Well, good luck. If you and Grete come back you must come to Berlin and stay with me. You know how beautiful the city is."

I nodded to her, remembering the deep blue of the Wannsee, the broad Kurfuerstendamm, the old majestic buildings. "Come, *Tante Gretel*, we have to go in."

The rays of the sun beamed through the arched, stained glass windows, and Grete's cheeks shone like wax. She wore a deep-blue suit and held a bunch of blue bachelor's buttons and white roses that shook through the entire ceremony. I kept glancing down at her to make sure she didn't disappear, that she wasn't just a mirage across some winter landscape. Her lips kept breaking into a smile and when she looked up at me her eyes glistened.

The preacher was about to begin his sermon when the door to the church creaked open. I turned and there stood Gusti grinning from ear to ear. I winked and smiled at her. I could have guessed that nothing would have kept her away from our wedding.

It wasn't until we said our final vows and I looked down into Grete's eyes that I felt I had arrived in a safe haven. Although I wasn't a religious person, even in those days, when the bells rang out and the warm sun shone onto our faces, I nevertheless felt solemn and touched by the ceremony.

We walked from the church to Grete's house, where her mother had prepared all kinds of fancy cold cuts, herring salad with beets, potato salad, cucumber salad, *Fleischsalat, Streuselkuchen,* plum cake and special cakes from the bakery.

Grete's Grandmother Caroline kept wiping her eyes with a lace handkerchief. "Don't worry, *Oma,*" Frau Doetsch reassured her. "Gretel will be back, you wait and see."

Grete's stepsister Lola rushed around pushing food on everyone, and her little cousin Alicia with long blond braids kept pulling my sleeve and asking me about Canada. Mathilde and some of Grete's other girlfriends were there, too, as were some of my old school chums.

When we were ready to leave for the train station, Grete's mother gave her some last-minute instructions.

"Now write if you need anything, Gretel. And when you want a return fare, we'll send it to you, do you hear? For now the rest of your money will be safe with us."

After Grete had paid our fare, and took money out of the bank for our trip, she still had three thousand marks left, a lot of money in those days. But her mother wouldn't let her take it along because she was convinced Grete would be back home in a year. We never saw a cent of that money again, and I don't need to say that there were times we were in dire need of it. Of course, after the devaluation of the currency in Germany in 1949, four years after the war ended, that money wasn't worth a nickel.

Our trunks were waiting at the station, packed with our feather quilts, warm winter clothing, boots, linens, cutlery, old pictures, a music box that opened to a dancing ballerina, from my Aunt in

Berlin. Grete had given some of her linens to her cousin Alicia because we were allowed only one trunk apiece.

When we left the house, Grete's mother put a silver broach on Grete's collar, an old silver Thaler piece that had been hammered and filigreed into a flower.

"Take it for good luck. This was given to me for a Confirmation present years and years ago."

At the station a band was playing all the old folk songs, "*Adieu, mein Heimatland* . . . Farewell my Homeland," and when our friends and family crowded around us, the tears began to flow.

Gusti took hold of my hands, her black eyes glistening.

"*Pauli*, promise you'll come back to visit. Promise. And let us know how you are."

Jette, always the more reserved, hadn't dared defy my mother's wishes and stayed behind at the *Sonne*.

As it turned out, those promises took decades to fulfill with everything that happened and the intervening war. As the train rolled away and Grete and I hung out the window waving, the band struck up one last song and everybody sang out "*Aber der Wagen, der rollt.*"

I could hardly believe how quickly my circumstances had changed and that I was once again on the road after only three months at home. But this time I had my sweetheart in my arms and we were on our way to a new life together.

19. Vancouver Island

WE ARRIVED THE NEXT DAY IN HAMBURG and stayed with Grete's stepbrother, Fritz Doetsch, a printer. On the day of departure, the 19th of August, we loaded our trunks and suitcases onto a horse-drawn wagon and headed for the harbour. That same day, Germans were going to the polls to approve Hitler taking over President Hindenburg's office. Even Hitler himself was in town. Nazi propaganda was pasted on every window and column, and the full regalia of red swastika flags and banners with "*Deutschland Erwache—Germany Awake*," lined the streets.

People paraded up and down the sidewalks carrying signs. "*Ja, Fuehrer wir folgen Dir—*Yes, Fuehrer, we follow you!" Or "Yes! Hitler Alone the Leader of the State!" Everywhere the S.S. in their black uniforms and black jack boots were visible.

We gave the agent our passports, tickets, and export permit, which was worth a thousand marks and all the cash we had was also in marks. Taking his time to check everything over, he creased his lips together and slowly shook his head.

"I'm sorry, but you can't leave without dollars. You have to exchange your money or I can't let you board."

"But the permit is as good as dollars!" I exclaimed.

He rubbed his fingers across a *Hakenkreuz* button that was pinned to his lapel. "That's no dollars," and with a cold, blank look told me he couldn't help us.

Then I whispered to him. "I can pay you."

His eyes narrowed and he leaned forward. "That is forbidden, do you hear?" he said, spitting the words into my face. "I can't give you dollars. Go try a bank." Then he looked right past me. "Next please."

Our boat was to leave that afternoon and we needed the money in a hurry. I went from one bank to another but no one would exchange our money. We were in a panic. They either had no dollars and said it would take a couple of weeks to get it exchanged, or they simply refused to help us. I pleaded with them and explained we were leaving for America, had a boat to catch, but our pleas went unheard.

All we could do was go back to the pier and get our baggage. The gangplank was up. The smokestacks spewed out black smoke, and the S.S. *Bremen* departed without us. That really knocked the wind out of our sails, and on top of it we thought we had lost our fare, but luckily we were able to exchange our tickets right away and make arrangements to leave on the S.S. *Europa*, departing from Bremerhaven a week later.

The harbour area was jammed with people and we soon found out they were waiting to hear Hitler's speech to the shipyard workers which was to be announced over a huge loudspeaker in the marketplace. We found ourselves standing among throngs of people listening to his shrill voice which sounded like some crazed religious fanatic, and every time he paused hundreds of workers cheered in unison with "*Sieg Heil's*" and "*Heil Hitler's.*" Masses of people were waving flags, shouting and saluting. Then Hindenburg's son spoke and asked all the German people to turn the office of President, which his father had held, over to the *Fuehrer* and Reich Chancellor. That was the day the Nazification of Germany was completely sealed and Hitler officially became Germany's *Fuehrer*.

A few days later I was down on my knees in front of the purser in Bremerhaven begging him to exchange our money.

"It is not possible for me to do such a thing," he said to me through his teeth and shuffling some papers. "Not possible. I simply cannot."

I looked around and slipped him a hundred marks. His fist closed quietly over the money, and without looking left or right he mumbled to us to come back in an hour. Sure enough, an hour later he had the money, but we knew that had he been caught he would have lost his job. By then the regime had made it as difficult as possible for anyone to leave the country. We were damn glad, if

Grete ready to board SS *Europa* on way to Canada, 1934.

not damn lucky to get out. By then many artists and intellectuals like Einstein, Bertolt Brecht, Thomas Mann, Lotte Lenya, just to name a few, had been forced to leave. Even Marlene Dietrich had left Germany by then.

Our cabin was in steerage, right over the screws, and our trip was noisy and shaky, but we were on our way and our honeymoon trip lay ahead of us. But neither of us had sea legs, and we both got so sick we didn't care whether the boat sank or stayed afloat.

Eight days later we arrived in New York Harbour. We clung to the ship's railing and gazed across the choppy water at the famous skyline which was veiled in pink-gray fog like cotton candy. The hubbub of tugboats and foghorns and the smell of oil and fish and sweating people, made us feel as if we were simmering in some giant mulligan stew. Someone pointed out the Empire State Building which rose above the fog like the finger of a giant. When we passed the Statue of Liberty, I told Grete we would climb right up into her crown. "You'll feel like a Lilliputian."

It took us hours to get through Immigration. We were pushed and jostled among the throngs of immigrants, and I would have traded the heat and humidity for ice and snow anytime. We had to swear an oath that we weren't insane, that we weren't spies, and that we didn't have syphilis. When our papers were cleared and we checked our baggage at the train station, I whistled for a cab to take us to Hans Spitzbarth's place who was a relative through marriage and also from Rehau.

He had been in the meat business in Rehau but had become a safecracker in New York. Every time a bank had problems with their safes, they called Hans. They took us to the Statue of Liberty and the Empire State Building, and we spent a couple of days at their weekend place in upstate New York.

As impressive as everything was, Grete and I soon grew tired of the towering skyscrapers where the sun shone a few short hours a day, and where the hot, sticky air smelled of fried onions. People and taxis filled the streets, which reminded me of Berlin, but I longed for some tall, green grass in a meadow beside a swift flowing river.

Every day the *New York Times* had news from Germany. There were headlines about a fear of invasion of Austria by the Nazis, and that Hitler was calling for a return of the Saar Basin to Germany. There was a list of the official Nazi Ten Commandments in the paper, one of them being that as a German male you had to choose a German woman or one of Nordic blood who was healthy and pure of body. In New Jersey a boys' camp was broken up because of alleged Nazi activities.

It was good to be in a free country, I can tell you.

We finally boarded a train which took us all across the northern United States and we had the pleasure of riding "first class." Of course, Grete had a hard time imagining that I would have dared to jump on a moving freight, but it was harder for her to believe the miles and miles of prairie we crossed with no living person in sight. She wasn't a very good traveller, I found out, because she didn't feel too well some of the time on our way across the country. We changed trains in Chicago and again in Everett, Washington, where we went north to B.C.

When we arrived in Vancouver around the mid-September we checked our trunks at the station and caught a streetcar to East Broadway where Arno then lived.

"Paul!" Arno shouted when he opened the door. "How's it possible you're back here?" He threw his arms around us. "*Und Mein Gott*, Grete. You too? Come in. Here, let me help you with your suitcases. Come in. I knew you two were getting married, but never thought you'd come back to Canada. Hey, Ida. Where are you? We've got company."

"So, you got yourself hitched too, eh," I said, giving him a pat on the back.

"You bet." Then he said to Grete with a wink. "How come you ended up marrying this *Sau Bayer* after all those years? Even I couldn't live with him. Just don't let him put any ideas into your head and whisk you off to some primitive little cabin way out in the boondocks."

We stayed up most of the night celebrating. Ida and Grete got along well right from the start. We spent a couple of days with them before deciding to go to Vancouver Island where Little Max, Big Max and Adam had settled. We went by ferry to Victoria, then took the bus to Westholme, which was nothing more than a whistle stop a few miles north of Duncan. Westholme was the only address we had so we enquired at the general store if they knew a Max Hopperdieztel.

"Sure, we buy fresh vegetables from him. Lives a couple of miles on up the road. You'll find it."

We left all of our baggage at the store and walked about a mile in the heavy twilight until we came to a small house. There was no answer and the door was locked, so I climbed through a window, figuring it had to be Max's place. But it was deserted. After passing several more empty houses, we finally came to a garage with a house in the back. The door of the garage was slightly ajar and after several knocks I pushed it open. On the table were a couple of photographs that I recognized.

"This is it," I said to Grete. "It's a picture of Rose, Max's sister. We may as well make ourselves comfortable until he gets back."

We were so tired we crawled into one of the beds and fell asleep. Well, sometime during the night Max finally came home. I hopped out of bed right away, not wanting a gun barrel in my face.

"It's me, Paul," I said laughing. It was quite a shock for him to find me there, and after he fumbled around and lit the coal oil lamp he had a double surprise to see Grete as well.

"So, you two finally tied the knot," he said, pushing the hair out of his eyes. Then he looked at Grete. "It's a good thing, too, the way he bellyached around like a half-sick moose all those years."

"So you guys got tired of the cold winters in the Okanagan, eh?" I asked.

"Got tired of not getting paid. The farmer had no money, but at least he gave us two horses. Big Max and me rode 'em the three hundred miles to Vancouver and then sold them. I ended up here and Big Max is in Victoria working at odd jobs."

The next day Grete and I moved into the deserted house in the back. It had a few pieces of furniture and some beds and we fixed it up for ourselves. There were a lot of abandoned places around in those years. If there wasn't any work, people just packed up and left.

There were times when Grete seemed pretty tired. I thought she was still recovering from the trip, but finally one morning when she was feeling quite sick, a light clicked on in my head.

"You're pregnant!"

She began to grin and nodded her head. "Well, I could be, you know."

I swooped her up and buried my face in her belly. "Why didn't you say something? How far along are you?"

She wiggled herself loose and then counted on her fingers. "I think maybe . . . August, September . . . " Her face and neck had turned a deep red and then she looked at me with her plump cheeks. "I had already missed my days by the time we left Germany."

"You mean we've had a blind passenger all this time and you never told me?"

"But how could I have known for sure?"

We were pretty excited and not for a second did we worry that we couldn't afford to have a kid or that we weren't ready. In those days they came when they came.

Adam John, who had come back down from the Yukon, worked on a nearby farm, then Big Max arrived from Victoria and moved in with us. Although Little Max had plenty of work selling his fall crop of potatoes, carrots, turnips and cabbage, there wasn't any room in the business for Big Max and me. So we went out every day looking for work and finally found a job splitting firewood for a couple of weeks, which earned us a total of $11.75. The money Grete and I had brought along was running low, but at least we had plenty of vegetables and lots of fish to eat. After Big Max and I finished cutting wood, there just wasn't any work to be found and we were getting down to our last dollar. Grete didn't seem to mind the hardship and was accepting the whole thing like an adventure. She was learning to cook, could make the best hotcakes in town by then, bake a good loaf of bread, and when she had time clacked away on her knitting needles.

I finally went to the Duncan City Hall and asked if they knew of anyone who needed some hired help for any kind of work. The clerk gave me a ten dollar-credit slip for groceries and sent me out to a dairy farmer who needed an extra hand. The farmer offered me $20 a month, and we were able to stay in the hired hand's house for free with a quart of fresh milk a day thrown in.

The farm was located right on the Cowichan River close to Duncan. The house was quite comfortable with a big kitchen and a living room with a fireplace. It was one of the nicer places we lived in during those early years in Canada. We had a good sturdy outhouse, carried water from the well, and made do with coal oil lamps. Grete fixed it up as best she could. The farmer's wife taught her how to can salmon, make quince jelly and to roll out a good pie crust. I was up early every morning to milk twelve cows, skim cream, separate the milk, shovel manure, and when the weather permitted, plough the fields with the team of Clydes.

Our first Christmas together in Canada was quite a celebration. We chopped down a fir tree which Grete decorated with ribbon, pine cones, and shells she had collected along the bay. She hung up fir boughs and a big red paper bell. Big and Little Max and Adam John joined us for Christmas dinner. The farmer had given us a nice fat goose and Grete made potato dumplings with lots of gravy. She made everything fancy with a linen tablecloth and candles, and with the fireplace roaring, the place was cozy all right. After supper, Grete took out her zither and we sang all our favourite Christmas songs. That was the first Christmas away from home that I really felt at home. Then we got into our stories about the North.

"You'd love walking across the frozen snow," Max said to Grete. "But it's so darn cold your nose can freeze up in a flash if you're not careful."

"Paul told me about the time he and Arno nearly froze to death rowing across the lake," Grete said, nodding her head.

"Never mind them," Max said laughing. "Adam and I almost didn't wake up one morning up there on the Babine. It was just luck that Paul and his Indian friend . . . ah Joe, came along and saved us."

"You guys should go up to the Yukon," Adam said. "That's the real north. In summer you can grow tomatoes as big as cabbages and in winter the rivers freeze over and the temperatures drop to 100 degrees below when the wind blows good and hard."

"I thought you went up there to mine gold," I said.

"Huh, the only way you can make money mining gold is working the dredges or growing tomatoes for the miners. But I'm thinking of heading up there again come summer. You're coming with me, aren't you, Little Max? There's some beautiful country up there, nice dry country. Doesn't pelt down rain all the time like around here."

"Well, here you can step outside in the middle of winter in your shirtsleeves."

We managed to scrape by over the winter and Grete really knew how to stretch the dollar. By then she could throw a thick, delicious fish-head chowder together and could make good flour dumplings and biscuits fit for a queen. She always had a pot of soup on the stove, and any spare time she had she knitted and crocheted or worked on her English, reading everything she could get her hands on.

We were quite excited about our big event and finally early one morning, the 16th of March, 1935, I took Grete to the Duncan hospital where George was born without a hitch. We named him after my father. Grete had fixed up her wicker trunk for Little George's bed, which was made to measure. It was about three feet long and lined in heavy white canvas. Grete had made a soft mattress out of goose down and lined the sides of the trunk with some soft flannel. Her mother had sent packages of knitted baby clothes from Germany, so we had everything we needed. We sure were proud parents and wrote home right away, letting our parents know the good news. I knew my old man would be proud that his name would be carried on.

Around the time George was born, I met Ben Nicols, a Dutch-man, who was peddling meat in the area. He had plenty of business and told me I could make myself a few extra bucks selling meat on the side.

I asked the farmer I worked for if I could get Sundays off. At first I had to borrow knives for cutting meat and borrow a car to deliver it. Business was brisk and I began to sell meat to the logging camps and the sawmills. But it was too much work for one day of the week, so I finally quit working at the farm and sold meat full-time.

Ben was a single guy and lived in a good-sized house across from the Catholic Church in Cowichan Bay, a little sawmill town on the water just south of Duncan. He had plenty of room so we moved in with him. Grete cooked for all of us, which paid the rent. Little George was a fat, healthy baby with red cheeks and I'd walk around with him in my arms, puffed up with pride. But I have to admit that I wished I could have shown him off to my parents. Grete wrote regularly to her mother in those days, and when she heard about our new son she wrote back wanting to know when we would return to Germany.

Grete and Paul with first born
son George, March 1935 at
Duncan.

"I don't ever want to go back," Grete said. "I'd feel trapped,
even if my mother says things are better."

We didn't get a newspaper on a regular basis, but on the whole,
there wasn't much local news about what was happening in Germany. We were struggling with our own lives and were so far from
home that we never gave much thought to any political ramifica-
tions. By the end of summer Grete was pregnant again, but I was
at least making a living and we looked forward to our second child.

The economy in Canada also seemed to be picking up, and that
same year Bennett, a Conservative, tried to push through a Canadian version of Roosevelt's New Deal to reduce farm debt and
establish unemployment insurance and a minimum wage, but all
it accomplished was to bring King and the Liberals to power with
prosperity just around the corner.

That fall Ben and I decided to go into business together instead
of competing against each other. We rented some property from
the Catholic Church right across the street from Ben's house, and
our business really began to roll. Big Max came to work with us
and we slaughtered about fifteen pigs a week and four to five head
of beef. It was just like back home again. We built a sausage kitchen

with a freezer, and it wasn't long before we had about $3,000 worth of equipment installed.

About this same time, an old, white-haired Dutchman by the name of Henry moved in with us. He had come over from Holland a few months before and couldn't get along with his son, so Ben, being Dutch, invited him to live with us. Henry couldn't speak any English or German, but he was like a grandfather to us and really enjoyed playing with George and helping Grete in the house. That's when Grete and I picked up quite a lot of Hollandish.

Our second Christmas together Grete must have cooked for a dozen people. Her mother had sent *Stollen* and packages of *Lebkuchen*, and knitted clothes for Little George. Gusti wrote with nothing but good news about the Nazi Party and sent us an article from a Bavarian newspaper which described her remarkable meeting with Hitler.

November 10, 1935
Lieber Paul, Liebe Grete,

It was so good to hear from you, and we are especially proud since Jette and I are now aunties. Mutter *and* Vater *were happy enough about the news of the baby, I guess, but you live so far away. And if you don't come back home, Little George will grow up to be a Canadian.*

I'm sending you an article from the paper that will surprise you. I think it will best describe to you the most wonderful thing that has ever happened to me and my Maedchen, my girls. Oh, Pauli, it was so exciting. Imagine me, your sister, a District Leader for the BDM, singing for Hitler *at his retreat in Berchtesgaden. I even shook his hand! He was very polite and friendly to us . . .*

Bayerische Ostmark—With the Accordion on Obersalzberg—A Rehauer BDM Girl tells her story—
13 aus der Ostmark beim Fuehrer

So "Wenn ich vo mein BdM sprooch, nochert muss ich schwaerma," *says Gusti in her Rehauer Dialekt. Gusti, District Leader and an outstanding sportswoman. She can play the accordion, whistle through her fingers and has a No. 3 Driver's Licence.*

"*Mit 30 Madla hammer aagfangt.*" *She began with 30 girls and now her group has grown to 400. They do sports together and go on hikes. Then Gusti had the idea to go to the mountains, to Berchtesgaden, and with some luck they would visit Hitler. Money was a problem, but the Mayor of Rehau gave them 50 marks for the trip and they found a reasonable place to stay. They hiked up to the Ulmhutte am Watzmann, 1600 meters, with backpacks, flags, and the accordion.*

"When we found out that the Fuehrer was in Obersalzberg, we rushed back to Berchtesgaden and phoned to find out if he was really there. They told me he would arrive late in the night, but I didn't believe that. I told them we are coming and we immediately formed marching columns and marched right through Berchtesgaden. I marched at the front of the columns and played the accordion. People watched from the sidelines and filmed and photographed us. When we arrived at Hitler's house, it was surrounded by a huge wall of people but the wall opened and let thirteen of us march through. When we couldn't get beyond the S.S. Post, we climbed over the garden wall and made ourselves comfortable sitting on the grass. Then we began to sing one song after the other. I played all the old soldier songs on my squeeze box until the Fuehrer arrived. When he heard we had come with music, he said, 'Bring the girls to me!' I stood in front of the Fuehrer and he asked where we were from. I told him Ostmarkstadt Rehau, twenty minutes from the border. The Fuehrer whispered in Obergruppenfuehrer Dietrich's ear. Then he tapped me on the shoulder, told me how much he enjoyed the singing and was sorry he had to leave because of a meeting.

Obergruppenfuehrer Dietrich asked how we stood with travel expenses. I was a little embarrassed that he would think we came up for money, but we really didn't have any money left. Then he pressed some paper into my hand.

Hitler waved to us for a long time as we marched away. Then I remembered the "Papierla" and when I pulled it out of my pocket there was a hundred marks. I can't describe to you the joy I felt, *net wega mir, bluass wega meina Madla* . . . not so much for me but for my girls, my Madla."

When I finished Gusti's letter I couldn't quite believe she had actually visited Hitler, The Fuehrer, but if anyone could have done it, it would've been my sister.

When Grete read the letter she tossed it aside.

"How can she and her *Madla* be so infatuated with Hitler? Bund Deutscher milk cows with sand in their eyes! That's what they are."

By January I wanted to buy land with Ben and build a proper facility. I couldn't see the point of paying rent every month to the Catholic Church. Most of our investment was in machinery which we could easily move, so we weren't going to be out much. Land was always a good investment and I guess it was in my blood about owning my own property. But Ben wouldn't have anything to do with the idea and then we began to disagree on other things too. He wasn't willing to extend any credit and if I didn't collect money from our customers right away we would get into a big argument.

So in early 1936 I sold out to Ben for $1000. By then I had decided it might be a good idea to head north to Terrace. I knew a lot of people up there and that part of the country was like a magnet for me. But I had to convince Grete that it was the right thing for us to do.

"There's still good homestead land up around there," I told her, "and I have good business connections all the way from Burns Lake to Prince Rupert."

"But we're just getting settled here. Can't you start up your own business in Duncan?"

"Sweetheart, I know you'd love the country up there. The scenery is like Switzerland and you'd get along with the people. Lots of Germans live in Terrace, too."

"But I get along here. We have friends here. And how can we just leave without knowing what's up there?"

"I know that country well and always wanted you to see the North. You'd like the winters, too. They're clean and dry . . . "

" . . . and if you don't find a job?"

"We don't have to worry. I'll find something, and if worse comes to worse, what the heck, we can always live off the fat of the land.

I could trap again. Look, it's still easy for us to get around. We don't have anything to lose, and we can come back down here if things don't work out."

George wasn't quite a year old and Grete was seven months pregnant. The more I talked the more curious she became, and finally she agreed that if we really wanted to go we should leave before the baby was due. I wanted to work with Ben until after the baby was born the end of April so Grete could go to the Duncan hospital, but she just shook her head.

"It's easier for me to get around before the baby comes. If that's what you want to do, then for heavens sake let's not waste our time. I want to be settled by then."

Then there was the question of Henry. He was like a member of our family and when we explained to him we were leaving for Terrace, he insisted on coming north with us in spite of his seventy-five years.

Maybe I should've thought things over and stayed in business with Ben, but we had reached a point where we could no longer work together in harmony. And maybe Grete and I should have stayed on Vancouver Island, but the worst of the Depression seemed to be over and I figured if business was picking up on the Island it would be okay in Terrace too.

So once again we were on our way with trunks and suitcases, Old Henry, Little George, and another blind passenger.

We visited Arno and Ida in Vancouver before we left on the boat to Prince Rupert and they were surprised, to say the least, that we were headed north and that Grete looked like she was due any day.

"You're not Catholic," Arno said. "You don't have to have a kid a year, you know."

"Well, what's taking you so long?" I asked him. "Ronnie must be lonely for a brother or sister."

He jerked his head toward Ida and with a big grin on his face whispered to me. "She keeps telling me the Pope won't send us to hell if we use rhythm."

"Well, we'll have to keep that in mind."

The water was fairly calm through the Straits, considering it was early March, but when we got past the tip of Vancouver Island and into Queen Charlotte Sound, the wind really blew. The ship rolled and vibrated and soon Grete and I were seasick, but it didn't bother Henry or Little George at all. Once we were among the shelter of the islands further north we felt better and spent a lot of time standing at the railing with the wind blasting in our faces. The gulls hovered above us, and sea lions sunned themselves on small rocky islands.

"If only I could paint all that," Grete said, looking out across the black rolling water to the timbered islands circled in misty gray fog. "You know, as a girl that was my dream . . . to be an artist. My mother would have laughed at me had I ever told her that."

"And I wanted to be a horse doctor, but you think I had an opinion? I was sent to Berlin to apprentice without being asked, not that I ever regretted learning a trade. I wonder what everyone is doing over there?"

"The same they've always been doing. My mother will still be shopping every day, filling her net with rolls and black bread, turnips, a quarter pound of beef, an eighth pound of ham. Our old friends will still meet at Cafe Horn, and the farmers will be out in the fields with their oxen getting ready to plant potatoes just like they've done for hundreds of years. I bet if you went back in twenty years you would find the same farmer with the same oxen. The only thing different would be the potatoes."

I put my arm around Grete's waist, giving her a squeeze. "Well, it won't take twenty years for us to get back."

"I'd like to go back home for a visit sometime, but I don't think I could ever live there again." Grete said. "I miss my mother, and sometimes I think of how Mathilde and I used to spend so much time at the movie house and the library, but there wasn't much else to do, especially in winter."

"Well, you'll soon have plenty more to do," and I patted her on her tummy and kissed her ear.

We arrived in Prince Rupert to a dark sky and a threatening storm, but by the time we boarded the train next morning for Terrace, the clouds had vanished and fresh snow lay on the mountain peaks. I couldn't help but see it as a good omen and that the third time around in Terrace would bring us luck.

20. 1936 Skeena River Flood

At FIRST GRETE WAS QUITE IMPRESSED with the snow-packed peaks and huge cakes of melting ice that clung to the sandbars in the Skeena, but after several hours of winding along the side of the river, where the heavily forested mountains came right down to the river's edge, she began to look at me with a question in her eye.

"Don't worry," I said to her, shifting Little George around who was sitting on my lap. I pointed out the window. "You can see there's no place to settle along the river here. That's why we have to go so far inland."

The fast-moving current had pushed piles of snags and drift-wood up against the beaches, and here and there small islands of bare cottonwoods and poplars seemed to grow right out of the water. "Once we get to Terrace there are plenty of settlements."

"Settlements?"

"You know, like I told you, small towns, Indian villages, just like down around Duncan. That's what I like about the country up here. Everything's still wild." I bounced George up and down on my knee. "Germany has nice forests, but they're so darned neat and tidy. And you can't hunt or fish unless you're rich. Here we're all rich."

"Yeah," Grete said, smiling and nodding her head. "Rich in dreams."

George began to fuss and cry and reached for his mama.

"*Hij heeft honger,*" Henry said, waking up from a nap.

I handed George to Grete. "Sounds like he's hungry."

She still nursed him and cuddled him close. "It must get awfully cold in the winter up here for that river to freeze," she said, rocking back and forth.

"There are a few cold snaps all right, but it doesn't bother you once you get used to it."

"I guess you can get used to anything if you have to," she said. "At least there's more than enough wood around here to burn. Mother turned every piece of coal over three times before she shovelled it into the stove."

When we arrived in Terrace, Grete probably expected more of a town after everything I had told her. In those days, Terrace was still a village. One main street, a few stores and that was about it.

"You'll like the people," I assured her. "Don't worry. They're one big happy family up around here."

Gus and Louise Gaensbauer, who had taken such good care of me when I lived with them, welcomed us. Their little boy and girl had long forgotten me, though. Louise took care of us like we were her own kids, and because the family spoke German, Grete felt comfortable right away. And Gus and Louise were happy that I finally got my girl.

Gus still worked at the mill for George Little, but the crew had been pared to a minimum, so there was no chance for me to get a job there. And Berth West, who had taken over the meat business from me when I decided to return to Germany, was barely making a living and didn't need extra help either.

"Maybe you should have written to the Gaensbauers first," Grete said to me one night in bed. "They would have been able to let you know there weren't any jobs."

"Don't worry. I'll find something, and we've got enough money to tide us over. I wanted you to see this country up here anyway, to see where I spent all those years apart from you."

Grete was probably right. Had I checked out the job situation, maybe we would have stayed on the Island, but I wouldn't trade those years around Remo and Terrace with Grete for anything, and as tough as times were, I know Grete would agree.

Not more than a week later Gus came home with some good news. He had put the word out that we were looking for a place to live. There was a farm for sale in Remo, a small place about seven miles west of Terrace, that had a house and barn and a few acres on good flatland.

"If it's cheap, I'm interested," I said to him, "but I still need a job."

"They're asking four hundred bucks for the place, but if you've got the cash, you can probably haggle the price down fifty dollars or so. And with summer coming you can get a good start on a garden, raise some animals."

The next Sunday we hopped on a speeder, a small rail car that drives independent from the train.

"I've been told the flat's been flooded a few times over the years along here," Gus said, pulling his hat down over his big red ears. A stiff wind was blowing and several inches of snow lay in patches on the ground. "But since the railroad's been built the grade acts like a dam."

A shallow slough about the width of a road ran between the railroad grade and the house, and on the other side of the grade flowed the Skeena. A small barn stood at the back of the property against a stand of gnarly-trunked cottonwoods. Gus kicked aside the snow and dug up some of the rich, red-black soil that was just beginning to thaw.

"Best soil in the world, like home-churned butter on bread," he said, crumbling it through his fingers. "Nice rich silt from all the flooding."

At least the farm would support us. Planting time was just around the corner, and important was getting the family settled and having a place where we could grow vegetables and raise our own meat. The house had three rooms and a lean-to that could be used as a bedroom for Henry. A veranda ran across the front. It looked pretty promising so I purchased the place for three hundred fifty dollars and we moved in.

We bought some second-hand furniture and Grete got to work right away sewing curtains and hanging mosquito nets over the beds. She had brought her sewing machine along from Germany and got that place spiffed up in no time flat. I bought a cow and a couple of young pigs and lambs and Henry wanted to raise some chicks. I repaired the roofs and turned over the soil for a garden when it thawed out enough. It was the first home we owned, and we really enjoyed fixing up that place. But it was a good thing we didn't know what was in store for us.

Grete became friends with Mrs. Russell, a registered nurse, who lived about a half mile away. She gave Grete plenty of good advice, and it was nice to know we could call on her for any emergency, especially since Grete was in her ninth month by then. I wanted Grete to go to Terrace the last week and stay with the Gaensbauers because at least Dr. Mills would be on call, but she only laughed at my suggestion and wasn't worried about giving birth at home.

Well, we didn't have long to wait. When Grete went into labour early in the morning on the 28th of April, I hiked down the road to get Mrs. Russell. Our second son, Thomas, was born red-faced and squalling, several hours later. We were very grateful to Mrs. Russell because she came by every day for the next two weeks to make sure Grete and the baby were okay and if there was anything that needed to be done, she did it without any questions.

George and Tommy were just thirteen months apart, and for years people mistook them for twins. We borrowed Tommy's second name, Floyd, from our good friend Floyd Frank, who still lives around Terrace. Tommy had the honour of being the first white child to be born in Remo.

The population of Remo in those days was something like thirty people, both sides of the river, which included the ferryman, the postman, a bachelor who raised strawberries, our friends the Froeses who had a farm across the river, and the Lindstroms who had a place on a knoll about a mile west of us where the Zimacord flows into the Skeena. And Jens Erlandson, the trapper, was back from his winter of trapping in the Zimacord Valley.

By the third week of May we had a vegetable garden planted with the usual peas, beans, beets, cabbage, carrots, lettuce, turnips and potatoes. Old Henry really pulled his weight around the place, too. He helped us plant and weed the garden, chop wood, play with the boys, and make himself useful wherever he could. It was

Grete with George and Tommy at Remo, 1936.

important for us to get a good start on the garden because we depended on a good crop to help pull us through the winter.

The weather was unusually hot for that time of the year. Even the nights were warm and we had to kick off our feather quilt. Grete had young Tommy outside every day, sleeping under the shade of a cottonwood, well protected with mosquito netting. The mosquitoes were beginning to hatch and hum along the slough where they thrived in the quiet, swampy water and soon became pests. George would start crying in the night because mosquitoes had crawled inside his net. We'd get up, light the lantern, get rid of the mosquitoes, but by the time we got him settled and back into our own bed, there would be a handful of the little buggers waiting for us. But mosquitoes were the least of our problems, and little did we know that the heat would spell disaster.

Although the snow level wasn't above normal that year, the unusually hot weather caused the snow in the bush and up in the mountains to melt nearly overnight. Water from the Babine, Copper, Bulkley and other rivers, including the Zimacord, all poured into the Skeena. When the Skeena began to rise, nobody worried about it because the river did a little flooding every year during spring runoff.

At first we didn't pay much attention to the high water either. The railroad grade was a couple hundred feet away from our house, and because it was about fifteen feet higher than the roof, I felt it was pretty good insurance for us against the river. When the Froeses and other farmers evacuated across the river, I still didn't worry because their property was wide open for flooding.

Every day we climbed up the grade to watch the muddy, churning water of the Skeena carry along trees and rolling logs and roots at a brisk pace. I felt a little uneasy all right, seeing so much water on the other side of the grade, but not alarmed. Then we heard that Usk, a village about six miles east of Terrace further up the Skeena, had been flooded and practically destroyed. Acres and acres of good bottom land all along the Skeena was being washed away, and thousands of acres were under water. Over a few short days, the water had risen so high that the river looked like a massive lake. I assured Grete that the more the water spread out the slower it would rise and that the level would start dropping any day. I just couldn't believe it would get any higher.

Then one morning a couple of days later, it was the beginning of June, Grete pointed toward the tracks. We had just sat down to her special sourdough hotcakes.

"It looks like people walking along the grade," she said, putting her hand up to her eyes.

I turned and looked out the window. "Holy moley!" I shouted, jumping up. "Those are roots . . . stumps of trees!"

I was across the slough and up the grade lickety-split. I couldn't believe my eyes. The water was about six feet from the top, boiling and churning and carrying along full-sized cottonwoods and broken limbs of trees, old stumps ten feet in diameter. I kept a close eye on the river for the next few hours, but still wouldn't believe we were in any real danger. Then in the afternoon Mr. Lindstrom came by in his rowboat.

"You'd better pack up a few belongings and as much food as you can carry. I've come to take you back to our house," he yelled from his boat. "It don't look good. The grade could go any minute."

"I'm not going," Grete whispered to me. "Tell him we'll be all right."

Mr. Lindstrom threw me the rope and I pulled the boat over to the bank. I looked at the grade and back at Grete. She shook her head again. "I don't know," I said to Mr. Lindstom. "I think we'll stick it out."

"Oh, no," he said, standing up in the rocking boat and shaking his arm. "You get your family in the boat right now, eh! The river ain't crested. It's plum too dangerous to stay."

When I finally convinced Grete that we had no choice, it was Henry who flatly refused to leave. He gripped the edge of the table. "*Nee. Ik kan niet zwemmen.* I can't swim," he said with puckered lips. "*Ik ben veilig hier.*"

I grabbed his arm. "You're not safe here!" I said in broken Hollandish. "And you don't have to know how to swim."

"*Nee, Ik blijf!*" he said, yanking his arm free and running his tongue across his dry lips. "I stay."

"The place is going to flood, Henry. The grade might go. *Kom nu,*" I said. "We've gotta get out of here."

He shook his head. "*Nee, Ik blijf.* You go with your family."

"C'mon, Paul," Mr. Lindstrom urged. "We don't have much time. Get your family to safety. You can come back for the old man."

Henry wasn't going to budge so we had no choice. When we got to the Lindstrom's place, which was on high ground, almost the whole village of Remo was there. Everyone had brought food and blankets and some people had strung up tents.

"I'm going back for Henry and I'll check the animals," I said to Grete holding her tight and kissing the boys. "And whatever happens, don't worry about us."

I rowed back to the house with the Lindstrom's boat. Henry was up in the makeshift loft, and like an old mother hen, was watching over his half-grown chicks in a cardboard box.

"What the heck are you doing up there?" I asked him.

"Somebody came by to rescue me," he said in Hollandish all excited and swinging his fist around. "But I showed him, ha. I pointed the shotgun at him."

"*Kom naar beneden*, Henry," I shouted. "We have to high-tail it out of here, and right now."

I went outside and climbed to the top of the grade again. To see whole trees whirling around in the roaring, swishing water made the hair on the back of my arms stand on end. The brown, muddy water had risen about three more feet. It didn't look good a'tall. A cold draft came off the water and the smell of mud and silt clung to my nostrils. A chicken coop floated by and I didn't have to put two and two together to realize that if the grade went our place would be gone.

I climbed back down and went into the house. "Henry," I commanded. "*Kom!* We have to hurry. I'm going to check the animals. I'll be right back."

I threw them some extra feed and hoped they could fend for themselves. Then I remembered the old rusted logging cable behind the barn which gave me the idea to secure the house with it.

"*Kom nu*, Henry," I yelled from the back door. "I need a hand."

Somehow that sparked something in his brain and he helped me drag the heavy cable over to the house and wind it around the shingled siding like a ribbon. Don't ask me how we did it, but the two of us heaved and tugged until we got the two ends clamped together and secured around a stump.

"All right, *oude* Man," I said, jerking my head in the direction of the boat. "Let's vamoose the hell on outta here."

He stood shivering on the steps with his jacket pulled tight around him. "*Nee. Ik wil niet gaan*," he protested. His thin body was hunched over and his eyes looked glassy. "I don't leave. *Niet zwemmen*. Can't swim. House is safe."

"*Stommert*, Henry! We can't stay here," I yelled at him. "You stupid bugger! If the grade goes we'll go down the river with it. Can't you understand that? And if you don't come you may have to swim."

"*Nee*, I stay," and he turned to go into the house.

I ran after him and tried to pick up his wiry frame, but he beat at me with his fists and fought like a cat, sticking to the veranda like a suction cup.

"*Blijf dan maar en verdrink!* The hell if I care. I'm leaving," I said.

I went down to the slough to get into the boat, yanking my toque down over my ears. When I turned around with some misgivings, Henry had disappeared inside. I decided I'd better check out the situation one last time from the top of the grade. In the time it had taken us to secure the house, the water had receded a few feet and things were actually looking calmer. I couldn't believe it and figured that the Skeena must have crested and the worst was over. I knew all along that the water couldn't possibly get any higher.

"Henry," I shouted bursting through the door. "The water level's dropping. It's going to be okay. *Jy kan blijven.* I'll stick it out with you overnight."

But I wasn't going to leave everything to chance. I tied the rowboat with a long rope to the veranda and left it in the slough. We couldn't do much about the furniture because there wasn't any high ground around the house. I checked the animals again and secured what I could.

We settled down and dozed off long before dark. Then about eleven I was jarred awake by a loud grating, roaring sound. I ran outside and grabbed the rail of the veranda. It was too dark to see, but I could hear rocks and water and boulders tumbling one over the other further down the grade. A gap was being cut! The warm, thick air smelled like swamp and I could hear the swift, rippling sound of water all around me. I stepped off the porch and icy water swirled over my bare feet. I rushed back into the house.

"Henry!" I hollered. "The grade is going. We're being flooded!"

Within minutes water was seeping into the house under the door. "Get into the loft," I ordered and hoisted him up. I piled the chairs on top of the table and threw clothing, pictures, guns, Grete's sewing machine and zither up into the loft with Henry. By then the water was knee high. I grabbed the hatchet in case we'd have to chop our way through the roof. I pulled the feather beds around Henry and me, listening vigilantly to the swish and swirl of water inside the house as it inched its way up the walls. A cold, earthy smell of mud hung in the air. The chicks peeped nonstop in the cardboard box, and Henry was shaking so hard his bones rattled against my side.

Suddenly I was on my feet. Another long, thundering roar and a horrible swoosh of gushing water was all around us. The house tilted and shifted. We're goners for sure, I thought, grabbing hold of the rafters. My lips were salty dry and my heart felt like it was jumping out of my ears. Henry hung onto my leg like a vise and didn't utter a word. I reached for the hatchet and quickly chopped a large hole in the roof. Logs and limbs crashed against the side of the house rocking it back and forth like a ship in a storm. We really were in a pickle.

"Just hold on, *oude* Man," I said. "If the water gets any higher we'll climb onto the roof. We'll be okay. I've been in worse scrapes than this one."

I talked half Dutch, half German and don't know if Henry understood anything.

I can't tell you how grateful I was that Mr. Lindstrom had come by that afternoon and taken Grete and the boys to safety because we were really up against it.

We huddled under our quilts hoping the water wouldn't rise any further. Every time the house lifted and rolled we jumped up ready to climb through the hole. Around three in the morning things quieted down a bit and the water began to ebb. Finally the house settled with a creaking slump.

At the first crack of light I figured the worst had to be over. I eased myself down into the waist-deep-icy-water, sucking in my breath. I pushed aside chairs and floating debris on my way to the veranda. Cold mud squished between my toes. At least the boat was still tied up. I pulled it in short then went back into the house.

"You're coming down now, Henry," I called out.

He shook his head in the dim light and clutched the cardboard box with the chicks.

"*Kom!* Bring the bloody chicks along. You have two choices, you hear me? Get on my shoulders or swim." I don't know what he understood, but without another word he straddled my shoulders. He squeezed my neck with one icy hand and balanced the box on my head with the other. I had to be careful with my footing but managed to get him and the chicks into the rocking boat.

The grade had held by our house, but fifteen hundred feet down the track, in the muddy light of dawn, I could see the outline of twisted ties and steel poking to the sky and boulders the size of a house lying alongside the grade in the deep water. The whole area was one big flood plain, but at least we were in the backwash of the main current.

I cut the rope loose from the house and we rowed over to the barn. It was quite a funny sight to see the lambs and piglets up on the hayloft, but old Bossy was really labouring in deep water. I heaved and tugged to get her outside and found some higher ground for her under some cottonwoods, leaving her with a supply of hay. I shoved the squealing pigs into sacks and tied up the woolly lambs and put them into the boat. They fought and bleated like the devil to get loose, and fear shone out of their white, glassy eyes.

At five in the morning we landed with our Noah's Ark at Lindstrom's. Even though it was early, Grete and some of the other farmers were standing on the bank when we arrived. When I jumped off the boat, Grete's arms were around my neck. The men tied up the boat and pulled Henry and the animals to safety.

"We thought you'd gone down the river with the house," she cried. "We saw houses float by upside down."

"I told you there was nothing to worry about," I assured her. "And we saved the house—tied a cable around it."

Later that day Mr. Froese and I rowed over to his farm to rescue their sow and piglets. Everybody thought we were crazy because the river was still wild and full of eddies, but Mr. Froese was worried about his livestock. In those days when nobody had much, animals were worth their weight in gold. We could hear the sand and silt grind against the underside of the boat and we both had to row like heck to keep on course. When we got to the farm most of their good bottom land was simply gone. Their two-story house had shifted a couple hundred feet and settled only ten feet from the river bank. Mr. Froese just kept shaking his head and swallowing, not believing what he saw, yet grateful that his house was at least still standing. In the barn six little pigs were on a platform that was

Paul in canoe during 1936 flood in Remo on the Skeena River.

floating around, and the old sow, blue from cold—and she really had turned blue—had found safety in the hayloft. We left her with food and water and shoved the squealing piglets into sacks and took them with us.

It took two weeks for the river to recede enough for us to move back into our house. Although it was in the same place and the cable was still wrapped around it, it had settled at a 45-degree angle. Mud was everywhere. Grete didn't say a word. She just kept shaking her head. She stepped gingerly onto the veranda and suddenly let out a scream. She was on her back in the mud. I reached out to pull her up and down she went again. By then she was covered in the brown oozing stuff. She began to laugh. Tears streamed down her cheeks and she just kept laughing. You know how she starts to laugh sometimes and can't stop.

I pushed open the door and the slimy brown mud was over a foot deep inside the house. The furniture had toppled and you could see the water line on the wall above the windows.

"Everything's ruined," Grete cried through her muddy brown, tear-stained face. "What are we going to do?"

"Don't worry," I said to her, putting my arms around her and kissing her tears away. "We'll get things cleaned up, and your sewing machine and zither are high and dry."

We didn't have time to brood. We moved all the furniture outside and got to work shovelling out the mud. We sloshed buckets of water over the furniture, walls and floors, and shovelled, scrubbed, and swept until the last of the silt was gone. Then we made a solution of water and disinfectant, which we got from the government to prevent the spread of typhus, and washed everything down once more.

Of course, that's all anyone talked about for months, and there was good reason because it had been one of those hundred-year floods. 1936 was a year not soon forgotten.

The blue sky and warm air seemed to defy the destruction that had taken place, and it was hard to believe how the force of the water could have buckled and twisted the rails and torn out nearly three miles of grade right there in Remo. The railway had to be completely rebuilt in sections along the Skeena and was closed to rail traffic until the end of August.

Every settlement along the river had been hit hard, and acres of valuable farmland had been washed away. We were lucky we still had our house, but it was too late in the year by then to plant anything. All the farmers had been hard hit. The community had run out of groceries and since the train wasn't running, supplies had to be brought in by boat from Prince Rupert. Rumor had it that the first load to come upriver was cases of beer.

The flood opened up a whole new line of work around the area. I rented a boat with a motor, and for a few weeks helped ferry people up and down the river day and night. The Canadian National Railway also moved in a crew to build a pile driver so they could construct temporary railway bridges. I was hired on and for awhile worked at two jobs.

The summer passed quickly. The neighbors helped each other out and we traded food and labour back and forth. There were plenty of wild berries that year and Grete and Henry took the boys berry picking nearly every day. They collected bucketfuls of huckleberries, blackberries, salmonberries, even wild currants. Grete canned the fruit and made all kinds of jam. She even collected wild rose hips and made jam from them.

In September, I heard about a defunct mining operation in Usk that had some horses for sale. I picked out a couple of sound-looking ones and brought them home. I built a makeshift corral for them, but they kept breaking out and heading back to Usk. One time the horses broke out and tried to cross the railway bridge over the Kitsumkalum River just as a train came along. The train was able to slow down enough to not hit them directly, but they both got badly torn up. I stitched them together and nursed them back to health, but they never regained their full strength.

Around that time Japan imported cottonwood and poplars from the Terrace area. Cottonwood wasn't good for much, but the Japanese used it for making matchsticks. There were thick groves along the Skeena and the tributaries. The price of the cottonwood was $22 a thousand board feet delivered at tidewater, which was about sixty miles down river near Telegraph Point.

It looked like a good way to make a few dollars, so I took a contract out for half a million board feet to be felled on the Kitsumkalum River and to be delivered by the middle of December. I received $10 per 1000 board feet advance from the government to pay for my expenses. I bought some private timber and some from the government, and even had a good supply on our own property. I also bought a surplus Cat off the road department to use for yarding or hauling logs. I soon found out, however, that a couple of good, strong workhorses were more efficient for hauling out some of the smaller logs further away from the river and not accessible with the Cat, so I had to rent a team as well.

I had quite a nerve-racking incident with one of the horses. I thought I take the team across the Kitsumkalum railroad bridge because the ties on the bridge were quite close together, and with their big feet I didn't think there would be a problem. The first horse made it okay, but the second one got his hind foot stuck between the ties. I tried lifting and pulling and shoving, but there was no way I was going to get that horse out of there without help. Then I heard the train whistle. My hair about stood on end. I didn't waste a second and ran down the track doing my Charlie-Chaplin skip across those ties hoping I could flag the train down in time.

The engineer stuck his head out the window and when he saw me frantically waving my arms he pulled the brake. Of course, I was worried stiff about the consequences for being on the bridge in the first place, but the engineer, the fireman and conductor, and even a few passengers got off the train and helped get that old Clydesdale unstuck without so much as a sour word.

I also rented a motorboat for towing the log booms down river and I hired Tom Wright, an Indian from Usk, to be my boat pilot and to help me manage the booms. It didn't take long for me to fell and limb enough trees for our first trip. We made up fifteen rafts with the logs, about twenty logs to a raft, and tied them together to form a long snake. We estimated that our trip to tidewater would take about ten hours. The unwieldy rafts were a little tricky to get moving, but we didn't expect too many problems. West of Terrace the Skeena wasn't as wild. It was late in the year, the water was low and the current easy.

We managed to maneuver around the log jams that would occasionally build up in the bends of the river, but we ran into some trouble with a shallow sandbar in the middle of the river. The first raft with the biggest logs scraped bottom and within a matter of seconds, logs were piled twenty feet high behind us. But we carried explosives in the boat for that very emergency. I jumped onto the pile of rocking, unsteady logs, tap dancing around like a moose on ice, trying to place the shot in a strategic position. I lit the fuse and jumped into the boat.

"Let'er rip," I yelled. Tom opened the throttle and steered us to safety. There was a huge blast and a geyser of water shot skyward. The whole pile shifted and floated free, but it took us a couple of days to collect and reassemble all the logs and form the rafts again. We learned a good lesson and after that formed the first raft with small logs.

Another spot on the river that caused us to panic was the Hole-in-the-Wall, just below where the Exchampsiks River enters the Skeena. The river makes a sharp bend there forming a giant whirlpool. On that first trip we had no idea what was ahead of us. Suddenly we were caught up in this black whirling current. I didn't say one word to Tom. Not a muscle twitched in his face and his black eyes focused dead ahead. He had that motor revved full blast but even with his expert piloting, we could not pull the log raft through. Every time we would almost get out of the current it sucked the raft and the boat back in. We finally got the boat to shore and cut the raft in half, making two trips.

As the weeks passed, we became quite efficient getting the logs downstream, and by the end of November I had filled my quota. I felt so successful that I filed for a second contract, knowing there wouldn't be a problem filling it. I was on to something big and was going to make some real dollars for a change. New winter boots, new jackets, brand new woollen underwear were on my list. We could stock up on decent staples without having to go on credit. Grete could buy material to sew new clothes, new slipcovers. Maybe we could buy some nice furniture, a rocking chair.

But my dreams of money didn't last long because there was one hitch. The cottonwood was never picked up. The Canadian government suddenly put a stop to all export of cottonwoods and poplars to Japan. There were other small outfits that had poplars piled up along the railroad grade, and it was all left sitting. There was nothing we could do, and it's needless to say that by the time I paid off Tom and all my other expenses, I was in the hole.

Then the forestry slapped me for a bill of $1,000 for timber that was felled but never sold. I felt pretty low and had no way of paying them off. Only years later, when we had settled in the Alberni Valley, did I finally pay off that debt.

Another incident occurred that fall that left me quite shaken. I had decided to take our cow to Floyd Frank's farm to get bred. Their place was about a mile above the Kitsumkalum River railway bridge. The only way over to the Frank's farm was to cross the river since the ferry crossing had been washed out by the flood. The river water was still low, but freezing cold, so with a stick in one hand for extra support on the slippery rocks, I took a good grip of the cow and headed across. We were nearly over when all of a sudden the current washed my feet out from under me. The lead rope tore out of my hand, and before I knew it the rushing water took me right into the Skeena River. The icy Skeena was the last place anyone wanted to be in late fall. My heavy logger's boots and thick woollen clothing pulled me down, and just like the incident in the Copper River, my arms and legs stiffened up so fast that all I could do was hold my head above water. But this time I had a family to think of. What would they do without me? Where would they go? The thought of leaving them behind terrified me. I began to swallow water and no longer had the strength to fight the current. Just when I thought I was lost with no way out of my predicament, my knees began to bump along some ground, and before I knew it, I was washed up alongside an exposed sandbar. My body had become so stiff that I could barely get on my feet, but I kept my mind focused on my family, and with my last bit of strength I could muster, pulled myself out of the water. I shook like the devil and kept stomping around until some feeling came back into my fingers and toes. But I still had another channel to cross before I would be safe. All I could do was plunge into the water and swim for my life.

Once out of the river, I took off like a scared dog on a stiff-legged run with about five miles to go. Of course, when Grete saw me with my frozen clothes and shaking body she had no idea what had happened. I can't tell you how relieved I was to be home safe again. She pulled off my clothes and rolled me into my warm feather quilt. With some hot soup down my throat I recovered quickly, though I couldn't talk for days. The cow came home on her own a couple of days later.

By December winter had really set in. Two feet of snow lay on the ground and the nights dropped to zero. We were well stocked with all the necessities, but if it hadn't been for the general store in Terrace extending us some credit we would have lived a pretty meagre existence that winter. To supplement our basics, we also had a big crock of sauerkraut. In the fall we had traded some pork with a farmer for a couple of crates of cabbages and got Henry busy chopping the cabbage and tamping it down in the crock.

I managed to pick up an extra dollar here and there by doing a little butchering around Remo and Terrace, which helped pay off our credit. And if the farmers had trouble with colicky or injured animals and couldn't afford to pay me, they always traded me some food for helping them out.

That Christmas both Grete and I received mail from our families. My sister Jette was planning to get married the following year, in 1937. Grete's mother sent us a parcel with warm clothes for the boys, a story book of Grimm's fairy-tales, and some precious *Lebkuchen.* She no longer asked when we were coming home.

Our winter evenings were long, and by then I think Grete was already getting sick of hearing me tell Henry the stories from my homesteading days or about the years when I was a boy in Germany. Of course, Henry enjoyed telling us his stories, too, but the more he talked about Holland, the more homesick he got. Sometimes he'd tell his stories with tears in his eyes.

Then I got to thinking about trapping again and how Jens Erlandson managed to make a living at it up there in the Zimacord Valley. Though the price of furs was still down, with some luck and a few mink you could still make a few good dollars.

"I found a real paradise up in that valley that time when I was recuperating," I said to Grete one night. "Nice open country, no mosquitoes, no blackflies, no no-see-ums. Wildflowers all summer long in the meadows as far as the eye can see."

"Every place you've been is a paradise," Grete said, looking up from her knitting. "I liked Duncan, but no, you wanted to leave for Terrace. You said Terrace was the best little town in the whole country. And here we are in Remo getting this place fixed up again and you're thinking of that valley!"

"You can see there's no way to make a living around here. But up in the Zimacord ... "

"Come spring we can plant a big garden ... "

"The soil's like hard pan since the flood," I said, throwing up my hands. "The economy has dried up around here. The export trade's dried up. The cattle business is worthless. There's just no work, Grete."

"Then why don't we move back to Vancouver Island?"

"That's easier said than done when we don't have two nickels to rub between our fingers. But that valley up there. It's a beautiful little valley and the trapping could bring us a few dollars. I've talked plenty with Jens. He has some good fur runs and he'd be our neighbour in the winter."

"And just how would he be our neighbour?"

"If we built a log cabin up there in the meadows, he would only be a mile or so away from us. And from here it's only a few miles up the river and you know I have to go into Terrace for any decent supplies as it is." I rubbed my hands together. "What do you think, Sweetheart," I asked, slipping my fingers through her hair. "We could try it for one winter."

"You must be nuts," Grete said with a frown, pulling her head away.

"You can live just like the pioneers did. It'll be the biggest challenge of your life and something you'll remember the rest of your life."

"What are we doing right now? Wouldn't you call this living like the pioneers? No electricity. No radio. No money. No nothing."

"That's just it," I exclaimed. "What do you say, Grete," I asked, leaning over and kissing her cheek.

Grete folded her knitting together and got up to stoke the fire. "What about wolves?"

I shook my head. "You wouldn't have to worry about them. It's only their howl that makes your hair stand on end."

"And bears?" she asked, throwing a chunk of wood into the stove.

"You know already they fear humans more than anything."

"And what if the boys get sick?"

"They can't get sick." When she started asking all those questions I knew I had her hooked. "Where there's no people, there's no germs. I never got sick out in the wilderness."

"What about all our furniture?" she asked, picking up her yarn and needles.

"You can take your sewing machine, your zither, your washboard, just leave the ice box and washing machine behind."

"As if I had one. And what about Henry?"

"Well, you know how he's been talking about home a lot lately. We'll worry about that when spring rolls around."

I wrote to the land office in Prince Rupert to apply for the homestead. January and February passed and we kept throwing different ideas around. Henry began to get restless and talked more and more about going back to Holland. We didn't have any money to help him with the fare, so I told him to write to his son. Sure enough, a month later a money order arrived for his fare back home. He still wasn't in any hurry to leave, especially with summer coming, not to mention that he was pretty attached to all of us.

By April Grete had finally warmed up to the idea of some real pioneering.

"It's our only chance," I assured her. "You won't regret it. Once the boys are older and ready for school, we won't be able to live like that anymore."

Henry, in the meantime, finally packed his suitcase and decided to go south. "*Nee*," he said, shaking his head. "No homestead for me. I want to die on my own soil."

His son was to meet him in Vancouver and send him on his way by train across Canada and back to Holland. We were pretty sad to see him go and Tommy and George cried like the dickens. He had become a real grandfather to them. He was a nice old guy and I could never understand why he and his son couldn't get along.

By the end of April we made preparations for our journey. We didn't have any money, so we sold our farm to pay off our credit and stock up on supplies. After the flood, the farm was practically worthless and we sold it for about half of what we paid for it.

We really weren't travelling far, but with no road into the Zimacord Valley, it was about as remote and isolated as you could get.

21. THE ZIMACORD VALLEY

YOU PROBABLY THINK WE WERE a little crazy for such an undertaking, but you have to remember that in those days it wasn't unusual for people to do that. For us it was better than bread lines and soup kitchens. During those Depression years—and remember it wasn't just in Canada where times were tough—people had to make do with what they had. And don't forget that I had enough experience with homesteading and wasn't at all worried about being able to provide for the family. When I homesteaded on the Babine I always felt that Grete might have enjoyed experiencing a pioneer way of life, though I doubted at the time she would actually have considered it. And now she was about to live it. She herself had said, soon after we arrived in Canada, that had she lived in the 1800s she would have been on the first wagon train that went west across America. I guess I had talked so much about my adventures on the Babine Lake that she was quite curious, too, and wanted to take up the challenge of some real homesteading.

We loaded up Mack and Dolly with our bedding, cooking utensils, guns, knives, and enough staples to hold us for about a month. Our destination was only six miles north the way the crow flies, so getting back out to Remo and up to Terrace for supplies wasn't a problem for me.

We were all in high spirits. Little George thought we were going to visit Henry. "Wo Henny? See Henny?" he kept asking. We still missed Henry, but homesteading with him would have been out of the question. As it was, life on the homestead turned out to be a lot tougher with the family than even I had expected. Tommy was just learning to walk by then. He'd crawl, pull himself up, take a few steps and fall flat on his face, and Little George, just over two, would clap his hands and laugh every time Tommy went down.

We rigged up some packs so we could carry the boys on out backs, and on that clear and sunny morning, just after Tommy's first birthday, we set off on our new adventure. With the last patches of snow rapidly sinking into the ground, we were prepared to accept everything nature had to offer, which at that point in our lives looked appealing enough, since we lacked most of the refinements of civilization anyway.

Our friends, the Froeses and the Lindstroms, promised to visit us over the summer once we were established. I led Mack and Dolly with George on my back, and Grete led Bossy, the cow, and carried Tommy on her back. We followed the trail single file along the rushing Zimacord River. The first lime tinges of green were beginning to show of the tips of the cottonwoods and poplars. At first the going was easy, but a couple miles up the river the patches of snow became broader and deeper. The forest was dense with spruce and balsam and cedar, and there were places where sunlight never touched the trail. By nightfall we found an abandoned log cabin next to the river where we decided to spend the night. I unloaded the horses and turned them loose in the clearing so they could rustle for food, but I rope hobbled them and kept the cow on a long tether in case any of them got some foolish idea to head back home. A little wind had kicked up, and with a shiver I pulled my jacket collar up around my ears. Even though it was late in the year, it smelled like snow.

We had packed along a tin heater which we set up in the cabin, so while Grete took care of the boys, I gathered twigs and broken limbs and got a good fire started. She had brought along some stew for our first night out. By the time we were bedded down the wind was blowing hard and the branches scraped on the cabin roof. I got up during the night to stoke the fire and check on the stock and when I opened the door, whirling bits of snow hit my cheeks. The ground was already white. By morning there was nearly a foot of the stuff and the thick chalky flakes were blowing sideways. A spring storm wasn't unusual, but we hadn't expected it that late in the season. We ended up being stuck there for a week until a warm westerly blew in and we could move on. I was kept busy collecting firewood and hunting for rabbits and grouse, though by the end of the winter they were almost too scrawny and tough to eat.

Dragging the horses and the cow through the swollen creeks and across fallen logs on our way up the river was quite an effort, and it took us most of the day to get to Jens Erlandson's cabin.

I stoked up a fire in the stove so we could get some water heated for tea. "When I was here a couple of years ago," I said to Grete. " . . . it was summer then. Remember I told you when I was so sick? All I could think about was you being here with me."

Her cheeks plumped into a smile. "I guess you got more than you bargained for," she said. "Now you have three extra mouths to worry about."

I grinned and gave her thick, shoulder-length hair a yank. "I came here to get my strength back, but I was so darned lonely at times you wouldn't have believed it. You know, I never feel home-sick anymore."

"I haven't felt homesick once since we left the Old Country," Grete said. She pulled out the silver Thaler piece which she had put on a chain around her neck and rubbed it between her fingers. "I haven't regretted leaving, even with the flood." She gazed out across the creek towards the mountain. "It would be nice, though . . . nice if my mother could see the boys."

"She'll get to see them. Once this country gets on its feet and I can earn a decent wage we'll take a trip back home. Or your mother could visit us. One day Gusti will come, too, you'll see. She'd love this country."

"I don't think my mother would come," Grete said, with a shake of her head. "She's never been further than Nuremberg. No, she wouldn't come. And I wouldn't want her to see us living in the bush like this."

"We won't be in the bush forever. One day we'll have a decent place. This is just the beginning for us."

The next day we made the last leg of our journey, following the Zimacord another mile before picking up a trail which led through thickets of greening poplars, willows and dark green spruce. It was quite a sight when we arrived at the beaver meadows.

They sloped away from the base of the mountain, which rose straight up about four thousand feet. High bluffs and jagged ravines broke through the heavy timber. To our left and right were the familiar glacial peaks packed solid with snow.

As I mentioned earlier, the open area totalled about seventy acres which was mostly dry. Pussy willows had popped open and new shoots of slough grass were beginning to poke through a green-brown tangle of last summer's growth. Mack and Dolly and the cow were already crunching and pulling at the new stocks. Across the meadow we could hear the drumming of a grouse.

"He's looking for a mate," I said to Grete, unhooking the straps on her back and setting Tommy down on the soft swamp grass. "Well, what do you think of it?" I asked.

She was never one for a lot of words. She turned and lifted George out of my pack. He stepped a few feet into the flattened grass then came back and threw his arms around Grete's pant leg.

She pushed her chestnut hair back out of her eyes and took a deep breath. "It's just like you said it would be. It's beautiful all right . . . peaceful. There must be a stream close by. You hear the water running? And the glacier look at it." She pointed, then put her hand on top of George's head, running her fingers through his blond hair.

"But there's nothing here," she continued with a shrug of her shoulders. "I don't know what I was expecting. But there's just nothing here. Where will we live?"

George began to cry and I picked him up. "Shhhh . . . listen to the jay squawking. *Horch mal*," I said pointing. "He's mad we're invading his territory." The gray jay jumped from limb to limb ten feet from us. "Sqwaaack . . . sqwaaack . . . sqwaaack."

"That's part of it," I said to Grete, " . . . starting with nothing. But if you look around, we've got everything here." I lifted my arm toward the mountain. "Look over there . . . the Sleeping Beauty Mountain in your back yard. Clear running creeks, fish from the river. In another month or so wildflowers, wild strawberries and raspberries, salmonberries, huckleberries, blueberries in August, cranberries in October, and we'll never have to worry about a supply of meat. Once you get used to this place you won't want to leave." I set George down and took his hand. "It's the only time in our lives we can do this—before the boys go to school. This is the real stuff out here, the real life."

Grete picked Tommy up and patted his back. "My mother would never believe this," she said, shaking her head. "I hardly believe it. And with two kids yet. I don't know . . . "

"You won't have to worry about a thing out here. You know the wolves and bears are afraid of humans and keep to themselves, and we'll never starve. If you know how to get along with Mother Nature she won't let you down."

"I guess this means real pioneer living."

"Yeah, you can say that, but you're already an experienced pioneer. And don't worry, we can walk out of here anytime. We'll find a spot for our cabin right now. No use wasting any time."

We hiked across the meadow toward an island ridge that was about three hundred feet long and a couple hundred feet wide. The ridge supported a good stand of young cedar and fir, which meant we had a ready supply of logs to build a cabin and barn. Spongy moss grew underfoot among ferns and trilliums and long strands of lichen hung from the trees.

"This looks like a good spot for the cabin," I said to Grete, turning toward the south-facing mountains. "Look at that view and all-day sun. In the meantime we can set up a shelter right here among the trees."

I felled some poplars that grew in thickets at the edge of the meadow and in a couple of days we had constructed a comfortable eight-by-twelve lean-to which we covered with tar paper. That was to be our home until the first snowfall. The weather was mild, and though the temperature still dropped to freezing overnight, the sun quickly burned off the frost and warmed up the days.

We had so much work to do that the subject of nothing being there or why we were there was never mentioned again. Jays and chickadees were daily visitors, scavenging for scraps. Robins hopped around the marsh and warblers flitted in and around the trees. In the early morning and late evening we would see deer across the meadow with their fawns. We discovered streams, promising huckleberry patches and highbush cranberries in the meadow that would bear fruit in the fall. There was a beaver dam at the lower edge of the meadow, and we found willows and poplars they had felled, leaving perfectly rounded, hewed stumps.

"I'll have to keep an eye on those sons-of-guns so they don't flood the place," I said to Grete. "Ten years ago they were almost trapped out and it was illegal to sell their furs. Looks like they might be coming back again."

"My mother had a muskrat cape. Are they like beaver?"

"They're smaller and don't have a flat tail. And they multiply like rabbits . . . good eating, like beaver."

"Pheewww. That would be like eating rats."

"The meat's a delicacy, just wait, though not the way the Indians cook it," and I told Grete about my first experience with eating cooked muskrat.

"And I won't cook it either," she said firmly shaking her head.

Well, I have to say that Grete ate her words. But by the time she had to meet that challenge, she had grown to love the wilderness and understood what I loved about it. Every day we went fishing in the streams and beaver dams for mountain trout or we went down to the river where we caught salmon. Even though I told Grete we didn't have to worry about bears or wolves, we never went anywhere without a gun and a knife. Salmon were plentiful so the bears weren't interested in us, and the wolves had found higher ground over the summer. There was one time, though, that a grizzly bear really gave us a scare, but I'll tell you about him later.

I started falling logs for our cabin right away, having learned by then the benefit of cured logs, and even if they only had three months to dry out, it was better than nothing. I cut some logs right there on the island and others up in the timber at the edge of the meadow, which I later hauled to the building site with the horses. Grete worked right along with me, chopping off the branches and peeling the bark off the logs. Sometimes we set up a makeshift play area surrounded by logs so we could keep an easy eye on the boys.

After we got settled and Grete felt comfortable about spending a night alone with the boys, I went back out to Remo with one of the horses to pick up more tools and supplies. I was pretty worried about leaving Grete and the boys alone, but she just laughed.

"I'm not lonely, and what's there to be afraid of?" she asked. "I've got a gun and there's nobody around that could bother us."

By then I had taught Grete to shoot and she was getting pretty savvy about handling a gun. Here I had brought her into the real wilderness where our survival depended totally on our wits, our skills, and on each other, and she had taken to it like a duck to water. She had long ago given up on manicured fingernails and fancy shoes and dresses. Now she wore longjohns and woollen pants, warm shirts and heavy boots. Her chestnut hair glistened and her cheeks were fuller and rosier than they had ever been.

"Remember we need a good stove and don't forget a butter churn and washtub." She wrote everything down because she knew darn well she couldn't depend on me to remember everything. "And we'll need all the canning jars you can carry, and seed potatoes," she added, " . . . and what about my sewing machine?"

Going with one horse was an easy two-day trip for me. But I still had to go all the way into Terrace for staples because there wasn't a store in Remo in those days. I didn't feel a'tall good about leaving them alone, so when I got to Terrace I scouted around for a dog and found a nice German-Shepherd-mix about a year old. He had a beautiful shiny gray-black coat and two black ears. I couldn't take Grete's treadle machine back on that trip because the stove, tools and staples were a priority, and there wasn't much she could sew at that point anyway. But the dog was a real surprise for them and Tommy and George were tickled pink. Grete named him Prince. He followed the boys everywhere and watched out for them day and night, though I can tell you they were never out of Grete's sight. They could have easily wandered off, especially George, who was curious about everything, and Tommy was into exploring by then, too. At their age they could have become bait for the bears or wolves, even coyotes, though for some reason we rarely encountered coyotes in the valley.

We had a lot of hard work ahead of us. By then it was the end of May, and we had to get the garden dug and planted. Yellow buttercups had burst into bloom among the mounds of marsh grass and pungent skunk cabbages. I had brought back a small tiller, so harnessed up Mack and ploughed up a patch of rich, black soil large enough for the garden. The sod was tangled and knotted and almost as tough as cutting through hardpan. When the garden was ready for planting, Grete went ahead and put in the seed potatoes, beets, cabbage, turnips, carrots, lots of onions and even sunflowers and daisies. But the only vegetables that really grew well in that sour soil were the potatoes and sugar beets, and we grew enough to just about hold us through the winter.

Grete learned to milk the cow that summer, too. The cow had a calf not too long after we arrived, so we had plenty of milk for the boys. Mrs. Russell had taught Grete how to churn butter and make cottage cheese, so there was always a cheesecloth full of curdled milk hanging from a tree over a small bucket. Her sourdough hotcakes and fresh bread were the world's best.

One day in late June she came running up to me with the boys straggling behind through the tall grass. By then everything was green and the garden seedlings were up. You could smell the spongy, moist heat seeping out of the earth. She was swinging a tin can with a wire looped through it for a handle.

"We found a patch of wild strawberries," she said puffing. "I've never tasted any so sweet. And look at the size of them." She picked several out of the can and with her red-stained fingers dropped them into my mouth. The boys' faces were smeared pink with juice.

"Hmmm, they melt on your tongue," I said grinning. "I didn't even know for sure there were any around here," and I pinched her cheek.

But cooking and berries aside, we really had to work against time that summer. At least I didn't have to worry about a fence around the garden as Prince chased off any deer that tried to come close enough to eat the vegetables, and I kept the horses and cow on tethers so they wouldn't trample down the garden and all the swamp grass.

I started work on the barn first since I was using green logs. Once I had the logs sawed to size and the foundation dug out—we had a real advantage there on the island because of the slope—we began the walls. I square-notched the corners of each log with axe and hammer and chisel, and slowly one row after the other went up. You'd think the two of us wouldn't have been able to get the logs up once the walls were a few feet high, but I just tied a rope around the log and then Grete and I rolled them up one by one on long poles that slanted away from the top of the wall. She pushed and I pulled. I saddled the logs over the corners, hewing them to fit.

After the barn was finished I began to cut firewood for the winter. We needed at least twenty cords of wood, so I fell poplars and alders right there behind the island. Where we planned to build the cabin I had cleared a twenty-by-thirty-foot area and dug out a good part of the hillside which would give us some natural insulation. Our building site faced south, and with all the open meadow space, we had full days of sunshine, at least during the summer months. Since I hadn't been in the valley in the winter, I didn't realize then that we'd be without a speck of sunshine for nearly four months when the sun was lowest on the horizon.

"And I want two big windows in the cabin, by golly," Grete said wagging her finger at me, "and a nice bear rug on the floor," she added with a laugh.

Anything to keep the missus happy was my motto, because for me life would have been nothing without her. When I came home from fishing or hunting and the smell of wood smoke and fresh-baked bread caught in my nose and the boys and Grete would be waiting for me, I had everything a man could want. Sometimes Grete and I would sit for hours watching the boys roll around with Prince in the tall, green slough grass. He would gnaw on their arms and they would laugh and hang on to his tail. That was some dog.

"I had my doubts when we first arrived," Grete said one evening after the boys were asleep. "I didn't think I could stand the loneliness, but there's no time to think about it and it's so peaceful here. The only sound you hear is the echo of the woodpeckers, the song of the birds. I don't even miss town. We have no worries, do we. We can do what we want."

We could do what we wanted, all right, but everything we did was out of necessity. The daylight hours were long during the summer with the sky getting pink by four a.m. The sun didn't drop behind the mountain until well past nine o'clock, and up there in the North, twilight lingered until way past eleven. The best part of all was that we weren't plagued by mosquitoes and blackflies. We didn't have to fuss with mosquito netting at night or fly-nets over our heads during the day.

One time during the summer Emil Froese, his sister Anna, and the Lindstrom boys came back with me after I made another trip out for supplies. Emil, a lanky, blond kid with a shy smile, and taller than me even at fifteen, packed in Grete's sewing machine on his back. We managed to bring quite a few supplies on that trip, including canning jars and a couple of windows. Emil knew a lot about wild herbs and showed us the different weeds we could use for salad. We found pigweed in the shade by the creek, miner's lettuce that had roundish leaves on a long stem, and of course the lowly dandelion. And there was plenty of wild yarrow to dry for tea.

By August we began to work in earnest on the cabin. The hardest part was cutting and splitting the cedars in half for the floorboards, and rafters. Sometimes I was able to make a perfect split using a wedge and a single-bitted axe. Other times we'd have to use the whipsaw. Once the floorboards were down and we started on the walls, we felt like we were making progress. It was tough work all the way. I had to be more careful getting the notches just right as I wanted the logs to fit good and tight. We concentrated on getting the main room built, which was about fourteen by twenty, before winter set in. Grete was kept busy chinking with damp moss and clay. The boys were always underfoot, but George, who was two and a half by then thought chinking to be the best game in the world.

"*Schau Mama, schau Dada,*" he'd say. "Look Mama." Even though my English was fluent by then, Grete and I still spoke German all the time, and naturally, that's the first language the boys learned.

I took several trips to Remo and Terrace that summer and fall to get all our winter supplies. Of course, I always checked for mail on my trips to town. We heard from Little Max that he'd gone up to Dawson in the Yukon to work on the gold dredges. Grete also received a package from her mother filled with delicious dark chocolate, wool for knitting, *Lederhosen* for the boys, magazines for us.

By late August the salmon were running and I set a net in the river. We would bring home as many as we could carry. Grete put up much of the salmon in jars and I smoked and dried the rest. Blueberries and huckleberries were in season and there were plenty of rose hips to collect, so Grete was kept pretty busy with canning and jamming alone.

We had a good run of hot weather that summer. I was out every day cutting swamp grass with my scythe, and the sweet smell of drying hay hung in the hot August air like sweet perfume. On the hottest days, Grete packed a lunch, which meant sourdough buns and homemade cheese. We'd hike down to the river about half a mile away and find a nice sandy spot in the shade where the water was shallow and the boys could safely play.

Bulrushes, bursting with white mounds of seed, grew along a swampy area close to the river. "They'd make perfect pillow stuffing," Grete said, stuffing the soft, puffy seeds into the knapsack.

One day when I returned home from a hunting trip, Grete came running to meet me all out of breath. "Dolly's stuck in the beaver dam. She's in deep. Hurry."

The horse was stuck in the mud right up to her stomach. I harnessed up Mack and got a rope around Dolly's haunches, but after an hour of pulling and pushing she still didn't budge.

"I'll have to get the gun."

"You can't just shoot her," Grete protested.

"We have no choice. If we leave her the coyotes'll make mincemeat out of her."

The first sharp frost sent us into the swamp to check if the cranberries had turned red.

"They smell like wine," Grete said, picking a clump and dropping them into her mouth. Her face turned sour and her eyes teared. "They'll make the best tangy syrup."

Paul with George
and Tommy on
Zimacord Valley
homestead, fall 1937.

Indian summer had arrived and alders and poplars were turning from orange and yellow to golds and bronzes. Geese and ducks
began to wing south, which gave us an opportunity for good roast
duck. You may think we had a lot of time on our hands and that
building a one room cabin wasn't a problem, but we had to use so
much energy just for survival that the days quickly passed and
suddenly it was the end of September and we still weren't in our
cabin. The nights were frosty cold and some days a raw wind
whipped a light flurry of snow across the meadows.

We pushed hard to get the roof finished and the windows
installed and by the time we had our first major snowfall the
beginning of November we were finally moved in.

I built a bed frame and bunks for the boys. We had stuffed
dried slough grass into covers Grete had sewn from sacking and
used them for mattresses. She had stuffed pillows with the bulrush
seeds and we had our extra-thick feather quilts from Germany to
keep us good and warm. Our cabin was definitely rustic, but by the
time Grete hung crocheted lace curtains on the windows, threw a

tanned cowhide on the floor and arranged our hand-hewed table and chairs, it was as warm and cozy as you could get. By then the days had shortened considerably, and already patterns of early morning frost clung to the window panes.

Our vegetables were stunted that first year because of the sour soil, but we had a good crop of potatoes. Grete really could do wonders with spuds and fish. She would fry up fresh salmon steaks and serve them with fried or boiled potatoes. From the leftovers she'd mix together the potatoes and salmon and prepare delicious, spicy salmon patties. We had a good supply of cranberry and sugar beet syrup which we used on hotcakes or as a relish with deer meat or even porcupine.

Grete had become quite a sureshot and went out hunting for blue grouse that fall. One time she came home in quite a tiff because she had shot a porcupine by mistake. Well, we didn't let anything go to waste, and it turned out to be quite a tender delicacy, tasting almost like chicken.

In late September I'd gone goat hunting with my .22. When you know the habitat of goats, it's not hard to get close to them. I climbed to the top of the mountain and down the steepest cliff where I knew they laid up in the daytime. When I came across several of them, I sat back for awhile and watched how they crossed a bluff, leaning their necks and stomachs tightly into the rock wall. Their hoofs, sharp as chisels, could hang onto anything. One pivoted right around on his hind legs on what looked like a sheer drop. The goats looked pretty surprised when I raised my .22. The real trouble was finding the dead goat after it had tumbled down the mountain a thousand feet or more, but the good tender meat was well worth it, some of which Grete also canned.

The boys were excited when the snow really began to fall in earnest. They stuck out their tongues to catch the big flat flakes. Grete caught them in her mittened hand.

"Look at the beautiful star crystals," she said to the boys, kneeling down in the crunchy snow. "Each one different."

"Let me see, let me see," George cried, pushing Tommy out of the way.

Grete stuck out her arm. "Here, you can catch them on your sleeve."

For Grete the hard work of preparing for winter was over and she could take time to play with the boys more. But she still had plenty to do everyday.

For me the winter meant trapping. I hoped to get some mink and marten and muskrat along the river, and if I was lucky I'd be able to snare a few lynx and foxes. There were plenty of muskrat trails and I even spotted some otter tracks, cagey little buggers that often collected the animals from the traps before you could get to them. I had prepared the best runs by blazing the trees along the line. The traps were cleaned and greased and I was ready for a winter of successful trapping.

By mid November, our world had turned into a thick blanket of white. Heavy gray and white clouds hung over the mountains, and on the days when we could see rays of sunlight stroke our Sleeping Beauty mountain, our valley below was left in shadow, and the stillness had become deep and muffled. We didn't get any direct sunshine for three more months, something I hadn't bargained for.

One morning I pulled out our snowshoes and we bundled up the boys good and warm and packed them on our backs. I fitted the lashings to Grete's feet.

"These are easy to use if you know how to dance," I said with a grin, looking up at Grete.

"Hummph . . . I can't even remember when I last danced."

"Well, you're about to now, and once you get used to them you won't know you have 'em on your feet. Now just follow behind me, but not in my same footsteps so we can make a good flat trail."

We needed to open up some trails so we could get out and around. Once the snow got over three feet deep it was pretty tough to make your way across the drifts, even in snowshoes. The snow was soft and heavy there in the valley, and if your webs sank down too deep you would have to lift each web straight up and clear the surface of the snow before you could move forward, and that was darned hard work. We had sore leg muscles the first few days, but after we broke in some good trails we would hike out through the snow in crisp weather, not feeling the cold at all. It was important for Grete and the boys to get out every day, too, except in the most severe weather, just to prevent cabin fever.

Grete was always surprised that we didn't have to wear more layers of heavy clothes, but you didn't need to when you were always on the move.

I took one more trip out to Terrace before the snow got any deeper. I had done some improvements on the trail over the summer and built bridges across the creeks, which came under the auspices of relief work which earned me $15 from the road department. I handed that money right over to the general store in Terrace where I loaded up with more provisions, including cod liver oil and some used books.

On my way home, just at the North fork of the Zimacord, Mack started to cut up. He yanked his head and backed away from me. When I got a clear view of the river, about a hundred feet away, there stood this monster of a grizzly on his short hind legs, sniffing the air. He let out a rumbling snort. It was all I could do to hang on to the horse, but I never took my eyes off that bear as he swayed from one side to the other. His little black eyes glared at me and I kept my eyes steady. I knew he wouldn't attack, especially if I didn't turn and run, but grizzlies were unpredictable and could be darned aggressive when they felt like it.

"Easy, old boy, easy," I said to Mack. Then the bear made a huff, dropped down on all fours and lumbered into the snowy bush. I let out a long breath and patted Mack's neck. But that wasn't the last of him, as Grete and I were to find out the following year.

"Well, I saw my old friend, Buster," I said to Grete when I got home.

"Buster?"

"A monster grizzly," I said grinning. Her mouth dropped open, but I calmed her down before she could object. "He just turned and ran. I scared the hell out of him, but you'd never want to tackle one of those devils. I hope you get a chance to see him one of these days. They're a beautiful sight, I can tell you, nice tan and brown fur.

"Oh, guess what?" I pulled a letter out of my pocket and passed it to her. "Arno and Ida have moved to Vancouver Island, to Duncan. He's delivering meat there. And they've just had a baby boy, after all these years. Named him Edwin. well, that should put them in good standing with the Pope."

"To the Island?" she asked, scanning the letter. "And he's working for Ben Nicols, the Dutchman?"

I nodded. "I guess he gets along with him okay, and it's steady work."

She finished the letter and laid it on the table. "Had we stayed we would be neighbours. I liked it out there along the bay."

"You don't regret leaving now, do you?"

She shrugged her shoulders. "No, but once we came north, maybe we should have gone into the real North, to the Yukon where Little Max and Adam live. It doesn't snow so much and you can still line your pockets with gold."

"Huh, if I thought there was money in gold I would've been up there myself long ago. Even during the gold rush days the only ones who ended up getting rich were the saloon keepers and the mule drivers."

I was still hoping I could line my pockets with some prime furs. Jens Erlandson was back on his trap line and visited us about once a week, always bringing a string of Dolly Vardens. We looked forward to seeing him as he was the only company we had all winter long.

"Yust like home ven I come and visit," he'd say in his Swedish accent.

Every few days I ran my own five-mile trapline, which I could easily do in the nearly seven hours of daylight we had, unless the weather got particularly bad and I had to camp out overnight. By then I felt like an experienced trapper, remembering all the lessons Old Sam had taught me. But it still was no picnic, especially when your fingers stiffened with frost, and the minute you stopped moving the iron cold would freeze your blood, and your back would ache from stooping and packing. I was actually quite successful on the trapline until the snow got so deep I no longer could get out to the lines.

The nights were darn long over the winter as it was pitch dark by four. To supplement the coal oil lamp, we used candles, which we had made from goat tallow. We had plenty of time to read and that's where Grete really improved her English. She read those cowboy books over and over, and used to write out pages in longhand for practice.

By December, winter began to bite down hard, and that's when the snow started to come down for days without stopping. It was nothing to look out and find three feet of new snow in the morning. I hadn't expected that either, as Terrace hardly ever got more than two feet of snow all winter long. With so much snow, the wolves came down off the mountain and began running in packs. Their long wails, especially on clear, moonlit nights, cut through the silence of our quiet cabin, and we would listen to their echoes along the mountain. At first terror crossed Grete's face, and the boys crawled deep under their feather beds, but eventually they got used to their howling. Sometimes, though, they came so close with their savage wailing and singing that even my hair stood on end. Prince would growl and whine and crouch low to the floor, and a ridge of stiff bristles would form along the length of his back.

Jens Erlandson dropped by at Christmas and we even convinced him to spend the night with us. We did our best to make the cabin festive, filling the room with pungent spruce and cedar boughs. We decorated a small spruce tree with cones, dried flowers and coloured bits of cloth. I had carved some wooden toys for the boys, and for Grete I had bought moccasins and some lavender cologne. She had secretly sewn me a pair of thick, woollen pants, and had knitted socks, mittens and toques for all of us. She had plenty of time to knit during those long winter evenings.

After a delicious dinner of juicy deer roast with rich gravy and thick, cranberry syrup and German potato dumplings, Grete played all our favourite Christmas songs on the zither. Even the boys sang along. Then Jens pulled a chess set out of his pack. He had carved all the figures out of cedar and made a board out of a piece of tanned leather. With candles, good company, a warm cabin, and music, we were about as happy and contented as anyone can get.

The first time I showed Grete the Northern Lights she looked up at the sky for a long time, pulling her thick jacket tight around her.

"They're so beautiful," she said quietly. Flashing streamers of pinks and greens and yellow filled the sky. "They look like bolts of shimmering silk and taffeta swaying in the wind. Now I understand why you couldn't quite describe them. And look at the stars, how close they are. Astronomy always was my favorite subject, you know. Look up there," she said pointing. "You almost can't see it, but there's the Bear and the Big and Little Dippers, and over there in the Milky Way—the Swan."

I put my arm around her. "And look at the outline of our Sleeping Beauty dazzled by millions of sparkling stars."

Winter deepened and snow continued to fall. Soon over seven feet lay on the ground. All that snow was a beautiful sight, piled up in drifts and filled with shadows and changing lights, muting all sound and raising our sense of isolation and solitude and seclusion.

But all that deep snow didn't come without problems. After every snowfall we had to shovel our way out of the cabin and I had to constantly shovel snow off the roofs of the barn and cabin and dig out the windows to let in light. We also ran into a major problem with the animals. I had planned to let them browse for some of their food over the winter, but with so much snow they couldn't step foot outside the barn. Although we had plenty of hay, that wild swamp grass didn't have enough food value to bring the animals through the winter. By mid March they were so weak they no longer had the strength to stand on their feet, so I had to destroy them.

I know it would have been best to just pack up the family and leave, but we were completely snowed in. And Grete didn't seem to mind all that snow.

"It's like living in a wonderland," she said. "The boys love playing in it and making snow caves, and it keeps the cabin warm. You don't have to leave on my account."

"Independent, aren't you."

"That's what my mother always said. *Gerade wie ein Hans-wurst.* You do what you want when you want."

With the boys underfoot all day and restless to get outside, Grete had her hands full. And getting the wash done was one of the worst jobs. In the summer you could do it outdoors, but in the winter it was an all-day inside job. And you had to keep woollens clean so they would heat efficiently. First you had to melt down all that snow to get enough water boiled for the tub. Then you'd have to scrub the clothes, wring them, rinse them, wring them, and hang them up outside. The cold air sucked the moisture right out of them. The wash would be stiff as boards with hoarfrost, but in a few hours almost dry. And don't think we changed sheets every week and underwear every day. But once a week we would heat water and fill the washtub for a good scrub.

Aside from all the chores, Grete had lots of hobbies and filled the long evenings with reading, knitting, crocheting, mending socks or playing Strauss waltzes on the zither. We played games with the boys, read our favorite books over and over and played lots of chess, too.

By late March the soft melting snow would freeze solid overnight so you could walk on top of it until at least noon. Since we no longer had a supply of milk for the boys, I took a trip into Terrace for canned milk and more staples.

"I'll be back tonight," I said to Grete. "I can make good time over the hard crusty snow and I should be able to catch a speeder into Terrace."

I bundled up my supply of furs and left at daybreak. I made good time into Terrace, but by late afternoon on my return trip, the snow had softened from the sun and I had to walk along the river, which meant crossing it every time I came to a cutbank. Sometimes the icy water came right up to my waist, and once out of the water, I really had to move fast to keep warm.

Although I had about eighty pounds on my back, I didn't run into trouble until I left the river to get into our homestead, which was about a half mile away from that point. The snow was still soft and I practically had to dig my way through four to five feet of snow. On top of it all, I had a torn ligament in my knee so couldn't use snowshoes, though in that much soft, heavy snow they wouldn't have been of much use. I didn't dare leave my pack behind because I was afraid that the wolves, hungry at that time of year, would tear everything apart overnight. The sweat from my face turned my eyebrows and beard into icicles as I pushed and dug my way through the snow. I craved to stop and rest, but I knew my feet would probably freeze into ice blocks or worse, that I would slip into a black sleep and never be able to pull myself out of it. By the time I stumbled through the cabin door, and I know you've heard this old story before, my strength was depleted. Tears streamed down my face and Grete, of course, had been worried to death because it was well past dark. I dropped the pack to the floor and Grete helped me undress. The boys were still awake and all over me. After some good, hot barley soup, though, my tingling body started to warm through again.

Then the snow began to sink into the ground almost overnight. The months of silence were broken by snapping buds, the echo of woodpeckers, and the trickling of mountain streams. Ducks and geese were winging their way north again. Grete brought pussy willows into the cabin, and the boys shouted and rolled around in the matted marsh grass with Prince. The long rays of the sun felt warm. Life was green again. I asked Grete if she wanted to spend another summer on the homestead or if we should give it up, but she was used to the place by then.

"We may as well stay the summer. Just get us another cow so we have fresh milk and butter for the boys."

So we prepared for our first family trip away from the homestead in a year. Our first stop was at Floyd and Aileen Franks' on the Kalum River where we wanted to buy a cow. The boys hadn't seen anybody outside Jens Erlandson in nearly a year and were so shy that we couldn't get them into the house.

My credit was still good, so we bought supplies in Terrace and Grete found some material she liked and wool for knitting. We bought new shoes for the boys, candy, puzzles, second-hand books. The boys stared at the candy jars, baskets of soap, and coloured bottles that stood on the counter, clinging to our pant legs for dear life.

We also heard the news that Hitler had crossed the Austrian border in March—that was in '38—and without a fight had taken control of the country. Only years later did I learn how cleverly Hitler had forced the surrender of Austria and all the countries that followed.

We had a busy summer ahead of us and put in another garden. By then we had plenty of manure to add to the soil. I also sewed Timothy seed into the meadow to enrich the swamp grass.

About that time two young fellows from the Prairies came by and took up a homestead further up the valley. I think they had about as much experience as I did when I first came from the Old Country, but at least they were used to long, cold Saskatchewan winters and wouldn't be taken by surprise.

We took a hunting trip together one day in early June and shot a few bush chickens. I was determined to get a goat as we had lived most of the winter on a diet of canned meat and fish. I pointed the way back to our cabin, and I climbed up the cliffs to find a goat. Well, it didn't take me twenty minutes to shoot one, but I had to drag that goat three thousand feet down the mountain. Since it was getting late in the day I decided to leave it at the treeline and take the liver along.

I was about a mile from home, following a bear trail, when I heard some movement in the brush. I stopped and held my breath. Suddenly, right there in front of me, a big black bear came ambling toward me. He didn't notice me until he was about thirty feet away. I had my .22 ready, and the moment he stopped I shot him right in the head. He dropped like a rock. Boy, did I feel proud of myself. Here I not only had a goat liver, but had just shot my first bear. Those two prairie chickens would pop their eyes when they saw what I had bagged.

My heart knocked and I headed for that bear thinking about the tasty meat and the thick hide. I grabbed the scruff of his neck. Suddenly he let out a huff and started to get up. It didn't take me a second to recover from my shock. I jumped on his back and cut his throat before he regained consciousness. But it wasn't enough to keep him down. He made an awful blood-curdling roar, struggled to his feet and ran another fifty yards before he actually dropped from loss of blood. Mind you, I had taken off in the other direction just to be on the safe side. I gave him time enough to bleed to death before I gutted him and took out his liver. When I got back to the cabin, and the fellows had arrived only ten minutes before I did, they thought I was pulling their leg when I told them I'd shot a bear and a goat—until I pulled out two livers. We had quite a feast that night, to say the least.

Just about that time Prince began to get real thin and it was hard to coax him to eat. He wouldn't drink anything and just lay there shaking. I knew he wouldn't pull through, but I couldn't put that dog down. In a few days he was dead from distemper. We all took it pretty hard, especially George, who was over three by then. The boys couldn't remember ever being without a dog. He not only had been good company and part of the family, but had also become a necessity to keep wild animals at bay, summer and winter, and we didn't have long to wait to find that out.

A month later Grete and I were sitting in the cabin. The boys were playing out front in the meadow. We had the door open so we could keep an eye on them. They were never allowed out of our sight. They bounced around in the tall grass and we could hear them laughing. Then I heard George "shooo, shoooing" something away. Grete was at the window in an instant. Her face went stark white. I looked out the door and there was this full-grown grizzly standing up on his hind legs, swinging his head back and forth just like I'd seen him on the river the summer before, but worse than that, the boys were walking toward him, trying to chase him away. That wasn't how I wanted Grete to experience a grizzly.

I looked at her and raised my arm. "Don't move." I grabbed my rifle and knife and quietly called to the boys. They were about twenty feet from the bear by then. The boys turned to me saying, "*Schau, Papa*, look."

Paul on homestead
in Zimacord Valley,
north of Remo. ca.
1937.

"Shhhhh," I said, and put my finger to my lips. Hot beads of sweat broke out on my face. "Come here," I whispered to them. "Slowly now."

I aimed the gun and waited for the bear to make the next move. I could tell from his markings that it was my old friend Buster. My heart banged like a drum, and even though it was my experience that bears were more frightened of humans than we were of them, in that moment that knowledge didn't help. The bear remained standing in that upright position for about two minutes, huffing and snorting and bristling his fur. Finally, he dropped on all fours and ambled off across the clearing, stopping once, as if to raise his cap, to take one last look at us. The boys, who were in Grete's arms by then, didn't even know what danger they had been in, but Grete was in tears and I suddenly felt a hundred pounds lighter. Although that little episode didn't last for more than three minutes, I felt as if it had lasted hours. After that we watched those boys like hawks. Had Prince been alive that devil wouldn't have dared show his face.

That summer Emil and his sister and the Lindstrom boys came to visit us again. It was always good to have company. You do get starved for company all right. Grete baked some blueberry cake which we ate with thick cream. George and Tommy were pretty shy at first, but they finally came out from behind the cabin and slowly made friends with them again. After our visitors left, we began to talk in earnest about whether or not we should spend another winter. We could see how shy the boys had become when human beings came around.

"The longer we stay, the harder it'll be for them to adapt to town life," I said to Grete.

"I don't mind living here," she said. "We've built everything with our own hands and we'll have a bumper crop of vegetables this summer. The boys aren't old enough for school yet anyway. And could you find work?"

"That's the trouble. Over the winter there's not much work and we'd have to do a lot of scratching to make ends meet. Out here we're at least guaranteed a few dollars from fur. Well, we still have time before the snow flies."

The summer passed quickly. We were settled, liked our easy way of life, and put off the days when we would return to civilization. That was weeks away. Then one morning in early September we found ourselves snowed in, and good. We weren't worried, had provisions enough, and thought the snow would melt overnight. As the days passed the snow piled up higher and higher, but we didn't mind being cut off from the rest of the world. Finally we decided to spend another winter.

I took a couple more trips to Terrace for supplies where I also picked up mail from Germany. There was mail from Grete's family and a letter from Gusti. She had married Hans Griesshammer, a postal worker, and was expecting. She wrote nothing about the Nazis. Jette and Karl had moved to Berlin where he had obtained a government position. And they had a baby girl, Erika, born in July.

I extended my trapping line that winter before the snow got too deep. Sometimes I'd be gone two nights. Grete was so independent and self sufficient by then that nothing worried her. The wolves were off the mountain again, but we were used to their daily howling.

We always looked forward to having Jens drop in on his round from the trapline, and sometimes he'd spend the night with us. Grete always had plenty to do, and the boys would exhaust themselves playing and tunnelling in the snow.

I have to admit that spring was a long time coming that year. We counted the days until the sun rose above the peaks and finally flooded our valley with sunlight the middle of February. We watched and listened for the first return of the ducks and geese and daily checked the snow level.

"You know," Grete said one morning, flipping hotcakes, "it's fine and dandy to live off the land, but it sure would be nice to crunch into a fresh apple, to smell an orange again. And I haven't talked to another woman in months." She plopped a heap of pancakes on my plate. "It's time we leave."

I looked out the cabin window. Yellow-green poplar and willows stood out against the dark forest of spruce. Sure, we could have continued to live there in the bush, but where would it have taken us? The isolation was beginning to wear thin and we had certainly proved to ourselves that we could stand up to the challenge of the wilderness.

"Anytime you want to go," I said to Grete with a nod.

"Go?" George asked. "Go to town?"

I patted him on the head. "As soon as the snow melts," then looking at Grete with a grin. "I said all along we could leave whenever you wanted."

So on the 18th of May, 1939, with patches of snow still sticking to the ground, we hiked back out to civilization. We left our cow and calf and most of our belongings behind, which I planned to pick up later. We had spent two full years out there on the homestead, but the time had come to find a more prosperous way of life.

22. Lake Cowichan

ALTHOUGH WE HAD ENJOYED THE CHALLENGE of living like pioneers in a remote existence up there in the Zimacord Valley, we were happy to get back to Remo and the luxury of civilization. Of course, luxury for us meant being around people again and getting together with some of our old friends.

We talked about moving back to Vancouver Island because Grete liked Duncan and the mild climate there, but before we could even consider it, I had to find work.

Clare Giggey ran a sawmill in Terrace, and when I talked to him about a job he hired me right away. We had moved into an abandoned cabin in Remo, and every morning I took the speeder to work. On my Sundays off I went back to the homestead to carry out the rest of our belongings and bring out the cow and calf.

I tilled the soil and we planted a small garden right away. The mosquitoes were terrible that summer, but they always were, there along the river. We didn't know what was worse, the deep snow in the winter on the homestead, or the mosquitoes, blackflies and no-see-ums in the summer along the Skeena.

The middle of August Mr. Giggey asked if I would help to manage the mill for him. I came home whistling and tossed my hat across the room, landing it right on Grete's head.

"What's the matter with you?" she asked with a grin, yanking it off.

"Giggey wants me to run the mill."

"Oh? And what's that mean?" she said, crossing her arms and leaning back against the sink.

"Papa, Papa," Tommy cried, grabbing hold of my leg. I picked him up and straddled him on my shoulders.

"It means I'll have a regular job with better pay. We could buy a decent place . . . get indoor plumbing. Our credit will be good and we could settle down once and for all."

She turned and picked up a dipper, plunging it into a bucket of water. "I thought we were going back to Duncan after we saved up enough money."

"Mama, *wasser, wasser,*" Little George said, pulling over a chair.

"It would be a good job, Grete. I'd be making fifty cents an hour."

She gave George a sip of water and took a drink herself. "Well, I guess you have to do what you have to do," she shruggd. Her eyes darkened and she smacked at the mosquitoes. "I'm sick of 'em . . . they're in your mouth, they're in your ears. Buzzing, buzzing day and night. Look at the boys. They're full of bites."

I put Tommy down and took a step toward her.

"Grete, if you really want to go back to the Island . . . "

"Isn't that what we've talked about doing?" She half turned away. "And sometimes I wonder what it would be like to see a movie again."

Back to Remo from Zimacord Valley, 1939. Left to right: Helen Lindstrom, Paul Hertel, Bobby Wiggins, Grete and boys (George and Tommy), Elsie Froese, Bill Lindstrom (behind Elsie) and Emil Froese.

"You've never complained," I said. I touched her thick, shining hair. "We can find a nice house in Terrace and I work there anyway."

She jerked her head and moved aside. "Would it make a difference? Terrace? Remo? There's no movie house in Terrace either," she replied, setting a hot pot of stew on the table.

"Look, I'll talk it over with Clare," I said feeling a little discouraged. "He was counting on me, but I guess I could find something on the Island, too."

Then Grete turned to me with that slip of her smile. "I already have enough saved for the fare, and some left over."

"You have! Then why didn't you tell me?"

"I wanted to surprise you, I guess."

Next day I told Mr. Giggey I needed a few days to think things over. I could easily have settled in Terrace as I'd put down roots years before and liked the people around the area. We were all in the same boat and everybody worked together helping each other out. It's a nice feeling when you live in a town and know so many people, but I guess Grete had had enough of the long, cold winters and was tired of all the deprivations, too. She had been a good sport, never complained, but I knew she always had a soft spot for Duncan, liked the mild climate there, the beaches around the bay, the salt water. And I had liked it there, too, for that matter.

So we sold the cow and calf and packed all our belongings into a couple of trunks and suitcases. When we arrived in Prince Rupert the first thing we did was see a cowboy movie with Hopalong Cassidy. George and Tommy stood up the whole time, clinging to the back of the seats with wide eyes. "Look Mama, Look Papa."

But headlines in the Prince Rupert newspaper that war was imminent and hopes for peace in Europe were getting dimmer by the day left us feeling a little edgy. Hitler had broken every promise he had made and only months earlier had invaded and conquered Czechoslovakia. And if Britain declared war against Germany, that would mean Canada would get mired into it as well, which wouldn't put us, as German immigrants, in a very good light. We had lived for two years without much news of the wider world and now we were being threatened with a war.

By the time we arrived in Vancouver, the first week in September, 1939, Hitler had invaded Poland and Britain and France had declared war on Germany. My old man had been right all along when he was concerned about Germany heading toward war.

When we arrived in Duncan, weary and a little travel worn, we visited our old friend Herman Kohler who let us stay in a cabin on his property. After we got settled we looked up Arno and Ida. They had three boys by then, all dark-haired, and the youngest one, Roy, was just over a year old. Tommy and George were three and four by then. Ida's brother, Joe Klein, who also lived with them made a living cutting cedar poles.

We all sat around the table enjoying Ida's cooking and of course the conversation turned to the War.

"Arno frets so much," Ida said in her Austrian dialect and gave her curly hair a toss. "I tell him not to worry. We're in a free country and far away from Germany. And we still go dancing on Saturday nights," she said rolling her shoulders. "We take the boys. Nobody minds. Sometimes Joe looks after them."

"It doesn't look good for us, Paul," Arno said. He still had a thick crop of black, coarse hair, not like my own thinning head. "I tell Ida, but she just laughs. There's nothing to laugh about, the way I see things."

I drummed my fingers on the table, thinking back on the days Arno and I had spent together up north. Pack up and go had been our slogan. At least Arno and his family had finally settled down, but there I was still packing up my family and moving from place to place, still looking for a spot we could call home.

I looked into Arno's worried eyes. "We haven't followed the news all that much the last couple of years," I said. "Up north nobody worried whether you were German, Swedish or a bohunk of any kind. Oh, there's always someone who's going to make a crack, but everybody's worried about making a living, that's all."

"Well, maybe you should have stayed up there then. The propaganda is only going to get worse, just wait. There's been plenty in the papers, even before the war broke out. I've already had problems being a German, you know. I just open my mouth and people give me dirty look."

"Did you take out papers yet?" I asked. "Nobody can touch you if you're a citizen."

"We never did," Arno said, shaking his head. "You know, the time just passes. Nobody ever cared."

"Well, I had to become a citizen when I applied for the homestead in Remo."

"It's too late for us. I don't think the government's going to stand on the street corner and hand out citizenship papers to Germans right now. Thank god the boys are Canadian. Joe isn't a citizen either."

"You own this house, don't you, and you have a pretty good business peddling meat, don't you?"

"*Ja, Ja,* naturally."

"Then you should be okay." I never believed for a minute that things would get as bad as they did for all of us Germans. "By the way, have you heard from Big Max?"

"Yeah. He's got a decent job in a butcher shop in Victoria. I don't think he's a citizen either. Victoria is quite a British enclave you know, and that could mean trouble for him, too."

The first thing I did was buy an old Model-T pickup for a hundred dollars so we could get around. I was hoping to start up a small meat business in Duncan, but it wasn't easy to break into a town where established businesses had a good foothold. Then I saw an ad in the *Cowichan Leader*. Three hundred acres of property was for sale at $1 an acre close to Lake Cowichan, about twenty miles west of Duncan. We drove out and took a look at it.

A one-lane road wound its way through the logged-off mountainsides where alders and fireweed had taken over the slash. Lake Cowichan was just a little village right on the lake, a logger's town with a general store, a beer parlour, a coffee shop, and a post office—but no butcher shop. The property we looked at was all stumps and blackberry brambles, ferns and fireweed, but I figured that once the land was cleared I could raise beef cattle. So I swung a good deal and managed to get credit. Next we had to find a place to live and when I mentioned to a fellow in the coffee shop that we were looking for a house, he told me he knew of an old twelve-room log house up on the lake front that was for rent.

"A Mrs. Doering owns it," he said. "It's quite a landmark. Built about 1914."

We looked her up and she didn't mind renting to us as she had a German name herself. We were pretty excited about the place as it was a beautiful two-story log house with large windows and two sleeping porches upstairs. A long veranda ran along the front and the sides of the house. A huge maple tree stood on the property and the leaves were just beginning to turn red and golden. Glints of sunlight from the lake shimmered through the trees.

"We'll take it," I said to her. "Twenty dollars a month you said?"

She nodded and smiled. "And you can help yourself to the wood in the shed. My husband loved to chop wood. Always went out after supper and chopped wood. I'm so glad to have somebody living in the place again. It's a nice family house. It's stood empty for awhile now."

"Looks like a shed or something burned down over there not too long ago," I said to her, pointing to a heap of black bed springs, bricks, a stove and chunks of charcoal and ashes a couple of hundred feet away from the house.

"Oh, that was the caretaker's cottage," she said lifting her chin. "Burned earlier on in the summer. An old man was living in it and keeping an eye on things around here. He came back from the village one day and it was gone. It's just lucky the house didn't go along with it."

The grounds had been well taken care of at one time. Climbing roses grew wild over the veranda, and on the side of the house hydrangea bushes hung full with faded blue and pink clustered flowers. We were pretty excited about finding that place, which was like a mansion to us. The boys ran up and down the stairs and spent hours playing hide-and-go-seek and cops and robbers in the empty rooms, hollering and squealing to each other and listening for their echoes. We bought a brand new three-piece chesterfield set on the budget plan for $49.90 and arranged them around the fireplace. Grete displayed her hand-crocheted snowflake doilies on

Grete and Paul, Cowichan Lake. ca. 1939.

the backs and arms of the furniture and bought unbleached cotton for curtains, ten yards for a dollar. She set up a few knickknacks and put fresh daisies in a vase. I found a second-hand dinette set for $5. The kitchen had a big wood-burning stove and we even had indoor plumbing. We were as excited about our place as any young couple could get.

"I finally feel like we're living in style," Grete said smiling, when we got everything moved in. "I'd love a house of our own like this someday. Look at the nice wallpaper and linoleum on the floor."

"Don't worry, you'll get your own house. Maybe not as big, unless you want a half dozen more kids, but once my business gets rolling I'll buy lumber and get our own place started."

Next I rented a little shop right there in Lake Cowichan and hung up a sign. I sold boneless stewing beef for 15 cents a pound, beef sausage for 10 cents, side bacon 28 cents, pot roast 21 cents. I bought all my beef from the farmers around the area. At first people were happy that a shop had opened and they could buy locally from me, but as the war propaganda machine heated up over the winter, my business noticeably slacked off. Maybe Arno had been right about the lower part of the Island being very British and anti-German. And every week the *Cowichan Leader* had something in the paper about Hitler. You couldn't even go to a movie without being reminded of the war. The newsreel showed the millions of Germans cheering Hitler, and films like *Confessions of a Nazi Spy* were popular. Recruiting was in full progress and the Red Cross was preparing for war activity.

By October all German citizens were required to register. One day an R.C.M.P. came into the shop.

"I just have a few questions, Mr. Hertel."

"How can I help you," I asked, setting down my knife and squaring my shoulders.

"I just need to know how long you been in this country."

"Well, let's see. It'll be ten years now."

"You a citizen?

"Yes, my papers are back at the house."

He nodded. "I'm sorry, but I'll have to take a look at them."

So I closed the shop and we drove back to the house. Grete looked worried when I came in with the police. I had to shuffle through some drawers to find my papers and when I handed them to him he said. "Your wife's not a citizen?"

"Not yet."

"Can I see your marriage certificate, please?"

I showed him the certificate which was in German, of course, but he didn't question it. "Well, as long as you're married your wife is okay, but we're asking all Germans, even if you're citizens, to register and be fingerprinted once a month. You'll have to go into Duncan for that. You got a radio in the house?"

"Can't afford one yet."

"Well, I also have to inform you that it's against the law for you to have a radio."

So there we were, enemy aliens. And because Arno and Ida weren't citizens they had to register once a month in Victoria. I read the newspaper closely, but there never was anything written against German immigrants except for a local fellow, a Canadian citizen who was born in Saskatchewan of German parents, who was accused of being a German Nazi. Would we be next, we wondered?

The only way we could write letters home was through the Red Cross, and we knew we probably wouldn't get any more mail from overseas until the war was over. But we also figured that it wouldn't last too long. Even though business was slow, and part of it was probably due to unemployment over the winter, we always had enough money to pay our rent. We enjoyed ourselves there on the lake and Grete knew how to stretch every nickel. I hired a carpenter real cheap, and in my spare time the two of us began to build a three-room house on our 300 acres. As much as we loved the log house, I hated the idea of being a renter.

The winter was unusually mild, but very wet. The end of November the rain started to fall and kept on falling day after day. It wasn't long before sections of the road were under water. Just before Christmas the river had risen and even the lake began to creep up the slope toward the house.

"You don't have to worry this time about flooding," I said to Grete. "We're high and dry."

"You've told me that before," she said, picking up the ballerina music box from my Aunt Gretel in Berlin and winding it. "Every day the lake gets higher. If all this rain were snow there would be ten meters of it."

"We've had over a foot of rain just this month," I said nodding, looking out the window onto the dripping porch. "But we're on high ground around here."

"Maybe the snow wasn't so bad after all," Grete said. "At least you can go out in the snow."

On Christmas Eve, Grete pulled out one of her fancy linen table cloths, silver candlestick holders, and our finest dishes. I cut down the biggest Christmas tree that would fit into the house. We put real beeswax candles on the tree and hung up candies for the boys. When they saw the tree their eyes just popped. I had bought them a train and a couple of toy trucks and Grete had knit the standard sweaters, socks and mittens for all of us.

By early January the rains finally quit and the water level in the lake dropped. We hadn't been in any real danger, but when you've been flooded out once, you gain a great respect for Mother Nature. By the second week in January it was so warm that the sap was running in the trees, snowdrops were flowering, daffodils were popping out weeks early, and cherry trees were blooming. Even the ducks and geese were flying northward. Then on the morning of the 24th of January we awoke to half a foot of snow on the ground. Grete and the boys were excited.

"I thought you hated the stuff," I reminded her.

"There's a limit to everything," she said. "Besides, this will probably be all gone by tomorrow."

I closed the shop early that day because the dark sky and chilly air threatened more snow. When I drove up to the house it was still light and the boys were outside throwing snowballs and rolling around in the snow. A snowman stood beside the front steps, holding a broom. He had a finely sculpted face. Grete's handi-work—a carrot for a nose. Tommy and George hadn't seen any white stuff in so long I think they'd forgotten what it looked like. I didn't see too much of them in those days as I worked such long hours, so when I jumped out of the old truck I chased them around and let them pelt me with snowballs. I only remember all that, of course, because the next day the snowman was gone and melted, and so was a part of our lives.

23. Settling in Port Alberni

I WAS IN THE SHOP EARLY the next morning because I had to prepare an order for one of the logging camps, though business in general had slacked off with all the anti-German war propaganda. By four in the afternoon I had hung the last of the meat and scrubbed the counters so decided to call it quits. I climbed into the pickup, wondering what Grete would have for supper that night. The little bit of snow that was left on the ground had turned to slush.

I drove across the bridge and onto the one-lane dirt road that led out to our house. It was just dusk. The sky had cleared and puffy clouds hovered over the trees, but unusually red. I marvelled at the brilliance of the color. Sometimes we'd get some pretty good sunsets there on the lake. I passed some leafless alders and maples and when the sky appeared again, the fiery-red glare against the sky seemed too bright, too close and the puffy clouds looked too much like smoke. I gripped the wheel and my heart began to knock. I pushed the pedal hard to the floorboard and when I came speeding around the last bend, red-orange flames were licking up the logs of the house and black smoke curled into the air.

Grete and the boys stood huddled in their feather quilts away from the burning house. Only one wall of logs was left standing. I jammed on the brakes and jumped out of the truck. The smell of soot and smoke stung my nose and embers were flying everywhere.

"*Mein Gott,*" I yelled, running over to them. I threw my arms around Grete and the boys. "You all right? What happened? Are you sure you're okay?"

Grete didn't say anything and just cried on my shoulder. Tommy kept screaming, "Mama's zebras, the glass zebras!" George grabbed my pants. "Papa, Papa," he cried.

Then Grete pulled away and held up her hands.

I grabbed her arms. "They're burned!"

"They're not that bad," she sobbed. Her face was streaked with black soot. "The cold snow helps. They're not so bad."

The last of the tinder dry logs crashed to the ground sending up an explosion of sparks and ash. "Come, get into the truck. I'm taking you to the hospital."

"No, I don't need any hospital," she said, shaking her head. "We're not going to any hospital. I can look after this myself. We've lost everything, all the papers . . . everything."

"It doesn't matter," I yelled. "Come, get in the truck." I rolled the boys into the quilts and lifted them into the truck. "Don't worry, everything'll be okay. Mama will be all right." I helped Grete in.

A car drove up and a few people jumped out.

"You folks okay?" they shouted.

"We're not going to any hospital," Grete said again in a cold whisper. She looked at me with tears in her eyes. "It's just my hands. They're hardly blistered."

The whole house and the woodshed was a smoldering heap by then. Only the garage, separate from the house, was standing.

"Yeah, we're all okay," I said, walking over to them. "The missus burned her hands a bit, but everybody's okay. The house is gone. Not much we can do now."

I got back into the truck and turned it around, figuring there wasn't anything we could salvage there.

"We'll go to Arno and Ida's," I said to Grete. "They'll put us up for a few days and Ida can take care of your hands."

"I was trying to light the gas lamp," Grete began. "How was I to know? It was empty so I put some gas into it. When I lit the match . . . " She paused. "When I lit the match there was an explosion."

"You and the boys are safe so don't worry about anything else." I had always made sure there was enough gas in the lamp so she wouldn't have to fool around with it. "I should have filled the lamp for you. I should have warned you about spilled gas."

"The curtains caught on fire. I grabbed the boys and the bedding. Everything's gone," she sobbed.

Paul, Grete and Arno
Michael at Duncan,
ca. 1940.

We were in pretty bad shape and it meant we had to start all over again from scratch. The house was insured by the owner, but we weren't covered for anything.

At first we were just happy that we were all safe and together. But it was, nevertheless, a shock. My citizenship papers were gone; and I had to go down to Victoria to get them replaced. All the photographs from the Old Country and the ones we had taken up North were gone, Grete's sewing machine and zither were gone. Not having a needle or thread or scissors didn't matter at first because we didn't have any clothes to sew buttons on, or cloth to sew clothes. Little things like that only occurred to us later.

But when we moved into our half-built, three-room house on our stump ranch with just the clothes on our backs, that's when the full realization of our predicament hit us.

Of course, Arno and Ida, and our friends, the Kohlers, all pitched in to help us. They gave us a few pots and pans and some bedding to get started, and quite a few people around the lake donated clothing, sacks of potatoes, rice and some canned goods. Every bit helped.

By spring there just wasn't enough trade to make a living and I couldn't carry any more credit, so I had to close the shop. I picked up a few jobs around Duncan and Cowichan Bay, but after a few days on the job they'd want to see my registration card. When they saw I was a German, even though I had my citizenship papers, they always let me go.

Then Grete was pregnant—with you. It was pretty happy news for us, even under the circumstances. The boys, after all, were four and five years old by then. She didn't even tell me until George's fifth birthday in March. She thought you were due sometime the middle of September. We scarcely had a nickel to our name, but we had a roof over our heads and were healthy and in pretty good spirits.

One afternoon we got a surprise visit from Little Max. He came driving up in a fancy Mercury with Frances, his girlfriend. Grete threw off her apron and ran a comb through her hair.

"Do I look all right? Is my hair parted straight ?" she asked, anxiously looking in the hand held mirror.

The boys pushed a box to the window and looked out at the car with big, round eyes, not saying a word. Max was twenty-eight by then. With a big grin he stepped out of the car, pushing back his hat. I grabbed him by the shoulders.

"How in the hell did you find your way out here?"

"Well," he said, sticking out his jaw. "Arno and Ida drew me a map." Then he leaned over and kicked at the car. "I hope I didn't break the springs getting here. How many years has it been since I've seen you."

"We got married in '34. Remember?" I opened the car door for Frances. "So how about introducing us to your girl." I reached my hand to Frances. "We're not too fancy around here," I said to her. "Watch for the puddles."

She had dark, round eyes and was no Bette Davis beauty, but she had a soft, kind face and didn't pinch her mouth together with any sort of arrogance because she was a city girl. She wore a gray suit, some sort of a plaid, with a wide-brimmed hat and long, black pointed shoes.

"She runs the boarding house where I've been living," Max said.

Frances stepped out of the car and looked over to the house and the surrounding stumps and slash. A few dogwoods were blooming and dark green ferns and salal had grown up between the stumps.

"Well, c'mon into our palace and meet Grete and the boys," I said to Frances.

At least by then we no longer sat on apple boxes. I'd bought some second-hand chairs and a table, and Grete had used flower sacking to tack up some curtains over the kitchen washstand.

"Hey, boys," I called. "Where are you?" I looked under the beds but they weren't there. "Those boys are so shy they must've run off," I explained to Max and Frances. "All those years in the bush. They're not used to fancy people anymore. They'll come around."

"Sit down," Grete said. "I'll make coffee."

"The Michaels told us about the house fire," Frances said, pulling off her gloves. "I'm always afraid of a fire in the boarding house with all those smokers around. I'm sorry. It must have been terrible." She looked around the room. There were no pictures on the walls, no linoleum or rugs on the floor.

"We lost everything," Grete said, "but we get by."

"We're expecting another baby in September," I told them.

A thin, wistful smile spread across Frances' face. "That's nice, real nice. I guess you'd like a girl."

We filled the afternoon rehashing the old days and getting caught up on all the news. Max had had enough of the Yukon, but Adam decided to stay up there permanently.

When the boys didn't show up after an hour, I went out into the bush and finally bribed them with the promise of some chocolate that Frances had brought along. That was their first introduction to Uncle Max and Auntie Frances, as they eventually become known to all of you.

We put in an early garden because of the mild weather. The fishing was good in Lake Cowichan, and for a dollar you could buy ten pounds of flour, five pounds of rolled oats, and a good supply of dried peas and beans. Somehow we made ends meet, and Grete always had George and Tommy dressed nice, too.

By June the weather had turned hot and bush fires began to break out. I figured the forestry might need men bad enough and would look past me being German. There was a big fire around Lens Creek about fourteen miles from Lake Cowichan.

"I've got plenty of experience fighting fires up north," I told the foreman. "Been in this country over ten years now."

He hired me and gave me a crew of twelve men. Altogether three hundred men had turned up to fight the fire. We started work at three in the morning as that was the time the fires were most inactive. We had water pumps and plenty of water. Before the sun came up we would soak down as much area as we could along the edge of the burn. Then we worked with picks and shovels, digging out any of the smouldering remains. We'd often lose ground during the heat of the day, especially if the fire climbed a standing snag, and the high winds carried the sparks way behind us where new fires started.

About the fifth day out, seven of us went up a side valley where a spot fire had broken out. We hiked along an old abandoned railroad track that was overgrown with alders. We climbed to the head of the fire and worked like dynamite all day digging a fire trench.

By dusk we started to make our way back to camp. The valley was completely filled with smoke and drifting ashes, and we had no idea how much the fire had spread below us further down the mountain. Our hands and faces and clothes were completely blackened. We came around a bend and saw that the fire had burned across our trail and moved up the mountain. It looked to us like only a narrow strip had burned, and even though the smoke was pretty thick, we decided to make a run for it. Everyone began to cough and wheeze and choke. The acrid smell bit into my nostrils and my lungs began to burn. Suddenly there was a shift of wind, and the smoke and heat and flying embers became so intense that panic set in and we ran back the way we came. One of the men fell and I tried to pull him to his feet. My hands and face felt like they were on fire, and I could smell the singe of shoe leather.

"C'mon, we gotta get oughta here," I croaked, putting my hands under his arms and pulling him up.

I was desperate for oxygen and my lungs felt like they were getting cooked. He finally dragged himself up, and a good thing, because I doubt I would've had the strength to carry him. We stumbled and choked our way out of there. The other guys were waiting for us further up the track, all of them down on their knees, coughing and wheezing. We found a stream and cooled off our burning hands and faces. There was no way back to camp except for a detour way around the mountain, so we spent the night in the bush and didn't get back to camp until eleven the next morning. At least Grete wasn't expecting me home that night, but when we didn't show up at camp the night before, all the guys had lost hope that we would make it safely out. Five of the men were sent to the hospital and treated for burns. A week later the fires were out and once again I was without a job.

During that spring of 1940, Hitler's army had pushed ahead for more territory, and Denmark and Norway quickly surrendered to his demands. By May the Nazis had stormed across the borders of Belgium, Holland and Luxembourg. In June they marched into France and hoisted their swastika flag on the Eiffel Tower. Mussolini also declared war on France and joined forces with Hitler. And the war propaganda increased in Canada which meant that the job situation for us Germans, and by then the Italians as well, would only get worse.

Then I heard that loggers were needed up in Oyster Bay, further north along the east coast of the Island. Since I could no longer get work around the Duncan area, we loaded up a trailer with our few meagre belongings and two goats and headed toward Courtenay. Arno and Ida and the boys had returned to the mainland by then where Arno found work in Vancouver in a meat packing plant.

When we arrived in Oyster Bay, I was hired right away, but when I showed the foreman my registration card he told me I didn't have to bother coming back. I always held off showing them my card as long as possible, hoping I'd get in a few days work. We had rented a little house on the Island Highway right in Oyster Bay and stayed until the end of July. I found other odd jobs, but they never lasted for more than a few days. My spirit was nearly broken by then and I finally quit looking for work. Fortunately, Grete was very healthy and carried you without a problem.

We practically lived off oysters that summer—oyster stew, oyster sandwiches, oyster burgers, raw oysters.

One day I picked up a conversation with a young man who lived right in Oyster Bay. He didn't seem to mind that I was a German and was actually quite sympathetic to our plight. He told me that his father had been hired on by Bloedel, Stewart and Welch Company, a lumber mill in the Alberni Valley and that I might have a chance for a job over there. So we loaded up again. It was quite an experience winding around that narrow curving gravel road by Cameron Lake. Around one bend a huge outcropping of granite the size of a house jutted out over the road. When we left the lake we found ourselves among giant old-growth firs eight feet in diameter. Tall, shiny green ferns grew thick along the ditch, rolling away in dark green waves as we passed.

"This looks like the way to the homestead," Grete said, leaning out the window to get a better view of the giants.

"Let's hope it's the way to a job or we may have to homestead again," I laughed.

I went straight to the sawmill down there on the Alberni Canal to apply for work. "I want to tell you straight off before you hire me that I'm German," I said to the foreman.

He lifted his hands and laughed. "Well, you sure don't sound like no Englishman. What kind of experience you got?"

"I worked in the southern Interior and up around Terrace in the mills, but I'm not going to start work and then be fired after a couple of days. I've got a family to feed."

"We don't worry about Germans much around here," he said, lighting up a cigarette. "Bloedel's one himself. Be down here seven o'clock sharp Monday morning."

We rented a place on Sproat Lake Road for $25 a month. We had no money left for food or gas, but a Mr. Stewart, who ran a grocery business on Third Avenue, gave me credit until payday, and Mr. McLean let me have some gas and a spare tire. I was really grateful they gave me a chance because most people I talked to turned me down.

It was August by then and Grete was due in about a month. One of the guys I worked with was a young Japanese fellow who planned to join the Canadian Army as a volunteer. He owned fourteen acres of land on Beaver Creek Road, just two miles out of Alberni.

"Good land," he said. "It has little house on it, very nice house. Grocery store right across the street. Only three hundred dollars."

"But I don't have that kind of money," I told him, holding up the palms of my hands. "I'm flat broke."

"Thirty dollars a month you pay me. Good land. You buy it," he said nodding and grinning. "I give you very good deal."

It was a nice piece of property and had a view of the mountains. Charlie Berry's Grocery was just down the road. Since we were already paying $25 a month for rent, I decided I couldn't lose, so by the end of August we moved again. But I started to build a decent house on the property right away. We picked up some good used furniture and a Singer sewing machine so Grete could sew some clothes and make curtains for the windows.

Then you were born on September 11th—in style at the West Coast Hospital. Grete shared a room with an Indian woman and when you were brought in for your first feeding, she told the nurse you were the wrong baby and that you belonged to the Indian woman. Your skin was so dark and you had so much black hair that Grete thought you had been exchanged by mistake. We sure were proud and happy to have a little baby girl. When I suggested we should name you Rosalie after your grandmother, Grete shook her head.

"That's too old-fashioned," she said, talking and cooing to you. She had you bundled up right next to her.

"What about Caroline, after your grandmother?"

"No. That's even more old-fashioned."

"Maybe Anna, after my mother, or how about Henriette, after my grandmother?"

She just smiled and kissed your dark-red face. "We're going to name you Rose . . . Rose Margaret."

The boys were crazy about you and fought constantly over who would hold you . . . for the first week or two.

Things began to look up for us. We made friends. At the mill I met Hans Irg, another German. His wife Justine was a Canadian and they lived about ten miles out Beaver Creek on Bland Road. The people around the Valley weren't as anti-German as farther down the Island, and there wasn't as much war news in the local *Advocate* as there had been in the *Cowichan Leader.*

Oh, there was talk all right about the Coast being invaded by an enemy power and how the West Coast was united in helping the Empire win the war. There was a push to sell "Help Smash Hitler" War Savings Certificates, and "Help Lick 'im!" stamps for backs of envelopes that had a mean, ugly face of Hitler. There were "Win the War" campaigns, free propaganda picture shows, and local recruiting was going on, but on a day-to-day basis things were pretty calm. Nevertheless, we had to register and get fingerprinted once a month, even as citizens.

That fall I drove eight miles up Beaver Creek Road to the Irgs' farm to buy a cow. Their house stood on a hillside facing the mile-high Beaufort Range which had two granite humps on top of the mountain covered with snow. To the east lay Mt. Arrowsmith, a dormant volcano. When I remarked how beautiful the area was, Hans told me that a farm was for sale down at the end of the road.

"About 350 acres," he said. "Some good fertile land with lots of good timber. Clarence Bland lives in a little shack right next to it. His old man used to own all that property—had three wives, imagine. When he died, Clarence inherited half of it and his brother the other half."

"Well, we've got a decent place now," I told him.

"If you're ever interested," he said enthusiastically, "he'd probably sell it to you cheap. C'mon, I'll show it to you just for the hell of it. We'd be neighbours."

We walked over to the farm, not more than a quarter mile away. A four-room shingled house with two long verandas was set back against some cedars. It was almost entirely overgrown with long, trailing rose vines. Meadows sloped away from it and a creek ran through the bottom land. The mountain seemed to grow straight out of the fields. Mt. Arrowsmith stood prominently in the distance, its peak shining in the sun.

"Soil is black as coal," Hans said. "Would've considered it myself, but didn't need all that land."

"It's a nice piece of property, all right," I said. "I've always wanted to raise some cattle and this would be the spot for it. Maybe I'll talk it over with my missus. See what she says, but I know she wouldn't move again."

"I don't want to look at any farm," Grete said, when I told her about the place. "And I don't want to live in the bush anymore."

And that was that. Well, I didn't have time to think too much about that place as I was finishing up the new house on our property and working every day, but every now and then my mind would wander and I'd think about the nice pasture land, the creek, and that mile-high mountain.

By Christmas our house was built and we moved in. The mill proved to be steady work and I was bringing home a paycheck every week, though it was just enough to scrape by on. I earned 65 cents an hour, which meant about sixty dollars a month take-home pay, and remember thirty of it paid the mortgage. Spring rolled around and we began to feel settled, but I'll be damned if we weren't hit with bad luck one more time.

I was at work at the mill stacking boards. All I can remember is that I had my back to a forklift that was carrying a stack of boards. Maybe the driver misjudged the width of the load, or I misjudged the distance he was driving, but the next thing I knew I was lying immobilized on the floor in agonizing pain. I was taken to the hospital in an ambulance where I was told I had a broken back.

So Grete was back to nursing me. I spent quite a stretch of time in the hospital and three months in a body cast. At least by then the government had benefits in place and I was covered by Workmen's Compensation. By the time the cast was removed, my muscles were weak as jelly and I still couldn't go back to work.

I had a little time on my hands, so I said to Grete one day that we should take a drive out to Beaver Creek and visit the Irgs. She was standing by the sink peeling potatoes.

"Hans told me we could come out anytime," I said. "You'd like the scenery out there. Reminds me of our old homestead the way the mountain range runs along the back of the property."

"Is that where that property was for sale?" she asked turning to me.

"I think it still is for sale," I said with a nod. "Maybe we could take a look at it once we're out there."

Grete waved a potato in the air. "I told you before that I don't want to live in any more bush. If you want to visit the Irgs that's one thing, but I'm not going out there to look at any property."

I leaned up against the counter and picked up a potato, tossing it up in the air.

"It may be a long ways out of town, but it's not bush. There's even a park close by. Stamp River runs through it and there's a big waterfall from what I hear. Hans told me visitors from as far away as California go there. And I heard talk at the mill that one day that road will go all the way through to Courtenay."

"I don't care where the road goes." Grete put the potatoes in a pot of water and set them on the stove. "We're settled here and we're close to town," she said, lifting the stove lid and throwing in a couple of sticks of wood. "It's not far for you to get to work from here and you know darned well you're no farmer. I don't know where you get your crazy ideas."

I put my arm around her waist and grinned down at her. Her blue eyes softened and she just shook her head. She still was the most beautiful girl in the world to me.

"You're right. I don't know where I get my ideas, but maybe this one isn't so crazy."

24. Beaver Creek

THE NEXT SUNDAY WE DROVE OUT Beaver Creek Road to visit the Irgs. The gravel road ran straight as an arrow toward the mountains. Dogwoods were in bloom and everything was lush and green from the spring rains.

About half way out of town we came to a few houses and a one-room schoolhouse. "That's where the boys would go to school," I said to Grete.

"They can go to school in town," she said.

"I don't want to go to school," George whined.

We passed Stamp Falls Park, swung by Bland Road and turned into a narrow, rutted road, overgrown with weeds which led to the Bland place. Rotted logs, covered with thick moss and broad green ferns, lay alongside the road under the shelter of cedar and maples. We came into an open meadow that was flanked on one side with fir and cedar and rolled away to an apple orchard on the other. Straight ahead stood the brown, shingled house covered in bare rose vines that wound around the veranda and up over the roof. Fresh snow was about a third of the way down the mountain, and the peak of Arrowsmith glowed pink in the afternoon light.

"That can't be the Irgs' house," Grete said. "The place looks deserted."

"The Irgs don't live far from here." I pulled up to the house and turned off the ignition. "I just wanted to show you the property so you could see for yourself what I've been talking about."

"I figured as much," Grete said, looking around with a skeptical look in her eye. "Where are the power lines?"

I stepped out of the truck and the boys scrambled out behind me and ran toward the house.

"Hey, not so fast," I shouted. I went around to the other side of the truck and took you out of Grete's arms.

"There's been talk that there'll be electricity soon enough," I said.

"Huh, there's probably no running water either."

"There's lots of running water in the creek. And there's a good well on the place—with a pump."

I pointed east and took a deep breath. "Look at Mt. Arrowsmith, a more beautiful sight you couldn't find. And over there, an orchard of mature apple trees in full bloom. We'll have plenty of apples in the fall."

"Listen," she said, wagging her finger at me. "Don't get any ideas about moving or picking apples. I'm not moving one more time. We've got a nice place now, it's close to town, and we can see Arrowsmith from there, too. I don't want to live out in the bush anymore."

"But this isn't the bush, and the house . . . "

"And the house? Look at it . . . an old, run-down shack overgrown with vines. Rats and bats and mice own it and it's probably rotted right through. Maybe there's some sleeping beauty in there waiting for you. But it won't be me."

Well, what could I say? You can't argue with a woman, especially a woman who's been bounced around one time too many. She finally walked around the front of the house, but refused to go inside or listen any further to my idea.

But I couldn't get that property off my mind. It was one of the nicest spreads of land I'd ever had an opportunity to buy, and I began to do some figuring. About three weeks later I finally said to Grete. "Listen, I know we could get $500 for this place, enough for a down payment on the farm."

"I thought we had settled that," she said, putting her hands on her hips.

"I'd like to take another look at the place."

"What are they asking for it?" she asked.

"Oh, about three thousand bucks."

She looked at me in disbelief, pulling her brows together. "And where's the money coming from?"

"Like I said, from this place, then forty a month."

She took a deep breath and crossed her arms. "It's just so far out. I can walk to the store from here. I can even walk to town."

"You'd have Justine for a neighbor and we'd get to know the other farmers in the area."

"How would I get around? Everyone lives miles apart out there."

"We'd go to town every Saturday. Besides, you can learn to drive and as soon as we can afford it, you'll get your own car."

"My own car? You can barely afford gas for the truck and you're talking about another car?"

"Well, down the road."

She shrugged her shoulders. "You can drop me and the kids off to visit Justine. You do your looking."

It was a warm June day when we went out again. I drove right past Bland Road, thinking Grete wouldn't notice.

"You've passed their road."

"We're almost there," I said, turning into the middle road that was overgrown with tall grass and dandelions.

Grete settled back into the seat and hugged you close to her, not saying another word. When we arrived at the place I shut off the motor and began to grin.

The house was in full bloom and covered with thousands of pink roses. Green, leafy vines had crawled over every window and door and had wrapped themselves around every post and under every loose shingle.

"It looks like a fairy-tale house," George yelled, bouncing up and down on the seat.

"Is there a princess in there?" Tommy asked, turning around and patting you on the head. "You want to see a fairy princess, Rosie?"

"Some fairy-tale, all right," Grete said, stepping out of the car.

"Can we go inside?" Little George yelled.

A sweet perfume hung in the air and bees hummed and whirred around the flowers. I stepped onto the veranda and broke off a cluster of small pink roses. I leaned down and tucked it into Grete's hair that glinted red in the sun. She had you in your arms and, you grabbed the roses and crushed them in your chubby little fingers.

Grete took a deep breath and shook her head. "Either I'm waking up after a hundred years, or falling into a deep sleep. I don't know . . . "

I had brought an axe along so we could hack our way through the rose vines on the veranda. I pushed open the door just like Fred MacMurray did in the movie *The Egg and I* when he'd bought a chicken farm for his wife, Claudette Colbert. Sunlight flooded the long, dark hallway. A damp, musky smell filled the air. Tommy grabbed my leg and began to cry. I picked him up. George pushed open a bedroom door and climbed up on some rusted bedsprings. He began to jump up and down.

"Now get off there," I said, "before the coils end up around your ears." There was another bedroom across the hall, and at the end of the hallway was a large living room which smelled of mold and mildew.

Grete began to cough. She took a deep breath and shook her head, pulling spider webs out of her hair. "This is the house that should have burned down," she said.

Yellowed wallpaper hung down in shreds and in a minute the boys had torn strips of it off the wall. The ceiling had big brown water stains and the linoleum was buckled. I looked through a small window caked with dirt and cobwebs. Big, puffy white clouds had settled on the snowy peak of Arrowsmith.

The kitchen faced some drooping cedars and was equipped with an old wood stove and a makeshift sink. Mouse droppings were scattered across the floor. We stepped out the back door onto another long veranda that faced the Beaufort Range.

"Well, what do you think, Sweetheart? It's a beautiful spot, isn't it?" I looked out across the fields. "See the creek down there, boys? You'd be able to fish everyday."

Your mother shifted you around in her arms. You were playing with the silver Thaler piece around her neck.

"It really does look like the homestead," she said. "But what about wolves?"

"You won't have to worry about 'em. I don't think there are any on the Island."

"And bears?"

George, Rosie and Tommy at
Port Alberni, ca. 1943.

"I know there aren't any grizzlies down around here—maybe
a few black bears, but they wouldn't bother us."

It was so quiet that the only sound you could hear was a low
hush from the mountain like the lazy breath of a giant. Ducks went
winging across the lower field. George cupped his hands and made
a loud quacking sound. An echo floated back from the mountain.

My eyes scanned the lower part of the mountain that had been
logged off around the turn of the century. Part of the slash looked
like a cat's face, and for years we had referred to it as the Cat's
Ears. I looked up to the bluffs on top of the range and followed the
ridgeline east to Arrowsmith. I breathed in the clear, fresh air. It
was a view I knew I could live with for the rest of my life.

Grete walked to the end of the veranda and looked out toward
the rolling hills of the apple orchard. Finally she turned to me. With
a half smile, a bit of a frown and a shake of her thick hair, she said,
"It sounds like you've already bought the place."

"I wanted you to make the decision."

So we sold our house and the fourteen acres and moved out
to Beaver Creek Road at the end of September, 1941. You were a
year old.

"And I'm telling you right now," Grete said when we finished hacking away the rose vines and had torn off the wallpaper and scrubbed the walls and floors before moving in our few pieces of furniture. "This is the last time I'm moving." Her finger was wagging. "I don't care what you do, but I'm staying put."

I felt a stupid grin spread across my face and took her into my arms.

"Now leave me alone," she said. Sparks of light flashed in her clear, blue eyes. "I mean business."

I ran my hands across her shining hair. "I know you do, and not over my dead body will you ever tear me away from this place."

Well, that's the story. I know I should end it here. That's what you wanted, isn't it—until we moved into the old place. But there are a few things I'd like to add, things you wouldn't know about or remember, things that happened during the war and afterwards. Can you give me a couple more minutes? I just want to tell you a little more about Grete and a few of the rough spots and that'll be it.

25. The War Years

WE WEREN'T IN THE PLACE MORE THAN A MONTH when Grete came down with pleurisy, a complication of pneumonia. She was pretty darn sick and didn't come home from the hospital for three weeks. I found a woman to take care of you kids. Couldn't afford to take time off work. When she finally came home, you had forgotten who she was and refused to go near her.

Then we heard about Pearl Harbor and the destruction of the American fleet in Hawaii on December 7th, 1941. Who knew where Pearl Harbor was? We hardly knew where Hawaii was. By that point Hitler had a good stronghold in Europe, and Canada was getting mired deeper into the war. At first Britain and France thought they would win the war without the use of heavy troops, but when France collapsed the year before and Italy joined with Hitler, Canada sent over half a million troops abroad.

When the Japanese bombed the U.S. military base at Pearl Harbor, Roosevelt declared war on Japan, and Canada, a strong ally of the United States, followed suit. Three days later the United States joined the war in Europe and with all the forces combined, Hitler was finally silenced, but not until May 7, 1945, three and a half years later.

We had lost contact with our families back home in Germany during those years. Grete had written to her mother after we moved into the house and sent along some pictures of you and the boys, but the Red Cross returned the letter and said we weren't allowed to send a letter with pictures. Well, that made Grete so mad she didn't write again for awhile. By then it was too late.

I came home from work one day, and I can still remember her cold hands and her face white as chalk. At first she wouldn't talk to me, but she finally broke down and started to bawl.

"*Mutter ist tot,*" she cried.

"But how do you know she's dead?"

No mail was coming out of Germany either, and I couldn't understand how she would have heard her mother was dead.

"I just felt it," and she made a fist across her heart. "I had this sharp pain and fell to the floor. I know it's my mother. I know she's dead."

I never doubted her, and sure enough, about a year later I got a letter from my cousin Hans Spitzbarth who was a prisoner of war in Baltimore. This wasn't the Spitzbarth we visited in New York in '34 on our way to Canada, but the one whose family owned the Kronenbrau brewery in Rehau.

I immediately left for Seattle where I boarded a train for Maryland. The poor bugger had been in one of Rommel's units in Northern Africa when he was captured. He had contracted malaria, and when I visited him he already had the shakes. He had been a good-looking guy with a straight nose and fine features, but his eyes were sunken into his head and rimmed in dark lines. He was well treated, with enough food and cigarettes and adequate medical care. He would have been okay had it not been for the malaria. He told me he had heard from his mother that Grete's mother had died of tuberculosis in the spring of '42. He didn't get back to Germany until after the war and died in '52 of malaria.

By early 1942 the Canadian Government had issued an ultimatum that all Germans who weren't naturalized citizens had to move three hundred miles from the West Coast by April 1st 1942, much like the Japanese who were put into internment camps. We were okay since I'd been a citizen for a number of years by then, but we knew that Arno and Ida and Big Max were in trouble. Months later we got a letter from Arno and Ida from Alberta.

Stoney Plain, Alberta
October 15, 1942
Dear Paul & Grete,
This place is further than 300 miles from the Coast, but we didn't have much choice. The police gave us twenty-four hours to

get out of Vancouver or they'd arrest us and throw us in jail. We piled everything we could into our Hup Mobil. We weren't welcome anywhere. In the Interior there were big signs, "Japanese and Germans Not Welcome here". I told you trouble was coming. You remember Ida's brother, Joe? He's in jail. Got into an argument one night in a bar with a guy who told him the British could easily defeat the Germans. You know Joe. He wouldn't leave it alone. Said the British are no good and that they wouldn't last. I told him he'd get in trouble if he didn't keep his mouth shut.

I hope this bloody war ends quickly. It's only October and already darn cold here with snow on the ground and the wind blows all the time—worse than in the North. Big Max ended up in Edmonton. You're lucky you had your papers. Don't bother writing because we're not allowed mail.

Viele Grusse,
Arno & Ida

The war dragged on and all imports were rationed—sugar, liquor, cigarettes. My back still troubled me, so I quit the mill and got back into the meat business again, and although there was a period I did quite well when the army was stationed in town, it was a tough time to be a German.

When the war finally ended in Europe, we had been away from the Old Country for over ten years. We had repaired our house by then and Grete added all the finishing touches, of course. She had put in a rock garden and we built a couple of goldfish ponds and put in rock walls and lawns. Weeping willows, that Monkey Puzzle tree, flowering cherries, holly bushes, lilacs and snowballs, rhododendrons, climbing roses, peonies, pansies, and in the spring tulips and daffodils were spread over about an acre. That was one of her favorite pastimes, looking after the garden.

We knew many of the local farmers by then. The Drinkwaters, Darbys and Plaunts lived a few miles from us toward town. North of us lived the Marlowes, the old Rands, Shannons, Kyles, Baynes, old Mrs. Lindsey, the Camerons and the Somers.

Shortly after the war ended, a white envelope with black edging arrived from Rehau. A letter like that always announced a death. I nervously tore open the flap and in a few words read that my father was dead. He had died the year before—1944. I remember the sting of regret that we had never settled things and that I hadn't been able to get back to the Old Country in all those intervening years to see him and the family.

Little Max and Frances also settled in the Alberni Valley the summer of '45 out there on Bayne Road. They never had children. Adam stayed up in the Yukon where he grew giant tomatoes in hothouses, and Big Max married Marjorie, a Canadian woman from Squamish. She was a widow with two children, Renee and Charlie, and they settled in Victoria.

Arno and Ida had moved from Alberta to the Okanagan and then back to Vancouver in 1947. They visited us several times on the Island after the war. Then there was that black day for them in '57. You must remember that story. What a shock after all Arno and I had been through together. I still remember when I heard the news . . . all I could think about were the tough times we'd survived up there in the North. You probably know more about it than I do.

Christmas, 1948. Left to right: Paul, Little Max (Max Hopper), Grete and Frances Hopper.

Paul's sister Gusti and her accordion in Gasthof "Die Goldene Sonne," Rehau, Germany. ca 1955.

In '54 I took my first trip back to Germany in over twenty years. It was quite a homecoming, but everything had changed. My father was dead, my mother was old and mellowed, with eyes full of tears and happy to see me. She wanted to turn all the property over to me, but the joke of it was, when she went to the bank, the only property left to speak of was the land the buildings stood on. Gusti was the same free spirit I remembered and still played the accordion and sang. She and her husband, Hans, had three children by then—Christl, Hans and Little Gusti. Gusti finally did come to visit us in 1978.

Jette had two daughters, Erika and Helga. When Berlin was bombed out in 1943, she and Karl returned to Rehau. Jette died in 1959 of a heart attack at age 51, and my mother died in 1967, right on my 57th birthday, at age eighty. So there you have the story, or a good part of it.

My life was no fairy-tale, even the later years. And I'm sure you yourself have found out by now that life never is. Regrets? Sure. Who doesn't have regrets after living out a life span, but except for a couple of major things that I wish would never have happened, I wouldn't have traded my life with anybody.

26. EPILOGUE: BEFORE THE END

THANKS, POP . . .
    I finally have a clear picture about your life through those long Depression years. Thanks for telling us about those years of gristle and grit, working and surviving, moving from one place to another. I understand now how it all happened and how Oma shouldered every bit of burden, faced every challenge with a stoicism and a level head that must have been familiar to all pioneer women.

Eventually we all visited the Old Country. I guess we needed to get back to our roots, your roots. Even Oma went back to Rehau with you in 1962 and made amends with your mother, or *Gross-mutter*, as we knew her. When I went over on my own in '61, I remember how Gusti hugged me and I cried. We felt a tight kinship from the moment we met. Her teeth were still white as china.

Over the years, Gusti and The Golden Sun had become synonymous and her voice and accordion were heart and soul of that Gasthof. When she died of a heart attack in 1986, the *Sonne* couldn't be the same again. It still sits there on the *Ascherstrasse*, you know, but the walls are now a creamy gold. The business has been sold and strangers run it. The *Stammgaeste* are gone.

About a year ago I had a long talk with Ron Michael and he filled me in on the details of that terrible accident his parents, Arno and Ida, had back in 1957. It was all over the newspapers. They were returning from a funeral in Osoyoos. Strangely enough, Ron knew about the accident before he heard about it on the radio and from the police. When the police described to him how a beer truck had lost its brakes on a long, steep hill, crushing and flattening his parents' car and killing them both instantly, Ron just nodded his head. "I know, I know," he said. His one brother, Roy, was only nineteen, his other brother, Ed, twenty. Ron was twenty-five.

Rose with Henry Joseph and son on the Sutherland River at the east end of Babine Lake, 1993. Henry's great uncle was Joe Hansen, who befriended and helped Paul out on the Babine Lake homestead.

Big Max died in 1988 and Little Max a year later. No one knows for sure what happened to Uncle Adam. He lost touch and disappeared.

Grossmutter doted on me when I met her for the first time in 1961. She still wore a black dress and heavy black shoes and her dark hair, streaked with gray, was pulled back in a soft roll. She limped a little and it took her a long time to maneuver those stone steps, but we liked each other.

So your life, the way it was, your children and who they are, and all the nine grandchildren and great grandchildren, what they will become, all stems, you know, from *Grossmutter* not wanting you to marry Grete. Think of it. Had you gone along with the scheme of things, we wouldn't be. And perhaps you wouldn't have been around long either. Had you been in Hitler's army you probably would have been on the front lines or shot for desertion.

So thanks, Pop . . . for the memories, for the windows to a life we never really knew.

BIBLIOGRAPHY

Allsop, Kenneth: *Hard Travellin'*. The New American Library, *1967.*

Asante, Nadine: *History of Terrace*, Terrace, BC: Terrace Public Library Association, 1972.

Baird, Irene: *Waste Heritage*, Toronto, ON: The Macmillan Company of Canada Ltd., 1939.

Bateman, James: *Animal Traps and Trapping*, Harrisburg, PA: Stackpole Books, 1971.

Bulman, T. Alex: *Kamloops Cattlemen*, Sidney, BC: Gray's Publishing Ltd., 1972.

Careless, J.M.S.: *Canada, A Story of Challenge*, Toronto, ON: The Macmillan Company of Canada,1963.

Central Carrier Bilingual Dictionary, Vancouver Public Library.

Collier, Eric: *Three Against the Wilderness*, New York: E.P. Dutton & Co. Inc., 1959.

Edwards, Isabel: *Ruffles On My Longjohns*, Surrey, BC: Hancock House, 1980.

Edwards, Ralph: *Ralph Edwards on Lonesome Lake* (as told to Ed Gould) Surrey, BC: Hancock House, 1979.

Frank, Floyd: *My Valley's Yesteryears*, Victoria, BC: Orca Book Publishers, 1981.

Geary, Steven M.: *Fur Trapping in North America*, Piscataway, NJ: New Century Publishers, 1981.

Handbook of North American Indians, Northridge, CA: California State University

Hobson, Richmond P.: *Grass Beyond The Mountains*, Toronto, ON: McClelland and Stewart Ltd., 1951.

"The Journal of American Folk-Lore," The American Folk-Lore Society, Los Angeles, CA: G.E. Stechert & Co., Vol. 47, No. 184–185, 1934.

Large, R. G.: *The Skeena, River of Destiny*, Vancouver, BC: Mitchell Press, 1957.

Lyons, C.P.: *Milestones on the Mighty Fraser*, Canada: J.M. Dent & Sons Limited, 1950.

Minehan, Thomas: *Boy and Girl Tramps of America*, Washington: University of Washington Press, 1976.

Payne, Robert: *The Life and Death of Adolf Hitler*, New York: Praeger, 1973.

Shelford, Arthur and Shelford, Cyril: *We Pioneered*, Victoria, BC: Orca Book Publishers, 1988.

Shirer, William R.: *The Rise and Fall of the Third Reich*, New York: Simon and Schuster, 1959.

Time Life Books: *The Nazis, World War II, Prelude to War*, Time-Life Books, 1976.

Turkki, Pat: *Burns Lake & District*, Burns Lake, BC: Burns Lake Historical Society, 1973.

NEWSPAPERS

Cowichan Leader, Duncan, BC, 1939, 1940.
Rehavan Tagblatt, Rehau, Germany, 1930, 1931, 1932.
New York Times, Glendale Central Library, Glendale, CA, 1934.
West Coast Advocate, Port Alberni, BC, 1940, 1941.

INDEX

70 Mile House 74
93 Mile House 74
100 Mile House 74

PRINTED AND BOUND
IN BOUCHERVILLE, QUÉBEC, CANADA
BY MARC VEILLEUX IMPRIMEUR INC.
IN OCTOBER, 1997